Stock Charts

by Greg Schnell, CMT, MFTA
and Lita Epstein, MBA

Stock Charts For Dummies®

Published by: **John Wiley & Sons, Inc.,** 111 River Street, Hoboken, NJ 07030-5774, www.wiley.com

Copyright © 2018 by John Wiley & Sons, Inc., Hoboken, New Jersey

Published simultaneously in Canada

No part of this publication may be reproduced, stored in a retrieval system or transmitted in any form or by any means, electronic, mechanical, photocopying, recording, scanning or otherwise, except as permitted under Sections 107 or 108 of the 1976 United States Copyright Act, without the prior written permission of the Publisher. Requests to the Publisher for permission should be addressed to the Permissions Department, John Wiley & Sons, Inc., 111 River Street, Hoboken, NJ 07030, (201) 748-6011, fax (201) 748-6008, or online at http://www.wiley.com/go/permissions.

Trademarks: Wiley, For Dummies, the Dummies Man logo, Dummies.com, Making Everything Easier, and related trade dress are trademarks or registered trademarks of John Wiley & Sons, Inc., and may not be used without written permission. All other trademarks are the property of their respective owners. John Wiley & Sons, Inc., is not associated with any product or vendor mentioned in this book.

LIMIT OF LIABILITY/DISCLAIMER OF WARRANTY: WHILE THE PUBLISHER AND AUTHOR HAVE USED THEIR BEST EFFORTS IN PREPARING THIS BOOK, THEY MAKE NO REPRESENTATIONS OR WARRANTIES WITH RESPECT TO THE ACCURACY OR COMPLETENESS OF THE CONTENTS OF THIS BOOK AND SPECIFICALLY DISCLAIM ANY IMPLIED WARRANTIES OF MERCHANTABILITY OR FITNESS FOR A PARTICULAR PURPOSE. NO WARRANTY MAY BE CREATED OR EXTENDED BY SALES REPRESENTATIVES OR WRITTEN SALES MATERIALS. THE ADVICE AND STRATEGIES CONTAINED HEREIN MAY NOT BE SUITABLE FOR YOUR SITUATION. YOU SHOULD CONSULT WITH A PROFESSIONAL WHERE APPROPRIATE. NEITHER THE PUBLISHER NOR THE AUTHOR SHALL BE LIABLE FOR DAMAGES ARISING HEREFROM.

For general information on our other products and services, please contact our Customer Care Department within the U.S. at 877-762-2974, outside the U.S. at 317-572-3993, or fax 317-572-4002. For technical support, please visit https://hub.wiley.com/community/support/dummies.

Wiley publishes in a variety of print and electronic formats and by print-on-demand. Some material included with standard print versions of this book may not be included in e-books or in print-on-demand. If this book refers to media such as a CD or DVD that is not included in the version you purchased, you may download this material at http://booksupport.wiley.com. For more information about Wiley products, visit www.wiley.com.

Library of Congress Control Number: 2017962794

ISBN 978-1-119-43439-9 (pbk); ISBN 978-1-119-43444-3 (ebk); ISBN 978-1-119-43442-9 (ebk)

Manufactured in the United States of America

10 9 8 7 6 5 4 3 2

Contents at a Glance

Table of Contents

Introduction

So you've familiarized yourself with the world of investing and you're ready to dive in, or perhaps you're already in the market but looking for more tools to improve your stock picking and portfolio management. Great! Charting gives you a way to visualize trends in the market. You can help improve your visualization with various tools that we show you how to use in this book, such as overlays and indicators. You also get to explore many different chart types, including candlestick charts, bar charts, line charts, and area charts, as well as discover the pros and cons of each chart type.

Beyond the basics, we introduce you to various strategies you can use to organize and manage your charts to make your stock trading easier and more successful. Yes, you'll still risk taking a loss when trading stocks, but with these tools we can help you minimize losses if one of your stocks takes an unexpected dive.

About This Book

First we introduce you to the basics of getting started in the world of stock charting. Then we take you on a tour of the most common charts that are used by traders. After you understand how to build these charts, we focus on chart settings and how the various options can impact your trading decision making. Finally we discuss how you can organize and manage your charts to trade more effectively and efficiently.

When you feel comfortable with stock charting, it's time to develop your own style. We show you how to put all you've learned into building a trading style using charts to improve your stock trading decision making.

You don't have to read this book from cover to cover (but we won't mind if you do!); simply find the topic you're interested in, read up on it, and put away the book until you need it again. And you can skip anything that's marked with the Technical Stuff icon or included in a shaded box called a sidebar; such information is interesting but not crucial to understanding a given topic.

Within this book, you may note that some web addresses break across two lines of text. If you're reading this book in print and want to visit one of these web pages, simply key in the web address exactly as it's noted in the text, pretending as though the line break doesn't exist. If you're reading this as an e-book, you've got it easy — just click the web address to be taken directly to the web page.

Foolish Assumptions

We've made a number of assumptions about your basic knowledge and stock-trading abilities. We assume that you're not completely new to the world of investing in stocks and that you're familiar with the stock market and its basic language. Although we review many key terms and phrases as we explore the basics of charting, if everything you read sounds totally new to you, you probably need to read a basic book on investing in stocks before trying to move on to the more technical world of charting.

We also assume that you know how to operate a computer and use the Internet. If you don't have high-speed access to the Internet now, be sure you have it before you try to trade stocks. Many of the resources we recommend in this book are available online, but you need high-speed access to be able to work with many of these valuable tools.

Icons Used in This Book

For Dummies books use little pictures, called icons, to flag certain chunks of text. Here's what they actually mean:

TIP

Watch for these little flags to get ideas on how to improve your charting skills or where to find other useful resources.

REMEMBER

We mark information that's particularly important for you to remember with this icon.

WARNING

If you read the charts wrong, mistakes can be made. A minor mistake can cost you a bunch of money, so we use this icon to point out particularly perilous areas.

TECHNICAL STUFF

We use this icon to point out information that's interesting but not crucial to your understanding of the topic at hand.

Beyond the Book

In addition to the material in the print or e-book you're reading right now, this product also comes with some access-anywhere goodies on the web. When you just want a quick reminder of charting basics, go to www.dummies.com and search for "Stock Charts For Dummies Cheat Sheet" in the Search box. There you'll find explanations on how to find key chart settings, various chart types you can use, key decision-making tools you can add to charts, and how to use charts for spotting trends.

Where to Go from Here

You're ready to enter the exciting world of charting. You can start anywhere in this book. Each of the chapters is self-contained. But if you're totally new to charting, starting with Chapter 1 is the best way to understand the basics. If you already know the basics, you may want to start with Part 3 on using charts to make investing decisions. Remember, though, to have fun and enjoy your trip.

1

Getting Started with Stock Charts

IN THIS PART . . .

Begin with the basics of building your stock charts.

Use charting to minimize your emotional response to the ups and downs of the market.

Chapter **1**

Brushing Up on Stock Charting Basics

You can find hundreds of books talking about technical analysis and stock charting, but if you don't build your stock charts properly to do that analysis, you could end up getting the wrong information. In this book we introduce you to the various types of stock charts out there, as well as the tools you can use to make these charts work even better for you when you're trying to make stock buying and selling decisions. This chapter gives you the basics.

Minimizing the Emotional Roller Coaster of Investing

Before you even start working with charts, it's important to understand how your emotions can help make good and bad stock purchase and sale decisions. In Chapter 2, we discuss the key emotional drivers of stock trading decisions and what economic forces drive those decisions (such as changes within a company and the effect of institutional investors). We also explain how building charts can help you track stock price changes and control emotions, and we provide some fundamentals on index charts and trends.

REMEMBER

Getting a better understanding of your own emotional reactions to these key factors that can impact the movement of stocks can help you make better business decisions based on facts rather than emotions.

Viewing Stocks from Varying Perspectives

Not all charts look the same or are meant to give you the same information. In Part 2 we introduce you to the key types of charts — candlestick charts, bar charts, line charts, and area charts. We show you how to build these charts using tools on StockCharts.com (www.StockCharts.com). Click the green button on the home page that says, "Free 1-Month Trial," and you'll have one month to try out the members-only sections of www.StockCharts.com for free.

REMEMBER

All chartists should know how to build these critical chart types:

>> **Candlestick charts:** These charts give you a detailed view of key stock information daily: open, high, low, and close.

>> **Bar charts:** These charts give you less detail than a candlestick chart does — only the opening price and the closing price — but they can be easier to read than candlestick charts.

>> **Line charts:** These charts show you the stock price trend with a simple line, which makes it easier to view a stock's trend over a long period of time.

>> **Area charts:** These charts show you the same information as a line chart, but they can be more dramatic because the area below the line is a solid color. They are most commonly found on TV financial news.

Discovering All the Tools You Can Use with Your Charts

As you become more familiar with the types of charts, you'll find out that many variables can make the chart look different and offer you different information. Some of the key variables include

>> **Time frames:** In Chapter 8 we discuss the critical time periods you can set for various types of decision making and how each of these time frames impacts the information you see on the chart. Choosing the wrong time frame for the decision you're trying to make could lead to a bad decision.

>> **Using a price chart:** With the proper tools, a price chart can help you determine the trends in the stock market. In Chapter 9, we show you how to spot uptrends and downtrends in a stock price, help you determine volatility and its impact on price, and give you suggestions about what to do if a stock isn't trending. We also talk about the various types of bases you may find in a stock chart and how these bases can impact your decision making. You'll also find information about determining whether a stock price is likely to start falling.

>> **Using overlays:** Overlays are powerful tools that make it easier for you to read a stock chart. We don't introduce every type of overlay, just the ones that are good for beginning chartists to use. In Chapter 10, we introduce you to some handy overlays to help you get started. One of the most common is moving averages. Actually, you can find overlays for many types of moving averages. We introduce the key ones and explain the information they can show when they are used. We also introduce Keltner channels and Bollinger Bands.

>> **Using indicators:** Indicators are another type of tool you can add to a chart. There are many types of indicators; we introduce you to the best ones for beginners in Chapters 11 and 12. You find momentum indicators and how to use them, as well as various types of indicators to determine the strength of a stock.

Getting Organized with Your Charts

After you're familiar with the various types of charts and tools available, it's time for you to start organizing how the charts can help you with your stock investing or trading decisions. Check out the following:

>> In Chapter 13, we introduce you to the power of organizing your choices by industry groups and/or sectors. This task enables you to improve your stock picking.

>> We show you how to keep track of what's going on with your stocks in Chapter 14. This task lets you better manage your stock portfolio.

>> Chapter 15 focuses on various types of indexes you can use in your charts to help you compare your stocks to the broader market. This task enables you to better analyze how your portfolio is doing versus the broader market.

>> Chapter 16 gives you strategies for doing a weekly check of the stocks you're holding or watching. This task helps you more efficiently track your portfolio.

Customizing Your Charts

After you have a good handle on what tools you like to use consistently for various types of decisions you need to make, you'll want to save these various chart styles to make it easier to use them again and again. In Part 5, we show you how to customize your charts and save the ones you like. You find out how to personalize your charts by seeing how various combinations of indicators and overlays can help support your personal trading style.

Putting Everything Together

Ultimately, it's time to take everything you've learned and put it all together to help you make better buying and selling decisions. We discuss some strategies in Part 6 that help you use your charts to gauge the market's direction as well as identify leading sectors and the best stocks in those sectors. You can use these techniques to narrow your focus to the sectors in which you want to invest or trade. We also show you how to build your charts to more effectively use these tools in order to improve your investing or trading results.

REMEMBER

We can't guarantee that you'll always sell stock for a profit, but we do believe using the tools we show you in this book will help you improve your buy and sell decisions. You find tips for how to pull together everything discussed to make good use of stock charts in the future and help you better understand how to use the information discussed in books like *Trading For Dummies*, 4th Edition, by Lita Epstein, MBA, and Grayson D. Roze and *Technical Analysis For Dummies*, 3rd Edition, by Barbara Rockefeller (both published by Wiley).

Chapter 2

Using Charts to Minimize Your Emotional Roller Coaster

To minimize the risks of owning stocks, you need to develop strategies for reducing your emotional reactions to the ups and downs of the market. Instead, think of your portfolio purely as a business at which you want to make money. Don't fall in love with any part of your portfolio. With the help of the fundamentals in this chapter, you can use stock charts to take the emotions out of your decision making.

Getting Ready for the Emotions of Owning a Stock

One of the hardest things to do is to watch your money invested in stocks drop in value on any given day for any reason. This emotional turmoil is one of the difficult parts of investing or trading in the stock market, especially for new entrants.

In the following sections, we describe two important actions you can take to prepare yourself for this turmoil: understanding a few basics of the stock market and arming yourself with information to level the playing field.

Understanding a few market basics

The benefit of the stock market is that you can make your stock work for you by managing your portfolio. After you get comfortable with the little swings in the market, investing gets easier. Investors are inclined to worry about big market drops as they can do tremendous damage to a portfolio. Interestingly enough, most brokers don't move you out of a falling stock market either. To compound that market turbulence, the news commentators try to report on stocks like they would any crisis every day, creating a lot of uncertainty. You need to find ways to address this uncertainty. One way to do that is to understand more about the markets and how to read the trends using stock charts. In the following sections, we explain a few things that can impact a stock's price movement and how you can address them with minimal emotion.

REMEMBER

By controlling your own investments or even following along with a broker's investment choices, you can have an understanding of the macro part of the economy. While you may not move out of harm's way when the market is set up to fail immediately, you can at least understand when to be more cautious. You may also recognize which *sectors* (different areas of the economy, such as finance or energy) of the economy are breaking down. This recognition can help you avoid these potholes.

News noise

If you turn on any financial TV show, you find people reporting news about stocks in almost the same way they would a sporting event. As you become more accustomed to working with charts, you'll find most of the news to be just noise, with maybe a few bits of information you can use as further research with your charting.

A great example of news noise is gross domestic product (GDP). *Gross domestic product* is how much economic activity is happening in the economy. You continually hear that an economy is growing fast or slow. However, the stock market doesn't speed up or slow down based on this news. When the economy and the stock market are compared side by side, it is clear that one does not predict or follow the other. In the United States, the GDP has ranged from positive 5 percent growth (which is huge) in some quarters, to negative growth in other quarters. The stock market does not reflect this huge variance.

If a country's GDP were soaring at 4 percent over two quarters, you would think the stock market would be too. If a country is sporting 4 percent GDP but the stock market has been going lower for the same six months, the GDP is not a timely clue for investors to use for investing. Over long periods of time, if the country's economic output is improving, the stock market is probably improving.

Changes inside a company

Stocks are also hit by other forces that you as the owner of shares in an individual company may be unaware of. Changes in government policy toward the company, internal problems in the company, or changes in sales of finished products for the company can have a positive or negative effect on the stock, long before any announcement.

For example, suppliers have insider knowledge about how things are going at the companies they supply. They can quickly determine whether a company is increasing or decreasing its order size. They may notice the first signs of a company in trouble, because the bills are being paid more slowly or the company is cutting down on standing orders.

The employees within the company may also have a better feel for what is happening inside a company or industry. While it is illegal to trade your own company stock or tell other people to trade with insider knowledge, there is no law against buying your competitors' stock just before a quarterly or annual report on earnings if you see the industry improving. These outside forces can be a long way from your scope of knowledge. The larger the company, the harder it is to know about all the pieces.

Reading reports by analysts may give you some hint of what they are expecting to see in the upcoming quarterly or annual company reporting. You can never know for sure what is going to happen until it is formally announced by a company, but the financial press certainly may alert you to the possibility of a major news story regarding a particular company or its stock.

Institutional investors

Institutional investors are large investors that buy millions of dollars of shares in individual stocks. They may be fund managers like Fidelity, hedge funds, large family trusts, or huge brokers with big clients.

With millions of dollars at stake, some investment companies go to extreme lengths to keep track of activity. Here are a few examples:

>> They interview every management member they can for clues. One concern about this is that the company leadership isn't going to tell you to sell the shares. They will always find something on which to put a positive spin.

>> Some large investors use satellites to track vehicle traffic at box stores like Lowes and Home Depot. If they think the volume is improving in various parts of the country, they've obtained powerful knowledge that the average retail investor doesn't have.

>> For holiday shopping seasons, institutional investors buy traffic-flow monitoring data from survey companies that place employees in malls to count customer traffic. They compare that store-level knowledge with the car volume from the satellite monitoring companies. Then they try to figure out who is getting the sales and who is not.

While a company stock may still jump up or down on an earnings announcement, lots of serious investors are willing to make sure they have a good idea as to whether the company is going to have a good number.

For an investor without helicopters, satellites, money, interview suppliers, and management teams to disperse, these tactics can all sound a little overwhelming, but don't let them scare you. You can level the playing field by being nimble and using different sources of data, as you find out in the next section.

Leveling the playing field

Framing a range of how well a company is doing can help an individual investor. Is the company doing better now than last month or a year ago? How can you gather that information? Are things improving? How can you follow this information? You get a couple of ideas in the following sections.

Tracking institutional investors

If large institutional investors are buying up the stock, that's probably a good clue. Conversely, if they are selling the stock, that is still a clue, just not a positive one. They're not really interested in telling everyone else what they are doing, but they do have to release their current holdings in a stock, and this information can be timely.

For a stock to move up in price, it needs the large institutional investors to start investing in the stock. If enough large institutional investors are trying to buy up the stock, this action pushes the price higher. As the price goes higher, most investors are happy to keep owning the stock because they are making money. Conversely, when large institutions want to sell their position and there aren't enough buyers, this pushes the stock down.

TIP

The key for tracking moves by institutional investors is trading volume. In Chapter 3, we talk about how to display volume on charts. When these investors are making a big move in a stock, whether buying or selling, the volume of trades goes up. If they are selling, you will likely see a downward trend in stock price.

If they are buying, you will likely see an upward trend in stock price. You find discussions about volume throughout this book.

Studying pressures on stock prices

When a stock sale takes place, a buyer is buying the shares from a seller. When more investors are trying to buy shares than sell shares over a short period, this pushes the price up. You may hear that there can't be more buyers than sellers — that the numbers are equal. But the number of people with the desire to buy can be higher than the number of people with the desire to sell. The way that comes into balance is through the buyer raising his bid to buy the shares. The imbalance is where you see the price forced to trade higher, so the seller is motivated to let the shares be sold to a buyer who is willing to pay more.

Understanding that stocks trading higher in price are probably moving higher because there are more buyers than sellers is an important piece of knowledge. You have a way to see that actually happening. Using a stock chart can give you this information.

REMEMBER

While you can't keep track of a stock price in your head for every stock in the market, you can use the history of the stock price, and this information can be shown on a stock chart. A stock price moving up is the sum of all known information about the stock at any given time by investors. Some may have more information or less information, but the price of the stock reflects a balance between buyers' and sellers' opinions. Throughout this book, we show you how to take advantage of the history you can see in charts to help you make better buying and selling decisions.

Building a Chart to Track and Control Emotions

Stock charts create a frame of reference for the current price. Is the price above the previous high prices for the last year? Is the price at the lowest price of the year? Is the price wobbling within a range and not really doing anything significant?

Throughout this book, we show you how to use various types of charts and their tools to help you better understand market trends and make better trading and investing decisions. Using charts not only helps keep your emotions in check as you invest but also helps you track emotions and opinions that investors have about particular stocks.

Figure 2-1 shows a stock chart using a price bar to represent the trading range for a day (see Chapter 5 for an introduction to bar charts). The top of the bar represents the high and the bottom of the bar represents the low. The little tab on the left is where the price started in the morning, and the little tab on the right is where the price closed at the end of trading. The stock shown is Cabot Oil and Gas (COG).

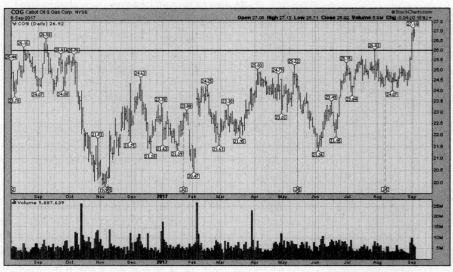

FIGURE 2-1:
A stock chart showing new highs.

Around September 1, 2017, the price pushed up above $26 to new highs. It had pushed up against this level a few times before and fallen back. Eventually, enough buyers took an interest in the stock to push it above $26. You can also see that the volume (depicted in the bottom panel) was around 5 million shares a day as a rough average for most of August. All of a sudden, the volume accelerated, and three trading days had a total volume of roughly 22 million, or more than 7 million shares a day. That extra volume of 7 million shares at $26/share is probably not a household investor buying shares. That totals over $182 million.

Using the chart, you can very quickly see the previous lows and highs on the chart. Because the stock is trading in the top right corner at fresh one-year highs, the stock looks to be hitting the ceiling of the chart.

TECHNICAL STUFF

Charting software fills the chart using the previous highs and previous lows. To do this, it adjusts the scale. As the stock price continues higher, the software adjusts the scale to accommodate the latest price information and fill the space vertically.

By using charts, you can see the broad picture of all the investors, and the price action shows you that they were buying more stock as the price made new highs. Without doing any investigating into the company's earnings or the products it's selling, your first clue is that opinions are getting more optimistic, a trend that is showing up in large institutional-size investing.

After you have a frame of reference for the price on the right-hand side of the chart, you can look back through the history to see other pieces of information. When and how did the stock bottom out? What was the size of the trading range for the year? Are the price bars changing in size? You can see that the stock has been moving higher on a jagged path since the lowest price in November 2016.

Checking Out Index Charts

Charts based on a particular index help you visualize how a group of stocks are affected by price changes in the market. Figure 2-1 shows a daily stock chart for one particular stock. Figure 2-2 shows the daily chart for a group of 30 stocks added together to represent an average. Making up this index are some banks; brokers; insurance, computer hardware, computer software, and energy companies; and others. This is called the Dow Jones Industrial Average (commonly called the Dow). The ticker symbol is $INDU on StockCharts.com. The companies in the index are chosen by the Dow Jones Company. By keeping track of the general price direction for some of the largest stocks in the United States, you can determine whether the stock market is moving higher or lower.

The chart of the index shows that the Dow has been rising quickly and moving from the bottom left to the top right. The last price on the right is near all-time highs. While the market doesn't go up every day, the general trend is up.

The chart of Cabot Oil and Gas in Figure 2-1 was not nearly as great-looking for the last year, but the recent price action is improving. As the economy rolls along, some sectors improve and others fall behind. Then management in those companies tries to get more efficient to improve the company performance. This cycle continues every day but takes time to play out. If all the companies are struggling to make higher profits, the index reflects this weakness in investor opinion. By keeping track of the index, you get a picture for the broader group of stocks.

The following sections provide just a few examples of stock indexes you can follow.

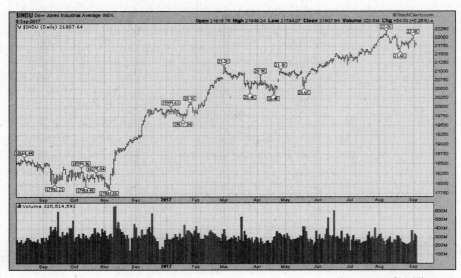

FIGURE 2-2:
An index chart.

Indexes around the world

You can track various indexes around the globe. Table 2-1 notes the key ones to track.

TABLE 2-1

Key Indexes to Track

Index Name	Ticker Symbol
Dow Jones Industrial Average 30 Stocks	$INDU
S&P 500 list of 500 major U.S. companies	$SPX
S&P 100 List of the Top 100 U.S. Companies	$OEX
NASDAQ 100 list of top stocks on the NASDAQ	$NDX
Index for all the stocks on the NYSE	$NYA
Index for all the stocks on the NASDAQ	$COMPQ
Russell 1000 holds the largest 1,000 companies	$RUI
Russell 2000 holds about 2,000 small-cap companies	$RUT
Canadian Stock Exchange	$TSX
London Stock Exchange	$FTSE

There are indexes for the entire world. There are indexes for each country and for each geographic region. There are commodity indexes, currency indexes, and bond indexes as well. There are charts for comparing currencies; for example, the $USDCAD compares the U.S. dollar exchange rate to the Canadian dollar. You can put together a chart of your favorite indexes based on the types of stocks in which you choose to invest.

Charts of the indexes can give you a sense of the value relative to the past. By using indexes around the world, you can evaluate the investor sentiment toward those asset classes without doing in-depth, fundamental analysis of resources written in a foreign language.

Commodity indexes

A commodity is any basic good that can be sold on the market, such as energy products (like oil and gas) and farm products (like wheat and corn). When you see the long-term price chart of 19 different commodities shown in Figure 2-3, what does that chart tell you very quickly? The scale across the bottom is measured in years from 1968 to 2017. The price is only the end-of-month price, which communicates what you want to know without the daily trading details. The price on the commodity index ($CRB) broke to new 45-year lows in 2016. Why are the commodities that the world has been built on at the lowest prices in 45 years? In one picture, the chart has probably altered your perception of what is going on in the world. Without doing thousands of hours of research into each commodity, you can see a significant change in the world based on investor attitudes to those asset classes.

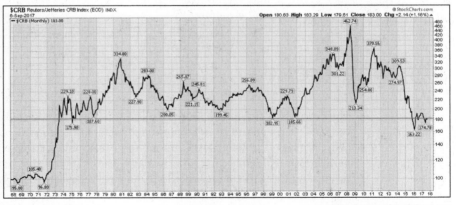

FIGURE 2-3:
The commodities
($CRB) index.

Chart courtesy of StockCharts.com

The S&P 500

The main stock index that all investors worldwide pay attention to is the S&P 500. This is really the best anchor point from which to view the U.S. market and the main index that all other markets are compared to.

What makes it such an important anchor is the number of companies inside the index and the broad cross section of the economy. Figure 2-4 displays three years of information, but each price bar represents one week. What also makes the S&P 500 information so valuable is that no specific sector of the economy is too large within the index.

FIGURE 2-4:
The S&P 500
($SPX) index.

REMEMBER

For investors, understanding the direction of the S&P 500 ($SPX) is the best way to gauge the broad economy.

Defining Trends

The contrast between the four charts in this chapter gives you a glimpse of the value of using charts to help you make trading or investing decisions. On each chart, there are trends where you see the price move in a general direction for a period of time. Trends can last a few days, weeks, or months. Understanding these trends and the direction in which the market is moving helps reduce your anxiety about trading and minimize the emotional roller coaster of investing. When you feel anxious about a trade, take the time to review your charts and determine whether the change you see in the trend differs from your original plan for trading the stock. Then you can make a less emotional decision about whether to buy, hold, or sell the stock.

On Figure 2-4, a trend line has been drawn in to highlight the uptrend. Making money using charts usually involves defining a new uptrend and recognizing the end of the trend. (See Chapter 9 for more about uptrends and downtrends.)

The horizontal line on the chart shows an area where the stock market couldn't make higher highs. Until the price broke above that area, the market was stalled. When the index started to make higher highs, you can see that the uptrend was strong and continued for a period of time.

The right edge of the chart shows the price rubbing against this slanted trend line drawn in by connecting the lows on the chart. With trends in stocks and indexes, you can use charts to help you enter and exit the market.

2

Viewing the Money Trail through Different Lenses

IN THIS PART . . .

Sort out the various chart settings you can use on StockCharts.com.

Light up with candlestick charts, which display price movement throughout the day.

Build a picture with bar charts, which show price movement but don't have as much price detail as candlestick charts, which can make it easier to find trends.

Check out the trends with line charts, which focus on closing prices.

Use area charts, which look like line charts but with a twist.

Chapter **3**

Focusing on Chart Settings

How you set up your chart enables you to get a clear picture of a stock's trend. In this chapter we show you how to use the flexibility of charting to build a useable display using three key components: chart attributes, overlays, and indicators.

In Figure 3-1 from StockCharts.com, you can see that the place for setting parameters, known as the workbench, is below the chart. You can access this tool for setting up charts online at stockcharts.com/freecharts/ under SharpCharts. You can then work through the steps online as we describe the process.

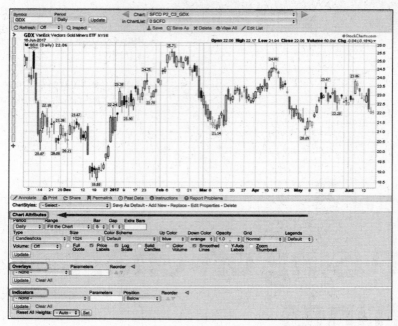

FIGURE 3-1:
Where to find
chart attributes,
overlays, and
indicators.

Chart courtesy of StockCharts.com

Choosing Chart Attributes

Chart attributes give you the primary choices for how you want to set up your chart. Chart attributes define things like the size and shape, the type of price display and color, and the background. Because there are different price display types like candlesticks, bars, and lines, each chart has different display requirements and choices. To show you how this works, we take you through the steps of seting up a chart in this section.

Some important decisions you have to make are the amount of data to display and how you want to display that data. These choices include the time period for the chart, the number of periods you want to display, the setup for the bars, and the type of chart. You also choose the colors and other appearance attributes.

Starting with the time period, range, and spacing

The first group of settings includes the time period for each bar, the dates you would like to see, and the spacing.

Period

When it comes to charts, the most popular time period for investors and swing traders is daily. This means that price information will be for one day. You can see how to set the periods in Figure 3-2. Common time period choices include

» Monthly

» Weekly

» Daily (shown in Figure 3-2)

» 1 Hour

» 5 Minutes

» 1 Minute

For this book, we focus on daily charts. In Chapter 8, we discuss when other time periods should be considered.

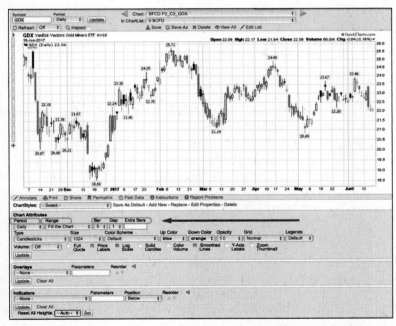

FIGURE 3-2: Period, range, and spacing selections.

Chart courtesy of StockCharts.com

Range

Range displays how many periods you want to display, which is an important choice depending on the information you seek. Stock charts show quickly, without a lot of description, where price has been for a particular period of time. When you set the range, you know the stock's movement for that period of time.

Some default range settings are

>> 1 day

>> 5 days

>> 10 days

>> 1 month (roughly 22 trading days)

>> 3 months (25 percent of a year, 63 trading days)

>> 6 months (50 percent of a year, 129 trading days)

>> 12 months (one year, 258 trading days)

>> 3 years

>> 5 years

>> 10 years

>> Year to Date

>> Select Start/End Date

>> Fill the Chart (as shown in Figure 3-2)

Traders or investors choose a time frame based on the type of decisions they want to make. For example:

>> Short-term traders select a three-month time frame most often, because they plan to exit in the same day or within a few days. The three-month time frame gives them enough information to see the trend visually, but not too much information that can make it difficult to see an exit point. These charts can be intraday to describe what is happening for the day. Using a chart with five to ten days broken into one-hour candles can show a stock starting to improve or break down.

>> Investors are less concerned with intraday movements and tend to select a one-year chart so they can catch longer trends. Because they will likely hold a stock for months or years, investors want to see how the stock has done over many years rather than just a few months. When they are trying to pick an entry or exit point, long-term investors will look to monthly charts.

>> Institutional investors tend to use 20-year charts with monthly time frames, but they will look at many different time frames as they make decisions for their portfolios.

The range selection has a relationship with the individual time period. Chart users will want to pair enough data to see the trend that gives them the ability to see the most recent information clearly.

Bar, gap, and extra bars

This area of the chart attributes changes automatically on StockCharts.com depending on which range you use. Set the range to Fill the Chart, so the software will calculate settings using three components. The software uses the width of each daily price bar, the space between the bars (gap), and the extra bars setting to pick the number of days to display. When you get more expertise, you may want to do your own fills, but that's more complicated than you need to get right now. In Figure 3-2, the width of each bar is 5, and the space between the bars (the gap) is 1.

The extra bars setting is a hidden gem. This setting allows white space on the right-hand side of the chart so the last price bar is not pushed up against the side of the chart. Typically, an extra bars setting may be 5 or 10 bars. You can set this manually by putting the number of extra bars in the Extra Bars box.

Defining the price display

Now take a look at the next area of chart attributes. Here you set the type, size, and color of price information (see Figure 3-3).

Type

Type refers to the type of display for the price information. Common display types are as follows (we discuss each type of chart and how best to use it in the chapters indicated):

>> Candlesticks (Chapter 4; this type is shown in Figure 3-3)

>> Bar (Chapter 5)

>> Line (Chapter 6)

>> Area (Chapter 7)

>> Performance (Chapter 12)

Size

People read charts on many different types of devices, including desktops, laptops, tablets, or phones, so the size of the chart is a personal decision based on the device you're using to view the chart.

FIGURE 3-3:
Type, size, and
color scheme
settings.

TIP

With the huge variety of display surfaces, individuals will want to optimize the chart to fit on the display they have. For example, for mobile phones, smaller charts are better. It makes sense to have specific lists of charts set up to browse on the various devices you use. You can set up custom settings for each of your devices to improve the percentage of the screen that your charts cover. In Figure 3-3, the size of 1024 is typical for a laptop.

Color scheme

Everyone has personal favorite colors. You can choose the colors for your chart display. Background color is the first critical choice. This parameter personalizes the chart and allows you to control the overall mood of the display. Using black or dark backgrounds for a change from traditional white space on presentation charts can grab attention. For printing your charts, white backgrounds are best. Using white with gridlines helps for printing, but various color backdrops can help make your chart your own.

TIP

If you're sharing charts on social media, black or dark backgrounds stand out in the scrolling but are harder to read. Lightly shaded backgrounds can improve the attractiveness of the chart while still providing uniqueness.

TIP

Accessibility options on the computer are very important, and many mainstream users find that some accessibility settings help them. The same is true in charting software. Depending on the quality of your vision, certain themes for the charts may be softer on the eyes. If you have specific vision issues, we recommend trying different backgrounds from the drop-down menu. For example, people with light sensitivity may want to use dark backgrounds, while people who need a lot of brightness on the charts may choose white or light colors for the background. You can also enhance the display choices of the data in front of the background to make the information stand out. When you change the background, it is very common to alter the price display so the two parts complement each other.

You may find the wide range of drop-down menus for setting colors daunting, so initially use the default settings to get you started (as shown in Figure 3-3). As you become more familiar with charting and your personal preferences, you can start playing with the colors of the price information to help you personalize your chart.

Up color and down color

Colors can also be used to show whether the stock is moving up or down. For example, you can use green for up and red for down, or you can set them to be the same. You may choose to use gold for both up and down on a chart displaying the price of gold. We go into the merits of using different colors as we discuss different decision-making strategies throughout this book. Figure 3-4 shows blue for the up color and orange for the down color.

Opacity

Opacity allows you to darken or lighten the price bars. A setting of 1.0 (as shown in Figure 3-4) means as bright as possible. An opacity of 0.0 makes the price invisible. The opacity tool is very nice for using area charts that you commonly see on TV. The opacity options are Auto, 0.9, 0.8, 0.7, 0.6, 0.5, 0.4 0.3, 0.2, 0.1, and 0.0. *Note:* This feature is available only for members.

Grid

Grid lines are easy to see on the screen. The grid setting allows you to adjust the look of the grid lines as well as the darkness of the lines. Your options are

>> Off

>> Normal (shown in Figure 3-4)

>> Dashed

>> Dense

FIGURE 3-4:
Additional color
and appearance
settings.

>> Normal (Dark)

>> Dashed (Dark)

>> Dense (Dark)

Note: This feature is available only for members.

Legends

This area controls how much information is shown in the legend. You can see the legend choices at the far right after the grid choices. The legend information is the amount of information about the stock(s) in the chart and is shown at the top left of the chart. Here are the options:

>> **None:** Removes all information

>> **Minimal:** Shows just the ticker symbol

>> **Default:** Includes overlays and indicator names (this setting is shown in Figure 3-4)

>> **Verbose:** Spells out the company name instead of the ticker symbol

Displaying volume and toggles

Volume, which measures the number of stock trades in a day, tends to be a supportive indicator. High volume at certain times can be critical for helping with price discovery. How volume is displayed is unique and not the same as other charting information.

Volume can be toggled on or off by using the volume drop-down menu shown in Figure 3-5 on the left side of the check-mark toggles. The options are

>> **Off:** No volume is displayed.

>> **Overlay:** The volume is displayed inside the price panel.

>> **Separate:** The volume is displayed below the price panel.

In Figure 3-5, the volume is set in the overlay position. If price is in the bottom corner of the chart, seeing the price or the volume can be problematic because they overlap. Using the drop-down menu to choose Separate moves the volume bars below the price panel into a separate display.

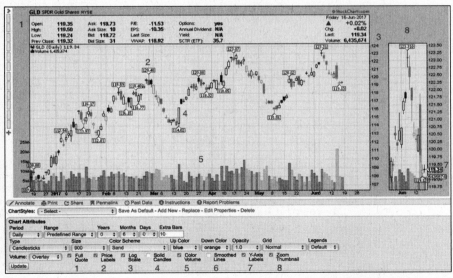

FIGURE 3-5: Volume and toggles.

Chart courtesy of StockCharts.com

Eight toggles are listed across the bottom of the chart, as shown in Figure 3-5:

1. **Full Quote:** Adds the Text panel on the top of the chart.

2. **Price Labels:** Puts the price label on the price bars at highs and lows.

3. **Log Scale:** Uses a percentage grid for long time periods where the price has moved substantially.

4. **Solid Candles:** Fills in hollow candles like the big one next to the "4." This is strictly a matter of user preference.

5. **Color Volume:** Shades the up days different from the down days.

6. **Smoothed Lines:** Makes the lines on line charts look smoother.

7. **Y-Axis Labels:** Adds the current price label onto the vertical axis on the far-right edge of the chart.

8. **Zoom Thumbnail:** Adds the box on the right with the last 18 price bars.

Setting Overlays

Overlays are display formats you add to a stock chart that help you understand price movement. You build overlays by clicking in the Overlays area below a chart. In the drop-down box where it says "None" (refer to Figure 3-1), you select a choice from the drop-down menu. The charting software automatically gives typical parameters. Each time you add an overlay, a new line below appears with "None" in the drop-down box so you can add another. We help you discover how to apply these overlays for making stock choices throughout this book.

The list of overlay choices is significant. Some of the common overlays are as follows:

» **Moving averages:** Helps you more easily spot a trend by smoothing out price action based on past prices

» **Horizontal line:** Enables you to more easily see the top and bottom of a trend

» **Price channels:** Helps you see the highest high and the lowest low on a chart

» **Bollinger Bands:** Shows the upper and lower limits of normal price movements

» **Keltner channels:** Shows the upper and lower limits for price movements based on an average of prices

» **Moving average envelopes:** Forms a channel using the simple moving averages

» **Events:** Marks important events such as dividends and stock splits

» **Pivot points:** Are used by short-term traders; the points at which the largest price movements are expected

TIP

Two other overlay choices that help you determine when to sell a stock are

» **Chandelier exits:** Helps you set stop-losses for selling a stock

» **Parabolic SAR:** Helps you see trend reversals

To give you an example of a common overlay, Figure 3-6 shows a simple moving average envelope on this chart of Apple Inc. (AAPL).

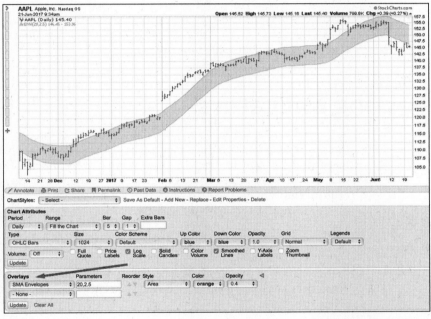

FIGURE 3-6: Overlay example.

Chart courtesy of StockCharts.com

TIP

Plotting things that have similar prices with the same scale (Bond Yield %) uses an overlay called "Price (same scale)." Viewing two stocks on the same price panel does not entail the use of an overlay. For two stocks on the same panel, you use the Indicators drop-down menu with a different display option (see the next section for more on indicators).

The Reorder option allows you to indicate the order for the various overlays you choose. Style lets you pick one of the following:

» Auto

» Solid

>> Solid (Thin)

>> Solid (Thick)

>> Dashed

>> Dashed (Thin)

>> Dashed (Thick)

>> Area

>> Dots

Opacity options are the same as those in the Chart Attributes area. *Note:* These features are available only to members.

Selecting Indicators

Indicators help you see price movement. These options are based on significant research done over the years by some very smart technicians to create indicators that help analyze price movement. Most of the indicators are derived from price, or price and volume. We help you figure out how to apply the indicators for making stock choices throughout this book.

Select an indicator by using the drop-down menu where the word "None" is in Figure 3-7. The MACD (Moving Average Convergence Divergence) is shown as the first indicator in the figure. This is a commonly used momentum indicator. The default parameters are put in, and when you click "Update," this indicator appears below the chart.

TIP

Guests at StockCharts.com are able to add indicators but not alter the display. Notice the arrow on the left where we point to indicators. This feature expands for members to set additional display features. Figure 3-7 shows it expanded.

Common indicators

Fifty different indicators are available. Some of the more popular indicators are as follows:

>> **Relative Strength Indicator (RSI):** Shows how strongly a stock is moving in its current direction, whether up or down

>> **Chaikin Money Flow (CMF):** Combines price and volume to show the movement of money in and out of a stock

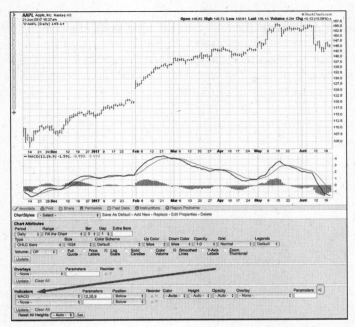

FIGURE 3-7:
Indicators.

Chart courtesy of StockCharts.com

>> **On-Balance Volume (OBV):** Combines price and volume to show how money is moving in and out of a stock

>> **Percent Price Oscillator (PPO):** The percentage-based version of the MACD

>> **Percent Volume Oscillator (PVO):** The PPO indicator applied to volume rather than price

>> **Force Index:** Shows the movement of price and volume

>> **Price Momentum Oscillator (PMO):** Tracks the stock's rate of change

>> **Stochastics:** Shows speed of stock price relative to past movements

>> **StockCharts Technical Ranking (SCTR):** Ranking based on a stock's technical strength

Volume and price as indicators

Two indicators need specific discussion (see Figure 3-8 to see the settings for these indicators):

>> Volume

>> Price

Using the volume indicator setting rather than the volume setting under Chart Attributes allows you to calculate unique things like a moving average of volume. Because volume offers clues in technical analysis, it is used more widely. You can position the volume indicator above the stock data, below the stock data, or behind the price by choosing one of three options: above, below, or behind price.

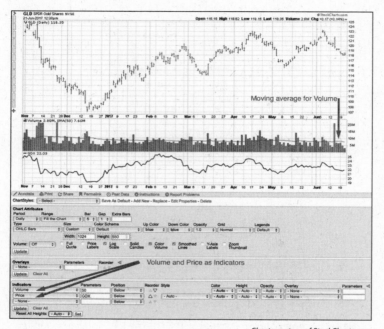

FIGURE 3-8:
Volume and price as indicators.

The price indicator is useful when you want to display two stock prices on the same chart. An example might be the GLD ETF for gold and the GDX ETF, which is an ETF that tracks a group of gold miners. By choosing GLD for the main chart, you can plot the GDX price underneath using the price indicator and add GDX in the parameter box (you can see this setup in Figure 3-8).

If you change the position to "Behind Price," the chart will display both GLD and GDX on the same panel. The scale for the indicator will be on the left.

TIP

An important note: If you're looking at more than one stock, where two prices cross is irrelevant when they are on different scales. Changing the number of days of the chart can change where they cross. There is no information to be gained by looking at where things cross when two stocks have different scales, because the charting software expands/contracts the scale so all the data in the time period fits on the chart.

Chapter **4**

Burning the Candle at Both Ends with Candlestick Charts

Candlestick charts provide users a graphic way to display price movement throughout the day on a daily chart. This type of display first became popular in Japan and today is one of the most popular charts in North America, especially for stock traders who need information for shorter periods of time, such as hourly or daily.

In this chapter, we break down the parts and colors of a candlestick chart, explain how to create one, and show you how to use one to make investing decisions.

REMEMBER

Each person has a different way of thinking about the market, which means different displays can be suited to different types of investors. Many longer-term investors find candlesticks too complex and would like to use something less detailed. You may find bar charts (see Chapter 5) or line charts (see Chapter 6) give you just the right information for what you need.

Deciphering the Parts of a Candlestick Chart

REMEMBER

The name "candlestick" was given to this type of chart because it has a body (or candle) for each day pictured in the chart. The chart reader can see the opening and closing stock price with a wider area in between called the body for each day with a wick strung through the body of the candle. The wicks sticking out from the candlestick bar show the extremes of the price movement throughout the day.

You can see an example of a candlestick chart in Figure 4-1. Each bar represents the price of Apple Inc. for a specific day.

FIGURE 4-1:
Apple Inc.
candlesticks.

Chart courtesy of StockCharts.com

REMEMBER

The important distinction is that the body of the candle reflects what happened during the day:

>> If it is hollow, the close was higher than the open. If it is filled in, the closing price was lower than when the markets opened.

>> On a hollow candle, the close is shown at the top of the body of the candle. On a filled-in candle, the close is shown at the bottom of the body of the candle. If the close is roughly the same as the open, the candle will appear to have no body, like on Apple's chart for May 2. This candle shape is called a *doji*.

Notice the closing price of Apple Inc. on May 3 was lower than on May 2, but the candle is still hollow. The filling of the candle doesn't reflect the change from the day before. It may coincidentally reflect the direction from the previous close. The hollow or filled candle style is a subtle change that makes the individual candles for each day stand out more than other displays we discuss in this book.

The following sections go into more detail on the parts of a candlestick chart.

The candle body

When looking at the body of the candlestick, pay close attention to the components as well as the shapes of the candles.

Candlestick components

Each candle body has several components, which you can see in Figure 4-2. These components provide various pieces of information:

» The opening price in the morning

» The closing price at the end of the day

» The difference between the two prices, which is the body

» Hollow candle moved higher through the day

» Filled candle moved lower through the day

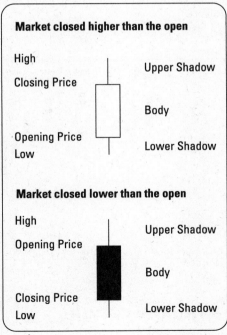

Market closed higher than the open

High

Closing Price

Opening Price

Low

Upper Shadow

Body

Lower Shadow

Market closed lower than the open

High

Opening Price

Closing Price

Low

Upper Shadow

Body

Lower Shadow

FIGURE 4-2: Candlestick components.

© John Wiley & Sons, Inc.

>> The highest price of the day, shown by the top shadow (the upper "wick")

>> The lowest price of the day, indicated by the lower shadow (the lower "wick")

Candlestick shapes

The body of the candle tells you whether the market improved or fell during the day. Its appearance gives you a feel for the price action throughout the day. You can visualize these differences in the candlestick shapes shown in Figure 4-3:

>> A long, hollow body suggests the price moved up significantly in a single day, with buying pressure pushing it aggressively higher. (1)

>> A short, hollow body suggests the market was positive through the day but change was not huge. (2)

>> A line across the middle of the shadow, referred to as a doji, means the market opened and closed at or near the same level, usually meaning the market is balanced at that price. (3)

>> A small, filled candle suggests the market was soft that day without a lot of momentum. (4)

>> A large, filled candle suggests selling pressure was evident as the price moved significantly lower. (5)

FIGURE 4-3:
Candlestick shapes.

Chart courtesy of StockCharts.com

Shadows on a hollow candle

The size of each shadow shows you how far the price moved away from the two key times of the day, the open and the close. You can see the differences in shadows in Figure 4-4. The shadows, or wicks, mean different things on a hollow body of the candle:

>> Long shadows above a hollow candle suggest very little support at the higher level. Bearish. (A bear market is a market in which stock prices are falling. People holding stock tend to begin selling stock.) (1)

>> Short shadows above a hollow body suggest the high was near to the close. Bullish. (A bull market is a market in which stock prices are rising. People tend to buy stock in this type of market.) (2)

>> No shadow above means the price climbed all day and closed at the highest price of the day. Very bullish. (3)

>> Small shadows below a hollow body mean the price tested slightly lower but then went up past the open to close at a higher level. Bullish. (4)

>> Long shadows below a hollow body mean the price moved significantly lower during the day, but then buyers came in and pushed the price back up above the open. Bullish. (5)

FIGURE 4-4: Shadows on hollow candles.

Chart courtesy of StockCharts.com

Shadows on a filled candle

As we note in the preceding section, the size of each wick shows you how far the price moved away from the two key times of the day, the open and the close. The shadows mean different things on a filled body of the candle. Shadow differences on filled candles are shown in Figure 4-5:

>> Long shadows above a filled-in body suggest very little support at the higher level. The price traded higher during the day and then dropped and fell below the open to close down on the day. Bearish. (1)

>> Short shadows above a filled body suggest the price tried to go higher after the open but then traded down, moved below the open, and closed down from there. Bearish. (2)

>> Little or no shadow above means the price opened and fell all day. The close was below the opening price of the day and couldn't go higher. Bearish. (3)

>> Small shadows below a filled body mean the price closed near the lows of the day. Bearish. (4)

>> Long shadows below a filled-in body mean the price moved significantly lower during the day. Buyers then came in and pushed the price back up significantly but not above the opening price for the day. Buyers stepping in and reversing the price back up is bullish. (5)

FIGURE 4-5:
Shadows on filled candles.

Chart courtesy of StockCharts.com

Windows

When the stock market opens in the morning, the opening price may not be the same as the previous day's close. News about the company, the related industry, or other news in politics may have come out after the market closed on the previous day, causing a gap between the previous day's close and the open the next day. The candlestick chart style does not try to connect the price points together. An example of this can be found on the Apache (APA) chart (refer to Figure 4-5) on April 27. On a candlestick chart these are called *windows* rather than gaps.

Introducing Color onto a Candlestick Chart

Introducing color on a candlestick chart is a method of quickly comparing the current candle's price to yesterday's closing price. The software uses the difference between a close higher than the day before or lower than the day before. For example, choosing one color that will show a close higher than the day before highlights an up day. Using a second color for a day when the market closes lower than the day before highlights a down day.

The majority of the time, the information from the hollow or filled candlestick coincides with the color code of the day:

>> A hollow candle that shows price moved up from the open to the close may also show that the price closed up compared to the previous day.

>> A filled candle shows price moved down from the open to the close. This closing price may also be lower than the close of the previous day.

TIP

While we can't show you color in this black-and-white print book, you can go to www.stockcharts.com and try it out yourself. In the create-a-chart box in the top middle of the screen, type in a stock symbol like BAC for Bank of America. This will show a colored candlestick chart of BAC.

You can see two distinguishing candles that show up when you use color to view the candles. Their unique qualities show up best on a color candlestick chart, but you can see the difference in the shading on a monochrome chart as well:

>> The filled candles show price action moving down between the open and close. This becomes even more distinct when color is used because when the price closes above the previous day, the computer will use an up color with a filled candle.

>> The hollow candles show price action moving up between the open and close. When you use color, if the price closes below the previous day, the computer will use the color you chose as the down color with a hollow candle.

Examples of these two unique candles are shown in Figure 4-6. The candles of interest are on March 8 and March 22. These candles show up infrequently but represent important information:

>> The March 8 candle closed below the open but above the previous day. It is a filled candle because it closed below the open, and the colored candlestick chart displays the color of an up day, meaning that it closed above the previous day.

>> On March 22 the intraday price action was up, so the candle is hollow, but the price closed below the previous day, so it is given the color of a down day compared to the day before.

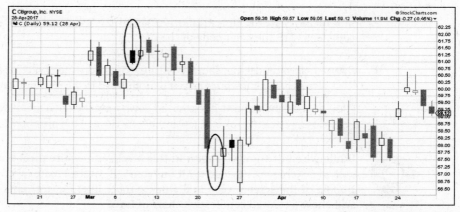

FIGURE 4-6:
Unique candles.

Chart courtesy of StockCharts.com

It does not always work out, but these unique candles sometimes mark turns in the market or important inflection points in the market. In the Citigroup example in Figure 4-6, they marked a short-term high on March 8 and very close to a short-term low on March 22. You can see other instances on the chart where these unique candles had no short-term influence.

Crafting Your Chart

You can set up your own chart with the price displayed using candlesticks. In this section we show you how to create a candlestick chart on www.stockcharts.com. To get started, go to stockcharts.com/freecharts/, enter the stock symbol you're interested in seeing under "Create a SharpChart," and click Go.

In the Chart Attributes area, you can create a candlestick chart by selecting Candlesticks in the Type drop-down menu. StockCharts.com defaults to a candlestick chart type for new visitors to the website. After selecting Candlesticks, you will need to click Update if the chart was in a different display format. You can see the tool for Chart Attributes in Figure 4-7.

FIGURE 4-7: Selecting candlesticks as a chart type.

Chart courtesy of StockCharts.com

TIP

There's no harm in trying some of the other selections for the chart. A good one to change is the size from the Size drop-down menu. For example, you can select Landscape or 900 from the Size menu and click Update. This expands the chart out to the right if you're on a landscape-oriented display, such as a laptop computer.

After changing some of the selections, click the Update button to show your changes on the chart. This action doesn't save the chart style that you create, but it does let you experiment with the settings. Members can save the chart style as a default. In Parts 3 and 4, we introduce all the possible options for creating your own chart style, and in Chapter 17, we show you how to build a customized candlestick chart.

Reading and Using Your Chart to Make Decisions

Candlestick charts are primarily for short-term trading decisions; longer-term traders or investors tend to use candlestick charts to pick entry and exit points. It is important to understand when candles matter most in stock buying and selling decisions; you also need to become familiar with some of the most common patterns. This section introduces those critical decision-making points.

Knowing when candles matter

Candlesticks are built based on intraday price movements, so daily candlesticks aren't typically used with long time horizons of a year or more. For shorter-term trading opportunities, though, candlesticks can be helpful. The following sections discuss short-term signs you may interpret from individual candles and candle groups.

Investigating individual candles

Candlestick signals typically have a life of five to ten candles. In Figures 4-3 and 4-4, the bullish examples show up more often in the direction of the uptrend. As you might expect, it is easier to find hollow candles with a small top shadow in an uptrend. In Figure 4-5, the bearish candles are plentiful in a downtrend. It is easier to find filled candles with small bottom shadows in a downtrend.

REMEMBER

As each candle is interpreted to suggest bullishness or weakness, it is important to realize the next move expected may not follow through on the next candle.

Looking at groups of candles

Individual candles may not be very reliable to trade with, but looking at candles collectively can be helpful. Looking across a few months of candles gives you more information, and trading in the direction of the trend is usually more profitable.

When a stock is in an uptrend, more hollow candles are present. When a break in a trend line occurs, you may experience heavy selling. On most charts, if you can draw a multi-month trend line, the candle that closes below the trend line is usually a big filled candle. (See Chapter 9 for more about trend lines.) An example of a trend line break on Consolidated Edison (ED) is shown in Figure 4-8.

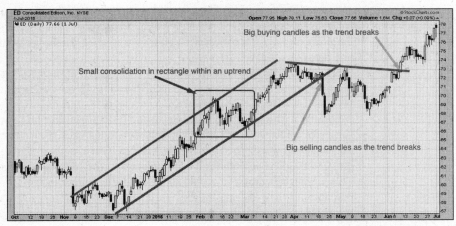

Chart courtesy of StockCharts.com

FIGURE 4-8:
Consolidation.

Pairing two or more candles can be a little more valuable to confirm a pattern within a trending market. How is that done? The first candle sets a bullish or bearish expectation for the next day, and the next day, investors watch to see whether the move based on the directional bias starts to happen. If it does, they investigate buying the stock on that basis and go through a process to decide.

Technical analysis tools work better when stocks are trending. A stock moving sideways for years is hard to profit from. However, a stock moving sideways for a month or so also allows you the opportunity to buy near recent lows. The term for a stock with price action moving sideways is *consolidating*. Consolidating happens when the price of a stock stays between two price levels and moves sideways. The stock shown in Figure 4-8 consolidated for three months between $67 and $73.

Conversely, a sustainable move above a previous consolidation range will usually need to be a larger hollow candle. The thinking behind the candle size is that if the price moves above a consolidation area, the new buyer has to be willing to pay more for the stock than at any time in the consolidation period. If only a few new buyers are willing to buy into the stock at a higher level, the chart is most likely to fall back into the consolidation range. Rarely are timid moves above a consolidation zone the best ones to buy.

Buying based on bullish candlestick patterns

Candlesticks carry a lot of information. Understanding candlestick patterns can be very beneficial to see a change in trend or typical price action that supports a move in the direction of the main trend.

In Figure 4-8, the period from February 26 to March 2 is a great example of seeing a bullish signal on a candlestick chart. First of all, the intermediate trend was up but had consolidated in a small range between $66 and $70 for about a month. After moving down hard on February 27 to the previous low of February 17, the next two candles got very small, showing a loss of downside selling pressure.

On March 2, the stock fell hard after the market opening, but by the end of the day the price had recovered above the previous close and above the open to create a long shadow under the first hollow candle. This shape of candle is a bullish candlestick called a *hammer* and is often seen at the bottom of a countertrend move. This is exactly what you would look for to end a downward move. When March 3 had similar price action (another hammer) and closed higher, this was very strong price action. The stock continued higher for most of March.

TIP

One reason to use a candlestick display is to help find bullish setups. StockCharts.com runs a scan every day looking for hammer candlesticks like the one described earlier and various other candlestick patterns. Using these tools, some investors find good stocks to invest in just using candlesticks. Figure 4-9 shows some of the other candlestick pattern names, and the number of occurrences is shown on the right side under each stock market. In Chapter 14, you find information on how to use and save scans.

Total		Candlestick Patterns	Equities						
			NYSE	Nasdaq	AMEX	OTC	TSE	TSXV	LSE
Bullish Reversal Patterns									
99		Bullish Engulfing	26	38	4	6	12	2	10
3		Piercing Line	0	0	0	2	0	1	0
0		Morning Star	0	0	0	0	0	0	0
25		Bullish Harami	6	10	0	2	1	0	2
5		Three White Soldiers	2	2	1	0	0	0	0
Bearish Reversal Patterns									
69		Bearish Engulfing	12	16	3	1	1	1	5
9		Dark Cloud Cover	1	2	2	0	1	0	1
1		Evening Star	0	1	0	0	0	0	0
20		Bearish Harami	6	2	1	0	2	4	1
11		Three Black Crows	2	2	1	0	1	0	0
Continuation Patterns									
15		Rising Three Methods	8	6	0	0	1	0	0
1		Falling Three Methods	0	0	0	0	0	0	0
Single-Candle Patterns									
7		Dragonfly Doji	0	0	0	0	2	5	0
0		Gravestone Doji	0	0	0	0	0	0	0
54		Hammer	6	10	0	7	6	16	4
38		Shooting Star	7	13	1	4	5	6	1
355		Filled Black Candles	101	76	16	41	28	15	49
270		Hollow Red Candles	39	53	12	63	22	9	55

FIGURE 4-9: Examples of candlestick patterns.

Chart courtesy of StockCharts.com

Chapter **5**

Spotting Differences with Bar Charts

L ooking at the price movement of a stock and trying to glean information from it can seem overwhelming for first-time users. In this chapter, we explore bar charts, which are one of the simplest forms used to view daily price readings.

Beginning with Bar Chart Basics

A bar chart is a chart type that is used for displaying price. When it is displayed in black, the price bars used today look a lot like the price charts from the business section of the newspaper. The following sections go over the structure of a price bar and different kinds of bar charts.

Price bar components

REMEMBER

A price bar has four main components:

» **Open price:** The price at which the stock opens (shown on the left)

» **High price:** The highest price of the day

>> **Low price:** The lowest price of the day

>> **Close price:** The price at which the stock closed for the day (shown on the right)

These four components make up a price bar, shown in Figure 5-1, and the name is abbreviated to a chart style of OHLC Bar (OHLC is an acronym for open–high–low–close).

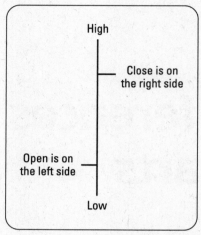

High

Close is on
the right side

Open is on
the left side

Low

FIGURE 5-1:
An OHLC bar.

© John Wiley & Sons, Inc.

Different types of bar charts

When placed day after day, price bars form a picture but do not have the pronounced look of candlesticks (see Chapter 4). You can see the four components of an OHLC bar chart in Figure 5-2.

Because the individual price bars look the same, your attention is not drawn to them, unlike the big down candles found on the candlestick chart type. In the Tesla example shown in Figure 5-2, your eye tends to see the trend more than the individual bars.

Another type of bar chart, which is less common, ignores the open on each bar and just uses the high–low–close (HLC) information. In the construction of the price bar, it places a line across the bar rather than just on the right-hand side. The format for this type of price bar is shown in Figure 5-3.

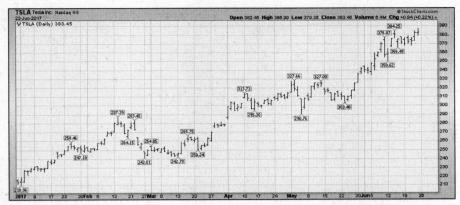

FIGURE 5-2:
An OHLC bar chart.

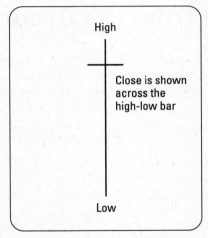

High

Close is shown
across the
high-low bar

Low

FIGURE 5-3:
An HLC bar.

The price bar represents the price movement and the closing price without the opening price information. You can see an example of this type of chart in Figure 5-4.

REMEMBER

As print clarity has improved, the OHLC chart is more popular than the HLC chart. We have experimented with both but migrate to the OHLC bar chart because we find the additional information of opening price valuable for understanding the daily price action. For this reason, the remaining charts in this chapter are OHLC bar charts.

FIGURE 5-4:
An HLC bar chart.

Chart courtesy of StockCharts.com

Building a Bar Chart from the Ground Up

The bar chart is a common type of chart display. Using the settings panel under the chart, users can change the display to show the variation in trading ranges. You can see the settings panel on StockCharts.com in Figure 5-5.

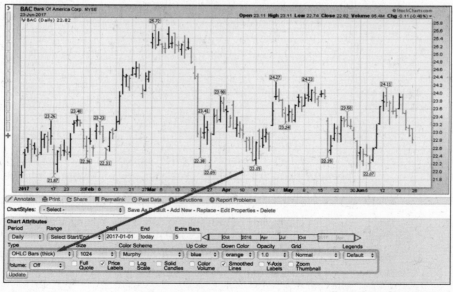

FIGURE 5-5:
Selecting OHLC Bars (thick).

Chart courtesy of StockCharts.com

TIP

You can access the tool for setting up charts online at stockcharts.com/freecharts/ and click on SharpCharts under Charting Tools. You can then work through the steps online as we describe the process.

Under Chart Attributes, select the OHLC Bars option from the Type drop-down list. You will need to click Update to get the bars on the display. *Note:* For clarity in the figures in this book, we have used OHLC Bars (thick) so the bars are wider and stand out more.

It is also possible to make the chart in color. Selecting the same color for both up and down movement is one setting. If you use a different color for up (blue) and down (orange), the chart will compare the current price to the previous day's close, and the color of the bar will be based on your color choice. In Figure 5-5, the type is OHLC Bars (thick); as you move across that line in the settings, you see the size is 1024, the color scheme is Murphy, the Up color is set for blue, and the down color is set for orange. It is easier for the eye to quickly pick out up or down days by using two different colors. (We discuss chart attributes in greater detail in Chapter 3.)

Putting a Bar Chart to Work

OHLC bars are nice to work with. The down price bars still draw attention when colored differently, but they do not have the ominous look of filled candles on a candlestick chart (see Chapter 4). Coauthor Greg uses bar charts for most of his work. He finds they draw his attention to the overall highs and lows, and he can add more days of information without losing clarity. They also draw attention to breaks in the price pattern.

Bar charts are less focused on the intraday price movements but still offer some level of detail for traders looking for intraday movements. Gaps, trading ranges, and market extremes are easy to see on bar charts, as you see in the following sections.

Gaps

The use of the word *gap* when visually reviewing a chart refers to the difference between the previous day's close and the morning open. In Figure 5-5, for example, March 1 was a gap up as the price moved from $24.52 to $25.29, while March 20 was a gap down from $24.78 to $24.50.

Gaps are emotional places on the chart. They indicate that a new piece of information has entered the market that causes sudden buying or sudden selling. Every transaction has a buyer and a seller. In the case of a gap up, buyers are clamoring to get the stock. In the case of a gap down, sellers are clamoring to sell the stock. These imbalances from information overnight or over a weekend cause the stock to gap.

Bank of America (BAC), shown in Figure 5-5, has two interesting gaps close together in March. On March 1, BAC gapped up. On March 20, BAC gapped down to below the level from which the gap up started on March 1. This leaves an image of an island, where price looks disconnected from the rest of the chart. Everyone who bought on the flurry of news from the gap up on or after March 1 is now trapped in a losing position.

REMEMBER

Almost every day, there is a difference between the open price of the day compared to the close the day before. If the price traded within the range of the previous day, the gap is not obvious. Note that even though the price gapped down on March 22 in Figure 5-5, the trading through the day of March 22 filled the gap. It's the open gaps between bars that are very noticeable and usually leave investors with some positive or negative emotion attached.

Short bars versus long bars

TIP

When a price bar is short, the market price of the stock is relatively stable throughout the day. It may close higher or lower, but the buyers and sellers are not eager to change positions. Long price bars show pressure throughout the day pushing the stock in a particular direction. If a long bar is your down color, you can quickly see downward pressure on the bar. Conversely, if the long bar is your up color, there is upward pressure on price.

Trading ranges, support, resistance, and breakout

Trading ranges can be short-term from a few weeks to a few months or even longer-term for three to four years. The ranges can be huge, making it profitable to buy low and sell high within trading ranges. Bank of America in Figure 5-5 traded between $21.87 and $25.72 throughout the first part of 2017. This is not what we mean by a trading range, however. A trading range is when price oscillates up and down, trading between two price levels.

Early in 2017, the price traded sideways between $22.20 and $23.40, with one exception on January 18. The next morning it went right back up into the range.

When chartists see this consolidating type of price action, they focus on where the lows for the stock are and where the highest price is. They look for three key types of signs: support, resistance, and breakout (see Figure 5-6):

>> **Support:** The traded range on BAC during January in Figure 5-6 shows information that has the stock supported at $22.20. We refer to the stock as "supported" because buyers are willing to step in to buy the stock after it had been higher. This pullback to a lower price is common. Institutional buyers that want to add to their positions or start new positions will start buying as the price is going lower. This stops the stock from continuing down and becomes *support* for the stock.

>> **Resistance:** When the price broke out of the trading range above $23.40, more buyers wanted to own the stock and existing owners didn't need to sell, so the price kept accelerating upward to fill the demand for the stock. Because the stock had stalled three times in the low $23 level, chartists call this level *resistance*.

>> **Breakout:** February 14 was the breakout day; you can see the stock accelerate higher above $23.40 with everybody loving the stock on Valentine's Day. After two huge days, the stock consolidated in a sideways range again for eight days. The new level of support was around $24 as buyers stepped in to own the stock when it dropped down to those levels. Then BAC gapped up on March 1 and consolidated again, which moved the level of support up to $25.

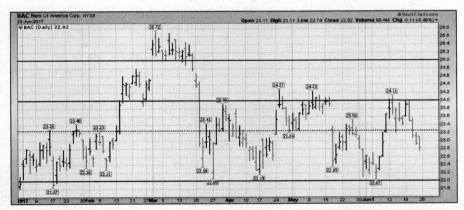

FIGURE 5-6: Support and resistance.

Chart courtesy of StockCharts.com

The stock had three approximate levels of support at $22, $24, and $25 where buyers stepped in when the stock was pulling back. It had three levels of resistance — periods of time when the stock price stops moving up — at $23.50, $24.80, and $25.72.

These support and resistance levels are some of the most important concepts in reading a stock chart. We use this concept throughout this book. Figure 5-6 has black horizontal lines drawn in at $22, $24, and $25 to demonstrate support.

In hindsight, chartists know that the intermediate high for BAC was $25.72. Following the price action, chartists watched to see whether the support levels drawn as solid lines would continue to act as support. March 15 violated support but closed above it. Then on March 17, Bank of America violated the $25 support and closed below it. This left everyone who bought above this level trapped in a losing position and starting to get nervous as they had bought after the stock had made a big move.

Then, on March 20, the stock continued lower after gapping below the March 1 breakout. Now some buyers who bought during the consolidation between $24 and $24.80 were getting uncomfortable with the stock because they had a lot of profit, and now that profit had disappeared. The next day showed the stock accelerating lower as more and more sellers tried to release the stock. It ended up finding support at $22 again after more disgruntled investors sold. Anyone who bought above $22 was not very happy.

Finally, the stock started rallying up from $22 support again, but the stock had trouble getting through $24, which was a previous support area. After April 1, the stock continued to trade between support at $22 and resistance around $24. This is how technical patterns are built from buyer/seller behavior.

In June the price made the lowest low in four months at $22.07 and then made a lower high at $24.11. Downtrends are formed by lower lows and lower highs, which also make investors nervous.

This concept of support and resistance is easy to see in Figure 5-6. The level of $24.80 is close to $25.00, so we would call the area around there a support/resistance area. The level of $24 is also a support/resistance area. $22 is a support area. We have placed a dotted line at $23.25. Even at that level, you can see how price gaps above and below between April and June.

Using lines to demonstrate support and resistance, chartists can see where a stock may have trouble or find support. When support breaks meaningfully, it usually means the stock will travel to the next level down and try to find support there, where interested buyers stepped in before. Resistance is the exact opposite of support. You need to find buyers who are willing to pay a higher price, moving the price above resistance. Those buyers are hard to find without some form of a catalyst.

Chapter **6**

Seeing What's Trending with Line Charts

re you the type of investor who is just interested in following the closing price for the day? Many investors consider that the most important piece of information. When they look at their monthly stock reports, the closing price gives them what they want to know: Is the price higher than it was the month before? The line chart gives these investors a picture of what is most important to them — the trend of the closing price over a particular period of time.

In this chapter, we describe the structure of a line chart, show you how to create one, and explain how to use one as you make investing decisions.

What Is a Line Chart?

REMEMBER

A line chart shows the direction of the closing price. This quickly gives the stock-chart reader a view of the price trend. A trend is established by continually lining up prices side by side and connecting the dots. Because the closing price for a stock is the most important price, the line chart connects closing prices rather than the highs from each day or the lows from each day. Figure 6-1 shows a basic line chart of closing prices for Bank of America (BAC) from January to June of 2017.

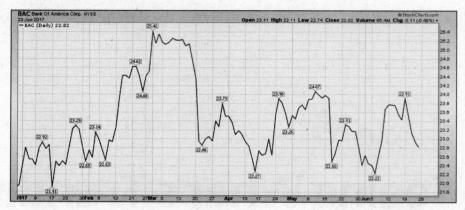

Chart courtesy of StockCharts.com

FIGURE 6-1: A line chart.

As you can see in Figure 6-1, a line chart is a clean, simple chart without a lot of busy information. Line charts are used frequently on financial news television channels like CNBC because it is easier for the viewers to read the data quickly on the screen.

In Figure 6-1, the chart has price labels showing the highest highs and the lowest lows of the closing price. The chart legend in the top left-hand corner tells you the current closing price of $22.82. Quickly scanning the chart, you can see this closing price is in the lower half of the chart. You can also see that the closing price has been oscillating between $22.25 and $24.00 for the last few months (from mid-March to the end of June).

REMEMBER

Line charts' biggest benefit for stock-chart users is that they enable you to view a lot more history, which gives you more insight into the long-term trend for the stock. You don't lose any information from a shorter-term chart, but you can get a feel for the stock price in a larger context rather than thinking short term.

In Figure 6-2, you can see a multiyear view of BAC from January 2015 to June 2017. The chart shows you that BAC made a huge move in 2016 and has been consolidating those gains for the last six months. At the end of 2016, BAC's closing price jumped from $14.94 to $23.01 and then consolidated in a range between $21.86 and $25.42. Investors like the longer-term understanding that line charts provide.

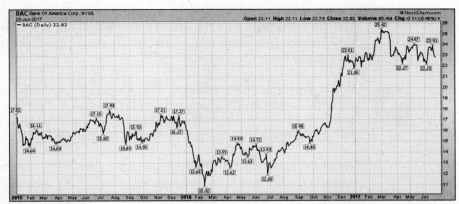

FIGURE 6-2:
A multiyear line chart.

Making a Line Chart the Easy Way

In Figure 6-3, you can see how to use the Chart Attributes area on StockCharts.com to set up a line chart. You can select the type, color, and time frame for the line chart. (For the basics of chart settings, check out Chapter 3.)

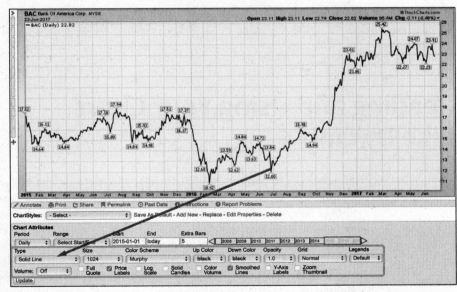

FIGURE 6-3:
Selecting a solid line chart type.

You can select from six different solid and dashed line types. The solid line chart type is in the drop-down menu. You can also choose Solid Line (thick) to help you see the line better.

TIP

One of the toggle boxes below the chart type is for smoothed lines. This is purely cosmetic and makes the chart look more professional. If there are a series of data points in a row that make the chart move quickly like the BAC chart in late 2016, this option will smooth the lines so they don't look pixelated.

We don't find using different colors to show price movements up and down that helpful on a line chart, because you can easily see whether the line is pointed up or down. You may prefer different colors, though. Select from the drop-down menus for up color and down color in the Chart Attributes area.

Another setting that works nicely with line charts is above the chart type but still in the Chart Attributes area. Within the Range drop-down menu is Select Start/End, as shown. Use the slider to the right where the arrow is pointed in Figure 6-4 to conveniently change the time period you want to see on the chart.

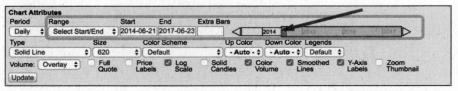

FIGURE 6-4:
Selecting the start/end range.

Chart courtesy of StockCharts.com

Reading and Using Your Chart Line by Line

As you can see from the figures in this chapter, line charts communicate price action very quickly and simply without any significant detail. One of the key benefits of line charts is that they don't show intraday extremes that may or may not be outside a trading range.

As a long-term investor, you want your price chart rising from bottom left to top right. That means the stock is rising in price over time. As a short-term investor staying in a stock for weeks or months, you still want the same price action, but you're looking to exit before the long-term investor does.

In the following sections, we show you how to add support and resistance lines as you read line charts, and we explain how line charts can be handy when you make investing decisions.

Adding support and resistance lines

In Chapter 5, we discuss the concepts of support and resistance. Support shows when there are more buyers than sellers and the price, which has been going up, turns downward. Resistance is the opposite; when there are more sellers than buyers, the price moves down, and at the point of resistance, the price moves up.

These concepts can be important when you're using line charts as well. Support/ resistance areas help you define points of interest on the chart. You can draw support and resistance areas easily on a line chart because they are so clean and simple. Figure 6-5 shows you how to use horizontal support and resistance lines to find the key trends. In addition to horizontal lines, you can also see places where trend lines that slope can be placed.

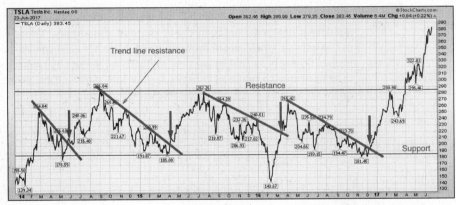

FIGURE 6-5:
Adding support and resistance lines.

Chart courtesy of StockCharts.com

Figure 6-5 shows closing prices for Tesla (TSLA) from January 2014 to June 2017. From Tesla's April 2016 high to its December 2016 low, the sloped resistance line shows you how the price steadily moved lower at each top. We call these sloped lines *trend line resistance.* When Tesla finally found support around $185–$188, it bounced through the trend line resistance and surged all the way up to the next level of horizontal resistance around $285.

Knowing when lines matter

New investors first starting to use charts seek to answer these two critical questions that don't seem intuitive:

>> Why would you buy when price is just above other high price points on the chart?

>> Why would you sell when price is near the bottom of the chart?

Those are both good questions, and line charts can help answer them.

REMEMBER

When price is breaking above former resistance levels or price is falling and there are previous support levels nearby, chartists will use these critical points on the chart to assess whether or not the stock should be bought or sold to maximize profits.

An example of buying at higher prices would be buying Tesla in April 2017 as it went to $290, which was a new high above $285 (see Figure 6-6). Everyone who owns the stock is profitable, and the price is moving to higher highs. Why would an investor sell a winner he already owns that continues to keep on winning?

Because most investors won't sell, there is less supply. Those who want to get in to the winner stock create more demand, which makes the stock continue to move higher. The stocks that make new highs usually start by making one new high and then continue to make new highs for a while. This critical point just above resistance on a chart is a good profitable area to watch.

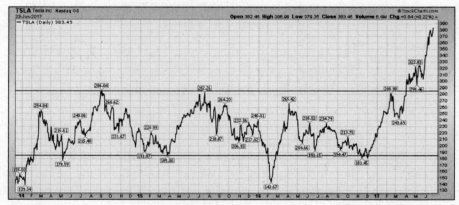

FIGURE 6-6:
Long-term support and resistance.

Chart courtesy of StockCharts.com

In the event of price moving below support, you don't know where it is going to stop next. In Figure 6-6, Tesla fell below support in February 2016. Everything on the right side of the chart after February 2016 was unknown at that time. Tesla continued to fall another $40 down to a level that was support in 2014. By selling near $185 (the support level), you can save a lot more pain by taking some losses. In this case it worked out, and Tesla rebounded. That is not always the case. If you choose to sell when a stock breaks its support level, you can still buy the stock again at some point in the future, perhaps when it is trending higher instead of lower.

TIP

We discuss strategies for using line charts in Chapter 19. Using line charts with horizontal support and resistance lines as well as trend lines can really improve trading results because they help you find the critical price moves.

Chapter **7**

Getting the Lay of the Land with Area Charts

Area charts are similar to line charts (described in Chapter 6) but look dramatically different. To replicate this chart type, which you've probably seen frequently on TV, you need to understand the unique settings for an area chart type. Without tweaking the settings, they can look overpowering and bold.

In this chapter, you discover how area charts compare to line charts, how to create your own area charts, and the best times to use area charts.

Comparing Area Charts to Line Charts

Area charts shade in the area below the line of closing prices, whereas line charts just connect the closing prices with a line. Area charts are also called mountain charts because they make a strong impression in the foreground against a backdrop, much like mountains against the sky. You can see an area chart in Figure 7-1.

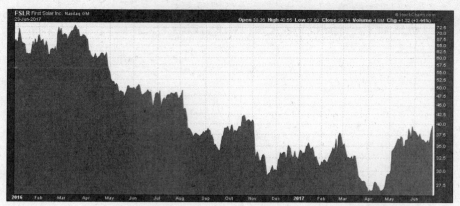

FIGURE 7-1:
An area chart.

REMEMBER

Charting a stock price shows you a picture of the stock's history. The difficulty in chart type selection is getting the type of display to tell the story you want to read. The key difference when comparing area charts to line charts is visual impact. The area chart highlights the lows and the highs and makes them stand out more noticeably. You can see how the trend of lower lows and lower highs becomes quite prominent on the area chart in Figure 7-1.

Business news networks use area charts because they have more impact. Many mobile devices have stock-tracking software and typically these use area charts to show the price intraday and for one week, one month, six months, and one year. Area charts more strongly depict the impact of trends in a couple of ways:

>> **Finding consolidation:** A stock that is consolidating sideways appears as a bumpy plateau on an area chart. A break above a plateau is excellent, and the dark shading helps that stand out. The shading under the move makes the price look strong at the new high. This helps the user because it's more prominent than a thin line on a line chart or a single bar on a bar chart (see Chapter 5 for details on bar charts and Chapter 6 for the lowdown on line charts).

>> **Eying changes in stock behavior:** Conversely, seeing the chart start to drop on the right-hand side helps the viewer understand the change in behavior as white space or background comes into the chart. Your eye can easily draw a subconscious line under the lows and compare them to the highs. A natural tendency of the eye to connect points in an image is valuable and a great reason to use area charts. With a candlestick chart (covered in Chapter 4), your eye is distracted by the candle colors and contrasts. Candlestick charts are rarely used on network television for this reason.

Making an Area Chart You Can Show Off

You can start a chart by going to www.stockcharts.com/freecharts/, typing a stock symbol under Create a SharpChart, and clicking Go. To create an area chart, locate the Chart Attributes area in the settings panel (see Figure 7-2). Using the Type drop-down menu, select Area from the list and click Update in the lower-left corner. This makes your area chart show up extremely bold, probably in black.

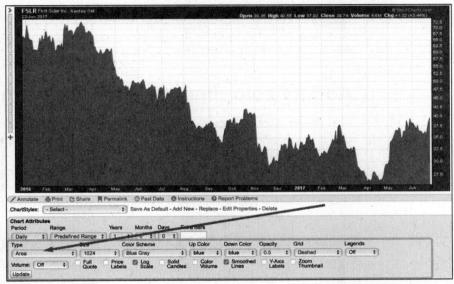

FIGURE 7-2:
Selecting an area
chart type.

Chart courtesy of StockCharts.com

After you select an area chart, two key things you can control are the darkness of the area and the color you want the area to be. It's simple and can have a strong impact on a TV screen or your computer screen. Legends and labels are also handy to include. (See Chapter 3 for the basics of chart settings.)

Strengthening or dimming the area display

If you would like to soften the darkness of the area, change the Opacity setting found to the right of the chart Type drop-down menu where you selected Area. Opacity affects the amount of the color applied to the chart. A low opacity has low color strength, while an opacity of 1.0 has high color strength. A setting of 0.0 will make the information invisible against the background. The opacity of the chart in Figure 7-2 is 0.5.

TIP

If the area chart isn't showing after you click the Update button, check your opacity setting. It may be too light.

Trying different colors

Charting doesn't have to enable a Henry Ford quote. Henry Ford was proud of his car factory having only one color for the Model T. He said, "Any customer can have a car painted any color that he wants so long as it is black."

While you are changing other settings, experiment with the Color Scheme drop-down menu and the Up Color drop-down menu. An area chart uses only one color, which you select in the Up Color drop-down menu.

Adding color lines to emphasize change

Area charts are better than candlestick and bar charts for looking at long-term trends. Some people prefer line charts to area charts. Seeing lines under the lows is a little easier in line charts (discussed in Chapter 6) than in area charts unless you use a bright contrasting line on the area chart. An example would be the gold line in front of a blue area chart on Figure 7-3. Charting software packages have annotation tools for drawing on the charts. We cover those tools in Chapter 17.

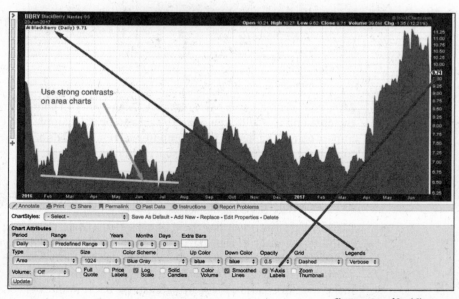

FIGURE 7-3: Lines, legends, and labels.

Chart courtesy of StockCharts.com

Looking at legends and labels

Legends are also helpful when you create an area chart because they detail what stock or stocks are being pictured. This setting box is found on the right-hand side of the Chart Attributes panel. The Default setting works well because it gives the key summary of all overlays and indicators used. We show the Verbose setting, which spells out the company name rather than just the ticker symbol, in Figure 7-3. The Minimal setting gives only the ticker symbol and price.

TIP

To see the exact level on the right-hand side of the chart display, a Y-axis label is nice. This label points an arrow at the exact price level of the last reading. If price breaks down hard in one day on a one-year chart, you may not see it as the line goes straight down. You can see this visually in Figure 7-3. BlackBerry had a bad day, and the drop was so steep it was not obvious. Turn on the Y-axis label by clicking on the toggle in the bottom row of the Chart Attributes. This creates the little price arrow with $9.71.

Adding a Personal Touch with Styles

A quick look at area stock charts being posted on Twitter shows a wide variety of styles. Play with the attributes to find a style that works best for you.

While color is helpful, not everyone sees color. If you experience any type of visual impairment, chart styles become more than just nice to have.

Setting up charts so they clearly show price movement against a backdrop is a personal choice. Area charts, for example, may need simple but effective alterations from the default settings to generate a contrast. Play with the settings under the chart. They can help you.

Some style ideas for your charts include the following:

>> Ten percent of the population is red/green colorblind. Age also takes a toll on eyesight. The Monochrome setting under the Color Scheme drop-down menu can help all these conditions.

>> Area charts can help if fine focus is an issue. Using the Price Labels toggle in the Chart Attributes area can help define highs and lows as well.

>> Area charts can help if you need reduced white space on your screen. Changing the background can help as well on other chart types.

After a while you'll find you have a few settings you really like. One of the reasons people sign up for stock charting software is for the ability it gives them to save *chart styles*. When you save a chart style, the software keeps the chart type, color choices, and size, to name a few.

When you come back another day, all your settings are maintained. When you enter a new ticker symbol for a company onto your saved chart style, it shows the new stock with all the settings you have previously chosen. The software also allows you to save more than one style. In Chapter 19 we discuss how to set up and save your styles for area charts.

TIP

Practice with different styles on the StockCharts.com platform. Use the 30-day free trial available on the home page to practice, and save charts that you have set up. This is one of the easiest ways to get comfortable with charting at no cost.

Knowing When Area Charts Matter

In later chapters, we discuss defining trends over different time horizons for investors. One of the keys to successful chart reading is recognizing downtrends and uptrends soon after the trend has started, and area charts make that easy. Area charts are very clean and simple to use. Filling the space below the price really highlights the trend for the stock.

The other advantage to area charts is the ability to see the big picture by extending the amount of history that is being shown. Much like the line chart, you don't lose a lot of information by adding a longer time period for the chart.

An area chart is a great chart type for people new to charting. It highlights the price action without complicating it. Long-term money managers like to use clean charts such as area charts to demonstrate the trend. Television channels consider the area chart style one of the best types to work with for their audience.

One of the main problems when using charts is understanding what matters. Because area charts have very little detail, they are for big-picture trading rather than day trading, for example. Trend lines as well as horizontal support and resistance levels are easy to see.

Stocks that have been trending up for years don't continue forever. BlackBerry phones are a great example of something being all the rage and then falling out of fashion. At one time the stock was over $145 per share. It lost half its value before the earnings per share started to decline. The changing trend in the long-term stock price almost always happens before the earnings decline.

REMEMBER

Stocks don't just grow to the moon and stay great forever. Stocks have growth phases, and then they normalize again. Some of these trends can last a long time, but eventually they stop. Investors want to catch the big moves up but need to sell to capture the gains when the stock stops rising. Area charts are a great way to see that big-picture change in trend.

3

Using Chart Tools for Decision Making

Discover the importance of charting different time frames.

Sort out pricing using charts.

Harness the power of overlays on your charts.

Find out how indicators improve your chart analysis.

Determine trading volume with relative strength indicators.

IN THIS CHAPTER

» Changing a variety of charts to
different time periods

» Looking at hourly, daily, weekly,
and monthly charts

» Examining multiple time periods
and closing prices

Chapter **8**

Charting Different Time Periods

L ooking at different time periods on charts is a lot easier with computing power. At a touch of a button, you can change everything. Chartists often look at different time periods to evaluate a stock, and great charting software helps with that analysis.

Using charting software, you can display differences for a selected period. The most common period for StockCharts.com clients is a daily period. (Most traders or investors check their portfolio when they get home from work, which probably makes daily charts the most popular.) When chartists refer to daily candlestick charts (see Chapter 4), each candle provides the information for the opening trade of the day, the high of the day, the low of the day, and the close of the day. Then the computer stacks these candles beside each other to create a chart. The chart may contain a year of candles (called the *range*), but each candle is showing the price action for one day, so the chart is called a daily chart. The *period* reflects how much time is in each candle, not the number of candles on the chart. As we discuss in Chapter 5 on bar charts, information can differ depending on the chart you select. Area and line charts (see Chapters 6 and 7) provide more of a summary than the detail you find in candlestick and bar charts.

In this chapter, we show you different chart formats in different time periods, and we provide pointers on when to use each type of time period.

WARNING

Charting one-minute candles during the day and putting money into the market based on these candles is particularly stressful trading that requires a precise strategy and discipline. The period is so short that it is called day-trading. This book is not designed for day-trading chart analysis.

Converting Candlestick Charts to Different Periods

You can use a candlestick type of chart (introduced in Chapter 4) to display different periods. In the following sections, we take a look at how the time period of a candlestick chart impacts the visual you will see. We use Amazon (AMZN) for June and early July 2017 to show how the periods you use to make up your chart can impact what you see.

60-minute to daily candle display

Figure 8-1 shows a 60-minute candle chart for the trading of Amazon on June 29 and the same date reflected by a single daily candle. The intraday candle closing levels don't seem very important when the day is over. Both views show a down day. The intraday candles open and close information isn't required to build the daily candle (but we still point out the closing price with a dotted line in Figure 8-1). Other than the high and the low of the day, the intraday candle information is dropped in the daily candle. But if you were day-trading, that 60-minute display would help you make entry and exit decisions.

FIGURE 8-1: Comparing 60-minute candles to one daily candle.

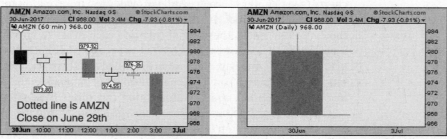

Chart courtesy of StockCharts.com

Daily to weekly candle display

The same information can be shown for the days of the week or the whole week. This information starts on the first working day of the week, so it may start on Tuesday if there's a holiday on Monday. If so, the weekly candle will include only four days. If Friday is a holiday, then the candle will use Monday's open and Thursday's close. The chart shows what happened for that week between the two weekends. Figure 8-2 shows the transition of information from a daily chart to a weekly candle for Amazon from June 26 to July 3, 2017; notice that the high and low of the week are included in the weekly display.

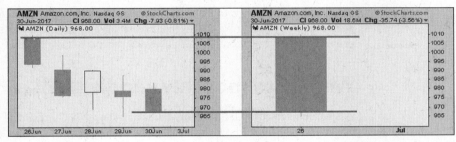

FIGURE 8-2: Comparing five daily candles to one week.

Chart courtesy of StockCharts.com

Note: If the week crosses over the month end on a Wednesday, the weekly candle ignores the month-end information. The weekly candle won't have any information specific to the monthly close.

Daily to monthly candle display

Monthly candles are different from daily and weekly candles. They use the start date of the first trading day of the month and end with the last trading day of the month for each calendar month. It doesn't matter what day of the week these candles start or finish on.

In Figure 8-3, June starts mid-week. The monthly candle selects the June 1 market open price to start the month. When you compare daily, weekly, and monthly candles, the highest closing price for the day or the week may not show as an important level on the monthly chart. June 5 is the highest daily closing price for Amazon in the month, but the solid monthly candle ignores that information.

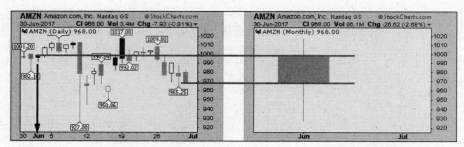

FIGURE 8-3: Comparing daily candles to one month.

REMEMBER

Having the monthly candle miss the highest daily close information may sound like a small difference to be aware of, but it does matter. Depending on the time period you're looking at, the highest close on a candle in a particular month will probably be different on the daily, weekly, and monthly charts.

Weekly to monthly candle display

It is difficult to compare a weekly chart to a monthly chart. If the start and the end of the month fall mid-week, finding the open, high, low, and close levels for the month on a weekly chart is impossible. Unless the market closed on a Friday for month-end at the highest level in the month, these levels will be different on the weekly and the monthly charts. Figure 8-4 shows why the charts have different values.

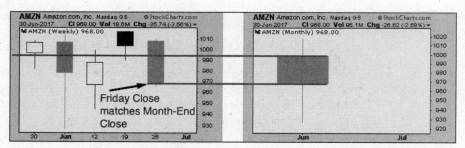

FIGURE 8-4: Comparing weekly to monthly candles.

REMEMBER

For one month, comparing the body of the monthly candle to a weekly chart can be confusing because the candles typically start and end on different dates. When every month has the same issue, the charts look different. This discrepancy is due to the computer using different start and endpoint information for the candles.

TIP

If you think you have looked at a chart before but you see a different value for a major high, like the all-time high for the stock, check the three different chart periods. We have found ourselves in similar situations.

Converting Bar Charts to Different Periods

Bar charts (which we introduce in Chapter 5) have traits similar to those of candlestick charts when switching periods. Again, we use Amazon for the month of June and early July 2017 to show you the differences in the following sections.

60-minute to daily bar charts

Figure 8-5 shows a 60-minute bar chart compared to a one-day bar. The intraday chart highlights the previous day's closing level with a dashed line. The chart conveys the same message as the candle chart in Figure 8-1. The 60-minute bars have a repetitive style, whereas the candle bodies appear to be more unique.

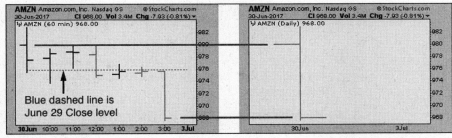

FIGURE 8-5:
Comparing
60-minute bars to
one daily bar.

Chart courtesy of StockCharts.com

Daily to weekly bar charts

Going from a daily bar chart to a weekly or monthly bar chart can work well. Figure 8-6 compares the daily chart to the weekly chart. Notice that the first day in June is included in the last week of May. Like the candlestick chart, it conveys the information between two weekends.

WARNING

Be careful about interpreting what the level for the first day of the month is on a weekly chart. It is lined up with the monthly header only if the first trading day of the week was the start of the month.

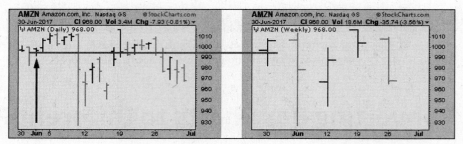

FIGURE 8-6:
Comparing 24
daily bars to 5
weekly bars.

Weekly to monthly bar charts

The variance between weekly bars and monthly bars is the same as that shown on the candlestick charts in Figure 8-4. Looking at the charts with the same range setting, the weekly chart populates differently from the monthly chart because a month can start mid-week, so this cannot be an apples-to-apples comparison.

>> The weekly chart on the left side of Figure 8-7 adds an extra week in the beginning of the chart, even though the dates requested are the same. So you can see that the chart on the left shows a price of 700 as the low, while the chart on the right has 725 as the low. You can see that a red circle highlights 725/700.

>> The deep low on the monthly chart that looks all alone is different on the weekly chart as the price move back up happened in the following week.

>> The price retracement at the top of the chart in June looks mild on the monthly chart, where price retraced most of May's push higher and was almost back to the price from the beginning of May. On the weekly chart, the price looks a lot more volatile with lower lows, then higher lows, and a final week of lower lows.

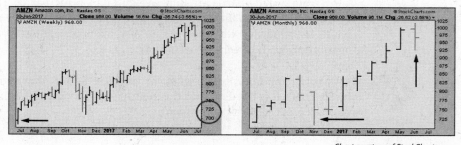

FIGURE 8-7:
Comparing
weekly to
monthly bars.

Converting Line and Area Charts to Different Periods

Moving to line charts (see Chapter 6) dramatically changes the information view by showing only the closing price. The closing price may be difficult to spot through the detail on the bar and candlestick charts that we discuss earlier in this chapter. You can spend a little time looking at each candle or bar to see the closing level, but the line chart in Figure 8-8 makes that level obvious. As area charts (see Chapter 7) shade the information under the line, the chart highs and lows are the same as those shown on a line chart.

Intraday data disappears as the price labels are based on closing prices only, not intraday prices. By eliminating some of the detailed price information, the chart conveys a similar look. A line chart gives you a different view of weekly and monthly information as it removes the little wiggles from day to day.

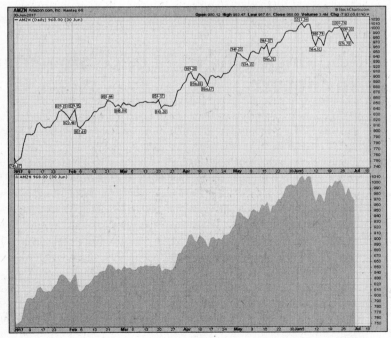

FIGURE 8-8:
Line and area (mountain) charts.

Chart courtesy of StockCharts.com

Taking It One Day at a Time with Daily Charts

Looking at daily charts — the topic of this section — helps you understand the mood of the market each day. Markets can be affected by news from various sources, but when investors think things are improving generally, they can ignore a lot of bad news. When market participants are worried, the slightest bit of bad news can add angst, and investors may drop their resilience of holding a specific stock through tough markets.

REMEMBER

Daily charts are the most helpful charts for seeing detail. Using any chart type, such as candlestick, bar, line, or area charts, can help you see what's going on. Being able to see the new annual highs or new annual lows is important, so if you're looking for that information, set the chart for a longer time frame, such as two to five years. Picking the chart type is a personal preference, but for most investors, charts that display daily periods are the best ones to look at in order to understand their investments. With daily charts as a starting point, some of the other periods have strong benefits too, as you find out later in this chapter.

Looking at the daily price movement in context

A daily chart gives you context for the current price and how it compares to recent history. This information is much more valuable than one day of information.

Figure 8-9 shows a one-year chart of Nike (NKE) using the bar chart format. The stock oscillated all year (from July 2016 to June 2017) in a range between $48 and $59. The right side of the chart is at the top end of the range, which makes the stock interesting now for everyone. Will it be able to move to the upside above the previous trading area, or will it fall back down into the range? If you own it, do you want to sell it and lock in your price near the high end of the range? If you don't own it, do you want to buy it here?

On just about every chart, you will see emotional gaps between bars. These erratic movements are not the daily norm for NKE, but the chart in Figure 8-9 shows these gaps often enough as sudden 5 percent moves that affect your capital. Nike is a Dow 30 stock, which is chosen by the Dow Jones Company as one of 30 companies in the Dow Jones Industrial Average Index. This is a prestigious list of strong U.S. companies that changes infrequently.

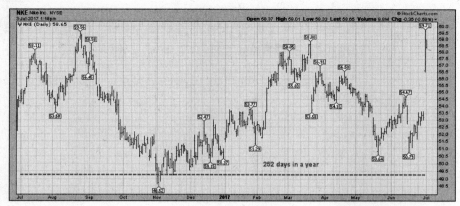

FIGURE 8-9:
Daily chart for
one year.

REMEMBER

It is important to understand that all stocks will move against you at some point in overnight trading and that each gap down should not be considered the end of an uptrend.

Daily charts allow you to see these gaps, whereas the gap has to happen on Monday morning to see it on a weekly chart. This is one key advantage of looking at a daily bar or candlestick chart when you're looking for critical price moves.

The daily chart shows the price moving between $48 and $59 over the period of one year. This sideways movement encompasses the whole chart. Strong stocks will start in the bottom left and go to the top right. Charts that are consolidating are hard to own because as an owner, you are in a range that is not generating new capital. Recognizing a consolidation range is helpful. If you like the stock for further gains, it gives you a chance to buy it somewhere in the range as the investing community has reached a balance.

TIP

The one-year view on the chart in Figure 8-9 makes the price bars compress together when it is formatted for a book. If you select Fill the Chart in the Range setting drop-down menu, it will maximize the clarity and fill the chart with as many candles as possible. As a computer screen is larger than the width of a book, a one-year daily chart may work quite nicely on your screen. (Flip to Chapter 3 for more about general chart settings.)

Using a range of one year (or more) with a daily chart

There are some compelling reasons to look at a range of one year in a daily chart. You can see

>> Consolidation ranges of a few months to one year

>> Annual highs

>> Annual lows

>> The price trading range for the last year

>> Breakouts to new 52-week highs (one-year highs)

>> Breakdowns to new 52-week lows (one-year lows)

When a stock is moving to new one-year highs after not being at one-year highs for a long time, investors take notice that this is a changing point in time. For the first time in a year, investors are willing to pay the most they have for the company stock.

Figure 8-10 shows Nike (NKE) in October 2009 moving to a new high for the first time in a few years. The chart has three years of daily information plotted in a bar chart format. While the price is squished together, you can see the stock move above previous prices. In October 2009, the stock goes to a new one-year high. Four months later in February 2010, the stock moves to new all-time highs. A lot of stocks were still very weak after the financial crisis and not close to new all-time highs. Seeing a stock do very well while other stocks are still recovering suggests strength.

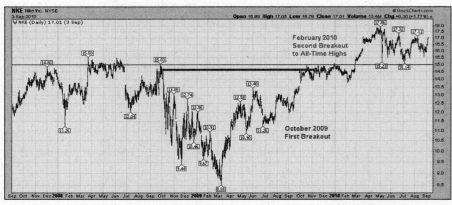

FIGURE 8-10:
Daily chart showing a stock becoming a winner.

Chart courtesy of StockCharts.com

If you look at stocks as they move to new highs after moving sideways, you need to consider what the current shareholder is thinking. All the investors within the last year are happy to hold the stock as it starts climbing.

REMEMBER

The best thing to see on a stock chart is a stock acting like a winner. The best way to have a winning portfolio is to own winning stocks. A common saying in the investment community is this: If you want to own a winner, buy one!

Owning Nike as it broke out to new highs was beneficial. Then the stock consolidated in the top right corner of Figure 8-10. Figure 8-11 shows what happened to Nike afterward. The stock continued to make new one-year highs for the next six years without making a new one-year low. The stock still had retracements of as much as 25 percent during the six-year run.

FIGURE 8-11:
Daily chart showing a stock staying a winner.

Chart courtesy of StockCharts.com

The disadvantage of looking at a long-term chart using daily candles or bars is that you can no longer see the individual price points. Having multiple years on the chart using different time periods (weekly or monthly) enables you to see the information clearly, but you lose specific information like gaps.

TIP

Converting to a line chart with daily information can help a little, as you see in Figure 8-12. The price labels for the highs and lows change with this type of presentation. Whereas bar charts and candlestick charts show intraday highs and lows, a line chart shows only the closing price highs and lows. Select Solid Line from the drop-down menu under Type in the Chart Attributes area (see Chapter 3 for details on basic chart settings). This cleans up the chart significantly and still allows you to see the trend.

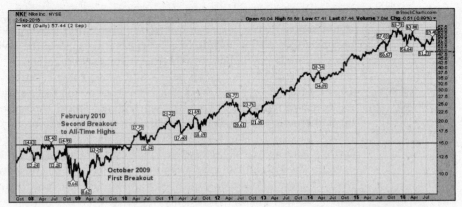

FIGURE 8-12:
A daily chart showing a stock staying a winner in line chart format.

Examining market capitalization with daily charts

You can calculate a company's market capitalization by multiplying the total number of shares by the current price per share, which is called *market cap* in most financial reporting. Companies are typically compared based on their market cap. While there is no standard or minimum/maximum in the industry, a few companies that create market indexes have created some rough measures that change over time.

Rough rules of thumb are as follows:

>> **Large-cap:** Greater than $10 billion

>> **Mid-cap:** Between $2 billion and $10 billion

>> **Small-cap:** Typically less than $2 billion

REMEMBER

Larger companies have more institutional ownership by pension funds and exchange-traded funds (ETFs), so their stock behaves differently than that of small companies. Small-cap companies can regularly bounce and fall 5 percent a day, whereas large companies don't have as many of those major swings. New investors would be well advised to resist the temptation to invest in small-cap stocks until they understand the wild price swings associated with these stocks.

When an individual investor has a portfolio of large-cap stocks, the portfolio behaves similarly to the *market index*. A market index is designed by a company placing a group of stocks bundled together to get an idea of the total price action of the companies within the index. The S&P 500 ($SPX) is a market index of the top 500 large-cap U.S. companies. The Dow Jones Industrial Average ($INDU) is another.

Because markets around the world are different and the United States has the largest market capitalization in the world, these large-cap groups are different sizes depending on the market you trade. Indexes for large-cap stocks are set up around the globe. Some of the most popular to watch include the following:

>> **United States:** S&P 500

>> **Canada:** TSX 60

>> **London:** FTSE 100

>> **Australia:** ASX 100

>> **India:** The Nifty Fifty

These indexes represent the most stable companies. A portfolio of large-cap stocks with diversification across business sectors typically mimics the movement of these indexes.

TIP

Some companies have dominant market capitalization. For example, Apple Inc. (AAPL) had a market capitalization in 2017 of over $700 billion. Websites like Google Finance or Yahoo Finance will quickly tell you the real-time market capitalization of a company.

Daily charts look different depending on the company's market capitalization. *Liquidity*, the ability to get in and out of the market fast, also is impacted by a stock's capitalization. The following sections take a look at the differences based on capitalization and liquidity.

Large-cap and high liquidity

Apple Inc. trades around 20 million to 30 million shares a day at $130/share. That means more than $2.6 billion moves every day in Apple shares. With that huge trading volume, the price moves smoothly by pennies each way throughout the day for the most part. Stocks that have high trading volumes are considered *highly liquid.* This liquidity is very important for large funds when they want to increase or reduce the size of their position by thousands of shares. The shares can still move up or down a lot in a day, but there are active buyers and sellers willing to own or sell at every penny move in each direction. This makes the stock more stable.

Figure 8-13 has the volume traded per day shown on the bottom of the daily chart. The higher the bar is at the bottom, the greater the volume.

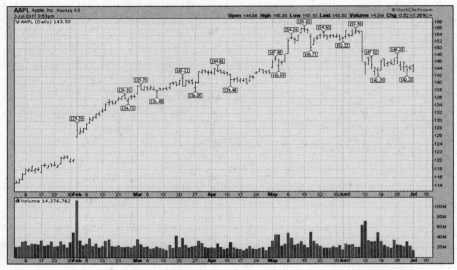

FIGURE 8-13: High liquidity share volume.

Small-cap and low liquidity

If you pick a small-cap company like Handy and Harman (HNH), as shown in Figure 8-14, you see that it broke out to a new high in 2017. HNH trades an average of 17,000 shares a day. It is very difficult for an institution to accumulate enough shares to influence its large portfolio positively. Conversely, when it wants to sell the stock, there are very few buyers for the number of shares it wants to sell.

While the price of the stock may move to new one-year highs, it is not nearly as liquid as Apple Inc. Large-cap, liquid stocks get large institutional investors buying large positions when they break to new highs. This is rarely true for small-cap companies.

Figure 8-14 shows the daily chart for Handy and Harman with relatively big volume as it moves to new highs, but the actual number of shares is still very small. For the first half of the month of May 2017, the stock traded less than 10,000 shares with no price movement for weeks. In February, it moved from a January 31 intraday high of $29.85 to $21.90. While the stock was dropping about 30 percent in three weeks, there was little to no buying interest.

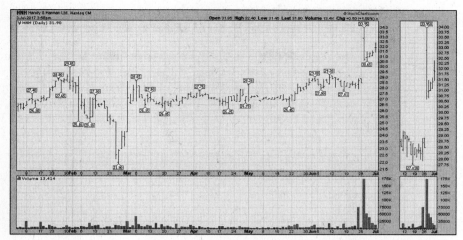

Chart courtesy of StockCharts.com

FIGURE 8-14:
Low liquidity
share volume.

This is the trademark of no liquidity. You are stuck holding the stock while it plummets. Handy and Harman may be a great company as it is breaking out to new highs later in the year. However, it will be hard to make money on the stock due to the lack of liquidity when you want to sell. If you can own a percentage of the daily float easily, it is probably worth avoiding. This is the type of stock a friend gives you a tip to buy. All stocks are easy to buy; they are harder to sell when you want to.

WARNING

Charts with low volume are notoriously hard to make money on because someone has to buy the shares from you in order for you to profit. Speaking from experience, this is not where the big money is made in the market, but it can be lost there.

Embracing Short-Term Thinking with 60-Minute Charts

When you've made the decision to buy a stock, your next step is to look for the best entry point. Conversely, if you want to sell, you also want to look for the best exit point. Sixty-minute charts can make the decision easier for you. Volume is a key factor in these charts.

Highlighting intraday price action

The majority of the trading volume happens in the first 1.5 hours of the day and the last hour. The two highest-volume time slots for buying and selling during the day are also at the most important time frames for bar and candlestick charts, near the open and the close. The volume is not consistent throughout the day, and this trend is quite obvious on 60-minute charts (like the one in Figure 8-15).

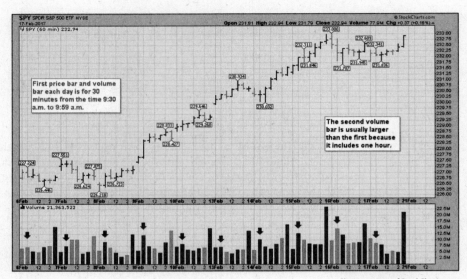

FIGURE 8-15: Intraday price and volume.

Chart courtesy of StockCharts.com

Some other clues can show up on 60-minute charts. While it is not always obvious, the market may open down slightly during strong uptrends but end up closing higher. On a 60-minute chart, the opening would start below the previous close. This typically shakes unfamiliar traders who may be worried they are going to lose their gains. Stocks ebb and flow. They get momentum to go higher, and then they pull back slightly. It is important to understand this give-and-take during uptrends.

REMEMBER

Being aware of the time of day and the volume can help investors either buy or sell their stocks when there is more liquidity.

Using 60-minute charts for index watching

News events throughout the day may make stocks wobble on an intraday chart. One display we like to use is a 60-minute chart of a market index or ETF so we can see how the large-cap index has moved over the last two weeks.

Figure 8-16 shows one such chart using the ETF that tracks large-cap stocks, the SPY. Using a range setting of 11 days with 60-minute bars, you can see that the market is making a series of lower highs and lower lows during late June 2017. Seeing where the market is relative to the preceding two weeks is helpful. In Figure 8-16, each time the SPY rallies, it is unable to make a high above the previous high. It is also making lower lows. If the trend starts to change to higher highs and higher lows, like in Figure 8-15, investors can see the price momentum start to improve throughout the trading days.

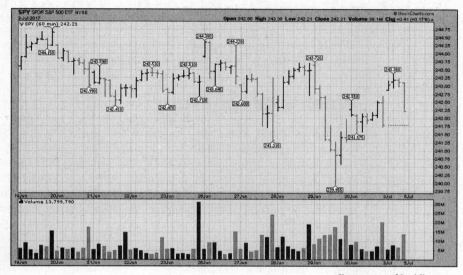

FIGURE 8-16:
Eleven-day,
60-minute chart.

Chart courtesy of StockCharts.com

REMEMBER

The same principle applies to stocks, indexes, and ETFs. As price ebbs and flows, investors looking to own a stock that has been consolidating can use 60-minute charts to evaluate the change from lower highs and lower lows to higher highs and higher lows.

If you want to be a short-term trader, you need to use short-term charts. A smart practice is to look at the daily chart to see the main short-term trend, and then look at the 60-minute chart to help you with entries into or exits out of the stock. If the daily chart is falling and the 60-minute chart is weak, you may need to wait until the trend on the larger period (daily) is improving. A pullback within an uptrend is the best combination to help on your entry. Trading results on 60-minute charts improve greatly if you're trading with the main trend on the daily chart.

It is hard to hold a winning stock for months to capture a big gain by looking at short-term 60-minute charts. Short-term charts are helpful only for short trades.

REMEMBER

By looking at short-term 60-minute charts, you can get a look at the investor sentiment for a very short-term trend. You can also use this shorter time frame to help expose the change from down to up, or up to down.

Seeing the Big Picture with Weekly Charts

Weekly charts are hidden gems for chartists. Understanding weekly charts is the best way to stay on the right side of longer trends.

Weekly bar charts

The daily chart of Nike (NKE) in Figure 8-10 earlier in this chapter looks a lot cleaner if we convert the daily bars to weekly bars. Figure 8-17 shows the same range setting on the chart with weekly bars instead. The legend in the top left corner highlights the period for the chart. With nine years of information on it, the chart is cleaner because one weekly price bar represents five daily bars. By removing 80 percent of the price bars, the chart is better. However, it is still very compressed.

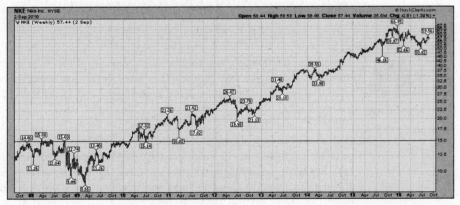

FIGURE 8-17:
A weekly bar chart.

Chart courtesy of StockCharts.com

The breakout above the $15 price line is easy to see on the weekly chart as well. It is not quite as easy to see the detail in price. This chart stops at 2016 to focus on the long historical trend rather than later price action.

TIP

When you're using a bar chart or candlestick chart, set the pixel size that is best for your screen. For example, we use a size setting of 1280 pixels and a range setting of 3 years of data, which is most comfortable to see on our screens. You may find that a different setting works for you. These parameters are set in the Chart Attributes area (see Chapter 3 for details).

Weekly line charts

Switching to a line chart improves the nine-year chart a little bit more. We have used a thick line chart in Figure 8-18. The color coding for up and down is not that valuable on historical chart analysis. Weekly analysis suggests looking at the general trend. Notice that as we drop detail from the chart, the number of meaningful price reversals also drops, as annotated by the price labels.

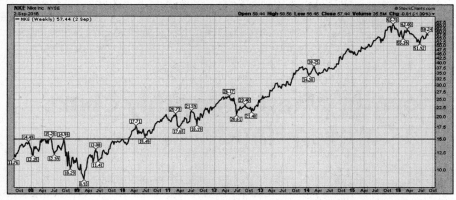

FIGURE 8-18:
A weekly line
chart.

Chart courtesy of StockCharts.com

TIP

With a line chart as the chart type, a typical pairing for your computer monitor is a chart size of 1280 pixels wide with the range set to five years of data.

The big benefits of weekly analysis

For investors trying to capture a longer trend, the weekly charts keep the big picture in perspective. Daily charts and 60-minute charts (both covered earlier in this chapter) give short-term chart signals that a longer-term investor would prefer to hold through due to a larger uptrend. Each year the market has some sort of a pullback. Investors trying to hold their positions may find weekly charts can help them hold through periods of weakness or consolidation.

Looking at the weekly chart to start with can help establish a directional bias. Knowing the larger trend before looking at the daily chart can provide a strong ballast.

Institutional investment houses use monthly and weekly charts to help stay with long-term trends. If the large institutions are holding through short-term pullbacks, it's probably wise for you to hold everything, too. By using the weekly charts, there is a major advantage to riding the trends longer with the support of institutions.

One of the difficulties of short-term trading is the constant tax payment on profits, reducing your working capital. If you can keep your money invested longer, like Warren Buffett, the entire amount will continue to build wealth rather than the after-tax portion. This subtle change is quite important.

TIP

Broader signals in the market usually show up before major damage is done to a portfolio. These signals can be part of your toolbox. Many of them rely on weekly chart information to understand the momentum of the market. These signals are covered in Part 4.

Knowing When a Monthly Chart Can Come in Handy

Typically, monthly charts are underappreciated. Monthly charts are not usually a key component for individual investors. However, monthly charts are the anchoring charts for institutional investors. For this reason alone, keeping track of the monthly chart is helpful.

REMEMBER

Monthly charts with long-range settings can really help investors. Gaining money by seeing a breakout above all-time highs or finding support for stocks that have dropped significantly is a strategy that monthly charts provide cleanly. They also help focus on the big picture rather than the small waves of shorter time periods.

Recognizing major long-term lows and highs

By providing long-term awareness, monthly charts allow you to analyze major historical highs and lows. Figure 8-19 shows a chart of Natural Gas prices reaching monthly long-term lows in 2016 that fell to the same lows back in 1999.

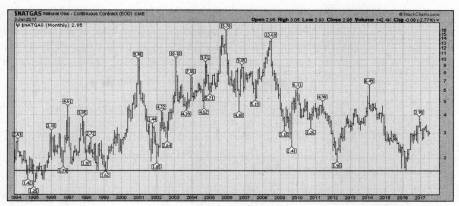

FIGURE 8-19:
Monthly
long-term lows.

In 2016 a lot of commodity prices dropped to long-term lows. Long-term investors aware of where each commodity had bottomed before made significant gains in many different commodity-related trades. By seeing where the long-term support was on Natural Gas in Figure 8-19, they started buying Natural Gas futures contracts or Natural Gas–related exploration companies near the lows. The gains in some of the exploration companies were 150 percent from February to December 2016.

Analyzing investor behavior

To continue the story of NKE, by looking through a monthly candlestick chart, you can see that Nike does not have a lot of major down months. That information is hard to capture from the daily or weekly charts. We have extended the Nike monthly chart to July 2017 in Figure 8-20. In July 2017, NKE looks like it is ready to turn higher as it makes new one-year highs.

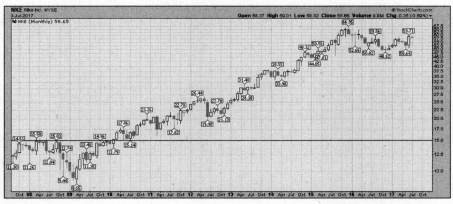

FIGURE 8-20:
A monthly
candlestick chart.

Using stock charts for investing is about improving the timing of investing to participate in major gains. This may not work out on every trade. NKE is a very strong chart, rising from bottom left to top right, and it has built an 18-month consolidation.

With the new one-year highs, the chart is signaling that it is ready to move higher. It could easily ramp up and make a sustained run to significantly higher highs. While it may not work out as a trade, being aware of major setups like this on institutional-size market-cap companies definitely improves your odds for finding strong stocks.

TIP

When institutions are trying to buy, they perceive the stock as having the potential to move higher. Institutional volume is usually required to make the stock move significantly higher in price. Looking for stocks that have a tailwind of institutional demand is a major key to investing success.

Picking the Right Chart for the Right Range

If an institutional investor likes the monthly setup and a hedge fund likes the weekly setup, they will both be interested in a stock. Investors trading the daily and intraday time frames are also tuning in and may find some compelling short-term signals. This merging of signals across various types of investors is very helpful. You can use this to your advantage.

REMEMBER

Look at multiple periods before placing a trade. First, look at daily, weekly, and monthly charts just to get a feel for the setup. The more investors you see looking at the same trade, the better. Sometimes the stock price is breaking through a down-sloping monthly chart. This is easily spotted on a short range. By understanding what is happening on the other period charts, you get a feel for the importance of the level.

TIP

There is a reason to discuss the principle of multiple periods depending on your trading style. Trading strategies are typically more successful in the direction of the next higher time period. If you want to trade based on a specific period chart (for example, daily), it is a good idea to use a complimentary period chart at least five periods higher for trading with the trend. As there are five days in a week, use a weekly chart to analyze the direction of the trend.

Other key multiple periods to watch include the following:

>> To trade a 10-minute chart, use a 60-minute chart for confirmation. There are six periods of 10 minutes in a 60-minute chart.

>> To trade from 60-minute charts, use a daily chart for perspective. There are 6.5 periods of 60-minutes each in a daily chart (9:30–10 a.m. is 0.5 hours).

>> To trade daily charts, use weekly charts for the trend. There are five daily periods in a weekly chart.

>> To trade weekly charts, use monthly charts. There are 4.3 weeks per month.

REMEMBER

The most important decision you need to make when looking at charts is what time frame you can sleep comfortably with. If you need to move to cash before the market closes every night to sleep well, you'll have to be a day trader. If you like trades that last a couple of weeks and you want to be very active in the market, you'll need to trade on daily and 60-minute charts. If you want to keep your trades three weeks to six months, daily and weekly charts will be your best choice. If you want to execute trades a few times a year, you may rely on weekly and monthly charts.

Shifting Your Focus to Closing Prices

Earlier in this chapter, we examine Amazon on different period charts. The information is the same for Amazon's daily closing highs on all daily charts. The monthly and weekly closing highs are probably different from those shown on the daily charts.

There are a lot of crosscurrents just discussing a new high for different periods. For Amazon in June 2017:

>> May 30, 2017, is the highest monthly close at $994.62.

>> The June 30 monthly close at $968 is not higher than May's monthly close, but daily new highs were recorded in June.

>> Monday, June 5, shows the highest daily close at $1,011.34

>> Friday, June 2, shows the highest weekly close at $1,006.73

>> The highest intraday price is the same on all period charts at $1,017.00.

Each chart period has a different closing high. We prefer to use daily closing highs rather than an intraday high. They are all different but correct.

The biggest advantage charts give you is the view from the perspective of buyers and sellers. The most important opinion on the direction of the stock can be seen in the actions taken by buyers and sellers with money invested in the stock. Charts can help you see what the collective group of owners think about the stock relative to what they were thinking a few months ago. If they are bidding up the price daily, they aggressively want to own the stock. If the price has been falling for months, the investor mood of optimism is declining.

A share of stock is worth what the next person is willing to pay for it. The underlying value of the company is based on variables such as growth prospects, stability of cash flow, ability to raise prices, debt, market dominance, new products, earnings growth, industry group, and access to markets, which all affect how different investors view the company. Because the markets have many participants, there is no single right way to value a stock. Here are some signals to look for in your charts:

>> The closing price each day is an important price. Whoever owns the stock is willing to hold it overnight. Holding it over a weekend is a bigger commitment. Holding it for years is a solid commitment.

>> For some reason, stocks seem to drop more often in the morning during an uptrend, and then rally up for the rest of the day. During a downtrend, stocks rally in the morning only to lose investor interest before the close, and the stock sells below the open. While this trend is hard to prove on every stock, you may find it helps you avoid selling into a morning pullback in a strong uptrending market.

TIP

Pay attention to the closing price of the day and the week. It is very difficult to get out at the top and very difficult to get in at the bottom. Intraday prices can be very difficult to watch. Sometimes the price will break out to new highs during the day but close the day slightly down. Closing above the breakout level and holding the breakout level for two to three days is an important signal.

» The concept of watching the price action to understand what is going on with the investors in a stock is more helpful than watching the news about a stock. When we wouldn't touch a stock because of the news around it, Warren Buffett was buying it. Price speaks louder than words.

REMEMBER

By looking at the daily price of the stock, you can see the mood changing over the near term. There are great companies you may have never heard of, but if the price of the stock is steadily rising on a daily chart, the investors are choosing to own the stock. Charting the stock price tells you the sentiment of the investors, not the sentiment of the president of the company.

Chapter **9**

Reading a Price Chart

Reading a chart is part art and part science. Charts give you the ability to analyze what investors are doing, which is better than just listening to what financial reporters, who may or may not own the stock, have to say about the stock. Analysts also fall into this camp. They place a buy or sell rating on a stock they don't own. When they have no money invested in the company, arm-chair quarterbacks can see whatever they want to see.

A great example of this phenomenon was Enron. The stock made its final high in August 2000. The topping structure was completed in November 2000. It took 11 months after that point for the first fundamental analyst to put a sell rating on the stock. By December 2001, two months after the first fundamental analyst downgrade, the company filed for bankruptcy. Two weeks before the bankruptcy, six fundamental analysts still had a strong buy on the stock and two reduced their strong buy to hold after the stock had fallen 95 percent.

Technical analysts can still make mistakes, but the premise of charting is to give traders a tool for finding new uptrends and recognizing downtrends, so they can exit stocks near the beginning of the fall. Getting those inflection points right every time is impossible, but working to find them can produce meaningful rewards as long as a good portion of them work out. This chapter helps you under-stand some basics of reading charts: uptrends, downtrends, consolidation, bases, topping patterns, and scaling.

Reading a chart creates an awareness of how uptrends and downtrends are created. The base is an important part of a price chart. Topping patterns are complex; an investor needs to use the shape of the chart to help define a topping pattern.

Running with Bulls and Sleeping with Bears: Uptrends and Downtrends

Most investors are afraid of losing money on a trade. That's normal. Using a chart to help you decide when to buy helps you set up levels. If the trade meets your expectations and is working as you expected it to, that's great. But if your expectations turn out to be wrong, you can minimize your loss, sell, and try again.

As you find out in the following sections, two important things are first, understanding what you want to see on a chart and second, understanding what you *don't* want to see on a chart.

In any chart you create on StockCharts.com, little price boxes appear on the chart next to the line by turning on the Price Labels toggle in the Chart Attributes area. These boxes can help new investors or traders see uptrends starting. (Flip to Chapter 3 for the basics on chart settings.)

Recognizing an uptrend

The definition of an uptrend for chartists is a series of higher highs and higher lows. As a chartist, you need to understand what that means, when it starts, and how it ends. When the stock is in an uptrend, the price will be moving higher up to the top right corner of the chart. You can see this movement in Figure 9-1. Price labels marking the highs above the line are at higher levels and price labels marking the lows are at higher levels.

On its way up, the stock for Advanced Micro Devices (AMD) is staying near the top right-hand corner and continuing to push higher. As the stock moves higher, it starts to run out of new buyers for a few days or weeks. To attract new buyers, the price falls to create a small pullback. Then, new buyers who have been interested in the stock find a place where they are willing to buy the stock. As part of the uptrend, new buyers come in to support the stock, purchasing at a higher level than previous support because they want to participate in the rise of the stock and don't want to miss the pullback in price.

FIGURE 9-1:
Defining an
uptrend.

Chart courtesy of StockCharts.com

This creates a staggered line where the trend is generally higher, creating an uptrend. Chartists draw a line underneath the rising lows defining the trend. Sometimes it is also possible to create a parallel line on the rising highs, creating *a trend channel.*

When the price stops rising and starts to drop for a few days or weeks, this is called *a pullback* within an uptrend. While the stock is moving up in price, everyone who owns the stock is happy to own it, because it keeps rising.

Spotting a downtrend

In a downtrend, the stock price starts to weaken and starts to make lower lows. Using the Price Labels tool on StockCharts.com, you can see a series of labels dropping toward the bottom right corner of the chart (see Figure 9-2). Downtrends are the opposite of uptrends. A downtrend is a series of lower highs and lower lows shown on a chart.

When the stock stops attracting buyers, investors who want to sell must accept a lower price to find new buyers. As other investors see lower lows, they too start to sell to preserve the capital in their portfolio. This works like an avalanche and builds on itself, causing further selling by other investors. Ultimately, this trend will attract people expecting the stock to fall, called *short sellers.* They borrow the stock from someone to sell it at a high price and then pay the original owner the lower price when they want to close the trade. This strategy works only when the price is falling, so short sellers are typically fast, short-term traders.

Prices seem to fall faster than they rise, so weak stocks can move down fast as the price action does little to attract attention from new investors. When the investors want to sell their stock and there are fewer buyers because of the downtrend, significant downward pressure pushes the stock price lower.

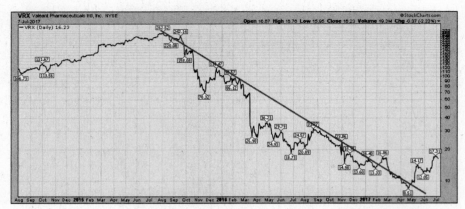

FIGURE 9-2:
Defining a
downtrend.

Bear market rallies are rallies that move the price higher in the short term when the primary trend for the stock is down. These can be sudden rallies that usually inspire some hope for investors holding the stock. Because there are people shorting the stock, when it moves up, it goes against their position. When they want to exit their short position, they have to buy the stock to close the trade. This creates buying pressure on the stock, and it rallies up. The counter-trend rally can be very steep but loses buying momentum after a few days or weeks. The stock plummets again and the cycle continues.

TIP

If you see a sudden uptrend in the middle of a downtrend, give it a few days before acting because it may just be a short-term rally.

The downtrend creates a situation where investors are less comfortable owning the stock and can be quick to sell if they make any gains during the downtrend. Others sell to minimize losses as the price gets closer to what they paid for it. Short sellers usually want to hold their short position briefly to profit from fast moves. This creates a volatile situation where the price moves in both directions quickly. While a stock is in a primary downtrend, there are fewer long-term institutional investors trying to buy a stock moving down, which causes the stop (the price set for selling the stock) to drop below its support levels.

These conditions make the stock more volatile as the price moves each day are usually larger in major downtrends. You can see this in Figure 9-2, which is the chart for Valeant Pharmaceuticals (VRX). Valeant wiped out the gains from a seven-year climb in 18 months. The scale on the right shows the price losing 95 percent of its value.

Bucking the Trend: When a Stock Isn't Trending

There are over 180 different industry groups in the U.S. market. At any given time, some of the groups are moving up fast, creating an uptrend, while others are being sold off, creating a downtrend. There are also groups that don't have momentum and can quietly trade sideways without trending up or down. This type of movement is called *consolidation*.

Looking at consolidation basics

Investors rotate in the market among the various different industries depending on the economic climate. A sector can gently move sideways or up without a lot of interest from investors who buy stocks for longer periods of time. Companies that tend to trade sideways often pay a dividend to keep their investors interested in owning the stock, but some investors may be frustrated by the stock's inability to trend higher.

For most investors, a sideways stock is uncomfortable to own. Depending on your buying price, you may be losing money or have a gain in the stock at any given time. As the price stagnates, fewer and fewer investors are interested, so the stock migrates down to the low end of the range. At that point investors see a price level where institutions have bought shares before and may buy more shares. This can create a level of support for the stock. These new investors may buy with an expectation of it going back up to the top of the range and sell it near the top. The cycle starts again.

For example, in 2016, financial stocks rallied hard off major lows in early 2016 after trading sideways for years. In the last quarter of the year, the exchange-traded fund (ETF) in the financial sector, XLF, broke out of the range and shot up 25 percent in a period of five months, topping in March 2017. XLF started to trade down. Four months later, the ETF continued to trade sideways between two levels but back at the top of the range. You can see this consolidation in Figure 9-3.

For XLF, the ETF had spent almost two years in a trading range that started in 2014. The lows of 2016 forced most investors to reduce their exposure or sell all the shares. When the shares rallied from the lows, the expectation of getting back to $20 might have been there, but the extension to $25 would have been a stretch to imagine.

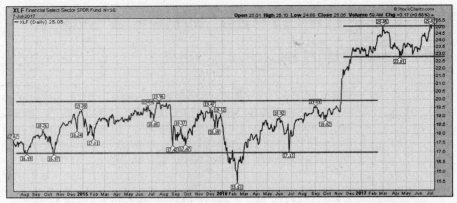

Chart courtesy of StockCharts.com

FIGURE 9-3:
Consolidation.

Seeing the ETF move 60 percent from the lows was a huge move in just over a year, from November 2016 to March 2017. If the price were to again tend to consolidate between $22.50 and $25.50, that would start to frustrate investors again.

Recognizing different periods of consolidation on a chart

REMEMBER

While consolidation is frustrating, these periods are also hard to spot until you have seen the range establish itself with multiple lows near a specific level and highs at another level. For this reason, chartists focus on previous lows and previous highs to see how price responds. If the price can continue higher, the top of the range will typically become support. If the price trades lower out of the range, there can be a lot of selling pressure as the price returns back to the lower edge of the previous range.

A great example of different types of consolidation can be found in the chart for Shopify (SHOP) in Figure 9-4. The stock came out as an initial public offering in May 2015, so investors had no historical information for the stock price. After a stunning first few days, the stock moved higher for a month with a high around $39. The stock built its first consolidation between $26 and $40.

Shopify opened at $25 on the first day of trading after pricing the offering at $17. After a few months, sellers were unable to find support at the lower boundary of the consolidation, so the price moved down considerably toward the initial IPO price of $17 trying to attract new buyers.

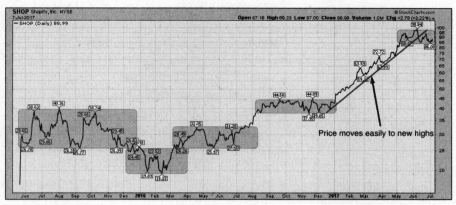

FIGURE 9-4:
Different types of
consolidation.

The stock started to find support again and spent two months trading at this level between $18 and $26. After getting back above the lows of the first consolidation range at $26, the stock consolidated again for almost five months between $26 and $32. From there, the stock moved freely up to $42. It consolidated for five months around the previous highs at $40 by oscillating between $38 and $45.

Then the stock broke above this consolidation to fresh new highs. Everyone who owned the stock was profitable and not really interested in selling. The stock moved unencumbered for months, easily surpassing prior highs with very small pullbacks as new investors stepped in to own the stock. The stock proceeded straight to $100. The stock started to consolidate at this new level for two months.

Reading investor behavior during consolidation

The different types of consolidation in Figure 9-4 are great examples of investor behavior:

>> In the first consolidation, the price ranged between the opening bid and the top of the first surge, testing both multiple times.

>> The second consolidation may have been built when large investors bought the stock from the original traders who were in a losing position on the stock. This is referred to as moving into strong hands.

>> The third consolidation was still working against the early investors by trading in the low end of the original range. The investors were starting to wonder whether that was all the stock was worth.

>> The fourth consolidation moved up to the high end of the original range and teased and tempted investors with higher prices. This level also worked the stock away from investors who just wanted to lock in the profits they had before.

Institutions typically like the sideways consolidation for building larger positions on stocks over a few weeks when they think the stock will go on to new highs. If they buy the stock all at once, they push the price higher. If they buy the stock on down days during consolidations in the price, they can accumulate more before the price accelerates away.

>> The final consolidation on the chart shown is where investors were locking in gains of at least 100 percent from the fourth consolidation.

REMEMBER

To book profits, you have to sell some of the position to record gains.

Leveling Out: It's All about the Base

When a stock moves sideways after being in a downtrend, we refer to the price action as building a base. The following sections describe types of bases and how to see the beginning of an uptrend from a base.

Types of bases

There are four different types of bases:

>> Double bottom base

>> Multiple bottom base

>> Rounded bottom base

>> V-bottom base

The following sections take a closer look at each.

Double bottom base

Figure 9-4 (shown earlier in this chapter) shows how Shopify (SHOP) built its base before moving higher. Shopify in Figure 9-4 made a double bottom base. In January 2016, SHOP made a singular low at $19.89 and then the price rallied. After the rally exhausted itself, near former support at $25, SHOP went all the way back down and tested the previous low around $19. When that low held, it was potentially a very important technical signal.

In the Shopify example, the price actually made a slightly lower closing low. That is still considered a test of the low because the price immediately bounced after going below the previous low briefly. This comparison of lows is one method of monitoring for support.

Many investors would have expected SHOP to hold at $25. The repeated testing of a level four or five times can be considered a sign of weakness. The more the support level is tested, the more likely it is to fail. A strong base usually has one test of the low, maybe two. When the stock price returns to test the base the third, or fourth, or fifth, or sixth time, each one is actually chipping away at supportive price action, and eventually it fails. This happens because buyers who stepped in at that level have probably spent their capital and it has not worked to support the stock. The price usually moves lower to find new interested buyers.

Multiple bottom base

The Advanced Micro Devices (AMD) chart in Figure 9-5 also built a base before accelerating higher in a large uptrend. AMD was in a big decline with a series of lower lows and lower highs before the stock finally found a level to build a base over a period of time. The final low on the chart is never known at the time it is made. As the price goes lower, more and more value investors start to invest in the stock. This creates the base, but the base takes time to form. Figure 9-5 points out a couple of interesting characteristics of the AMD multiple bottom base.

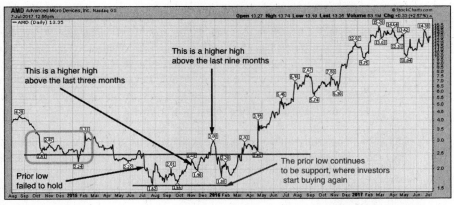

FIGURE 9-5:
Creating a base.

Chart courtesy of StockCharts.com

A base is developed as the stock price stops going lower and starts trading in a sideways consolidation. While the base is under construction, you still don't know whether it is going to resolve higher or continue down. When you start seeing higher highs and then higher lows, you can start to take some comfort in the assumption that the price is going to move higher.

As the base is built, the stock continues to attract value investors. As the stock starts to move to new highs, the momentum investors who like to buy higher highs start to move into the stock. As the stock starts to outperform other stocks, it attracts relative strength investors, who look to buy stocks that show strong performance. When the stock is moving rapidly, it attracts day traders looking for big percentage moves during the day. The continued improvement in the stock's price action is what starts to bring these different investing styles together.

REMEMBER

Rather than focusing on the day of the extreme low, chartists typically wait for the development of the base and look for the price action to improve.

The multiple bottom base can still have very wide price extremes. As AMD continued to find resistance around the $2.50 level, the stock sold off and continued to test the low-price area around $1.60. The breakout to nine-month highs suggested something was changing in the price behavior. From the lowest price to the highest price in 18 months for AMD, the stock doubled. On the final stab toward the low, the stock bottomed at $1.80, which was a higher low. It was still hard for investors to have the confidence to invest when the stock fell from $3.00 to $1.80. As the stock accelerated back up above $2.50, where there was a major support/resistance level, this helped show that the stock was changing character and trying to go higher after being there recently.

In the AMD example in Figure 9-5, the price made one test of the low within a few months. The first low was $1.62, and $1.66 was a test of that low. The spike down a few months later to $1.80 was not part of the original base, but the January 2016 push down coincided with weakness across the stock market. The monitoring of the base is important on each stock, but broader trends can disrupt the accumulation of stock by investors. In this case it resulted in a wider base with the $1.80 considered as another retest of the lows.

REMEMBER

The confirmation of a base is difficult as it is happening, but investors don't need to catch the exact low to find profits in the market. A little hindsight can be okay.

Rounded bottom base

While almost every base has a slope down and a slope up on the other side, a *rounded bottom base* gently makes a saucer over time. Where the AMD chart in Figure 9-5 earlier in this chapter showed a double bottom and then came down to create another major low on the right-hand side, some charts are smoother and create a uniform rounded bottom. Chipotle Mexican Grill (CMG) in Figure 9-6 shows a smooth rounded bottom base. This style can be quite common.

FIGURE 9-6:
Rounded bottom base.

A rounded bottom base just indicates that it is taking a longer time for a stock to break out and go back upward.

V-bottom base

Bases can V-bottom. If the base V-bottoms, it probably coincides with overall stock market weakness that finally started to rally. Usually it takes time to develop the change in trend with multiple tests of the low or at least one test down near the previous low. In the case of a V-bottom, you don't get that luxury of testing a prior low.

TIP

While commodity prices and commodity-related stocks can create V-bases, it's not uncommon to see a commodity-related stock bounce off the lows and then build some sort of a consolidation before going higher. Commodity-related stocks include stocks for agricultural and energy products, such as oil or natural gas.

For chartists, finding support at previous lows is very bullish. When you don't have a previous benchmark at or near a level and the price just bounces seemingly off thin air and accelerates back up, it's difficult to decide when to invest capital. An untested low is difficult for chartists in most cases, so chartists have to use other techniques to help establish conditions for a tradeable low. Figure 9-7 shows an example of an untested low for Devon Energy (DVN) stock.

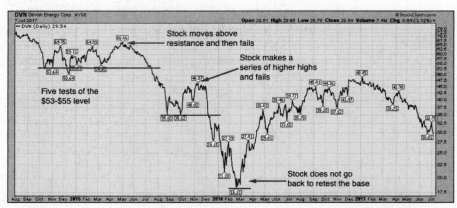

FIGURE 9-7:
V-bottom low.

Chart courtesy of StockCharts.com

You can see that the price stayed near the low for a few days and then moved higher. A tested low usually takes a few weeks to a month before the test happens for a better confirmation.

REMEMBER

Major long-term basing patterns usually include some sort of major selloff that exhausts the investors' expectations. We have all been a victim of waiting for a test of the lows that never comes. The market accelerates away from you while you await the test. We don't usually think of investing capital as easy. Chartists try to put rules around trends, bases, and tops to help protect capital in downtrends and invest based on common setups. Improving your odds by using charts doesn't mean a sure thing.

The start of an uptrend from a base

REMEMBER

When looking for the start of an uptrend from a base, you look for two features:

>> The stock stops making new lows. The previous lows hold as support within 1 or 2 percent.

>> The stock starts to make a higher high for the first time in a long time.

Then you patiently watch for higher highs and higher lows:

>> If the stock makes a higher high but has not made a higher low, then you want to watch the next pullback to see whether the prior low holds as support.

>> If the stock keeps finding support at prior lows, then you want to watch for higher highs.

As this happens, a *base* ends up being created. In Figure 9-5 earlier in this chapter, the first push to fresh three-month highs was a potential clue that things were improving. The second surge to nine-month highs that broke the downtrend and pushed above previous resistance was a confirming clue. Eventually, when a stock starts making new one-year highs, the uptrend is usually underway.

Reaching the Top: Muffins, Spires, or Something Else?

Looking for the end of a trend is one of the most difficult parts of charting the market. The end of the trend is difficult if not impossible to spot on the day of the final high. On the final high, investors love the stock and are happy to own it because it has been very profitable in their portfolio.

Stocks that make new highs can continue to make new highs over and over. Stocks without earnings can move higher quickly with the promise of something great. Stocks with great earnings can get stalled because the investors start to believe the stock's best days are behind them.

One of the reasons for using charts is to participate in the main runs on a stock and avoid the rest of the time, including the down-cycle moves. While this does not lend itself to listening to what the president of the company wants you to think about, it does lend itself to watching what investors are doing with the stock.

Commodity stocks are notoriously volatile. They don't treat buy and hold investors very well. While the stock may run up and pull back over and over, the most profitable investors are the ones who get in near the lows and out near the top over and over. The rest of the investors are left with very average to low returns as commodity cycles come and go.

Other stocks have a longer-term thesis. Amazon, for example, has reported little to no earnings relative to its huge revenue base. The management team keeps reinvesting the profits back into the company to increase revenues and attract more users. While the stock may be vulnerable to big swings, Amazon continues to have a road map to larger revenues from new areas in the market. In 2016, its revenues grew $29 billion in one year. Each year, the revenue has continued to accelerate.

While Amazon may be successful, others in the retail space are getting wiped out by the success of online retailing. Various electronics retailers, department stores, and trendy retail boutiques have been forced into bankruptcy, and more seemingly happen every month.

REMEMBER

It is this dichotomy within the market that various investors can participate in. Owning what is working and avoiding what is not working is a critical component to achieving investment success. While it is important to ride the trend, it is also important to have an exit strategy to capture profits. Unfortunately, there is no signpost on each stock saying: "This is the top!"

One of the methods that chartists use to find market tops is to use historical price patterns. Using examples of how stocks have historically topped can give you some clues. When you see subtle changes in the same patterns over and over, it gives you an idea of what to watch for. There are multiple ways a stock can top out:

» The rounded top (muffin top)

» The spire

» The parabolic run

» The double top

» The range trading top

The rounded top

The *rounded top,* also known as the muffin top (see Figure 9-8), is typically one of the most difficult patterns to spot. The stock slowly loses the interest of new investors. As the stock goes from being an aggressive performer to a mild performer, investors assume they just need patience to ride out the consolidation before the next move higher.

FIGURE 9-8:
A rounded top.

Chart courtesy of StockCharts.com

In Figure 9-8, which shows the stock for Fastenal (FAST), the investor is clearly in love with the stock heading in 2013. The stock has been on a tremendous run for years and looks set to continue. As the stock approaches the previous high, everything looks great. The upsloping multiyear trend line was breached, but the stock has bounced back above it and is testing the all-time highs. Then the stock fails to break through to new highs. It starts to trade in a range from early 2013 to late 2015. Then it starts oozing lower lows into 2016. It finally starts to climb higher in April 2016 but falls again through October 2016, when it enters another upswing. The highs start to diminish slightly as well in April 2017. Eventually the stock just continues to slowly make slightly lower lows and slightly lower highs, establishing a rounded top over a long period of time.

Years go by, and the stock has not done anything. These stocks are very hard to exit for longer-term investors because of the beautiful run they had and the expectation that the run will resume at some point. The price action does not weaken significantly, but it does not trend higher either.

The spire

The *spire* is our analogy for a price move that bolts out of nowhere and goes ballistic. Spires are frequently seen on new initial public offerings (IPOs). Shake Shack (SHAK), a burger restaurant, had a soaring IPO in 2015. Figure 9-9 shows the Shake Shack IPO that moved from $21 to $50 to $96 in a few months.

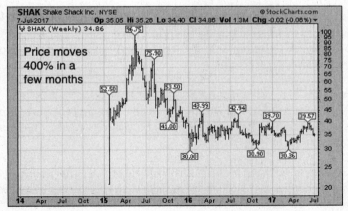

FIGURE 9-9:
A spire.

Chart courtesy of StockCharts.com

Typically, these types of moves are exhaustive with no new buyers coming in, and the price collapses as quickly as it moved up. There may be an attempt at a retest of the high, but that usually collapses quickly as well.

These spires are notorious for huge moves intraday. If the price of the stock is moving more than 5 percent per day — and some days 10 percent — the stock may continue to soar, but being ready to exit is usually prudent. Making annual returns in one day does not usually last long.

TIP

While the stock may be new, keep your normal chart settings for range on StockCharts.com. They will help you see these ballistic moves a little better. Because charting software changes the vertical scale as the price goes higher, you will need to be aware of the change. The later section "Scaling for Profit: It's Only Money" explains this in more depth. (Flip to Chapter 3 for an introduction to chart settings.)

TIP

While we mention that IPOs can create this spire chart pattern, biotech stocks can have some remarkable results when they get FDA approval. The chart shoots up instantly on the news but runs out of buyers at the price extreme. It usually pulls back to build a base at a higher level, which may take months or years.

The parabolic run

A *parabolic run* is when a stock starts building momentum over a period of time. As the story spreads about how great the company's products are, the increased investor attention continues to rise, creating an improving stock chart. The price continues to accelerate, with the price moves gaining in size. On a weekly chart, it looks like an extreme ramp-up. These can be very profitable to own, but are subject to violent corrections.

In Figure 9-10, the price for NVIDIA (NVDA) stock in early June 2017 moved from $140 to $168 to $140 all within two weeks. A 20 percent move is quite shocking, in both directions. That was not even an earnings week, which provided the huge move earlier in May.

Parabolic runs make it difficult to pick the top. Another company usually copies or subtly changes a great idea to compete with the success of its peer. When another company invents something that starts to affect the sales and revenue, the investors will leave the original stock long before the revenue is affected. A parabolic run can also be a collapse in the industry. A great example is Cisco Systems (CSCO) in 1998–2000. Cisco made fabulous products that helped the world move data. The stock went up 1,500 percent in three years, and once the top was in, the investors stayed away for years. Figure 9-11 shows Cisco's parabolic run and subsequent collapse.

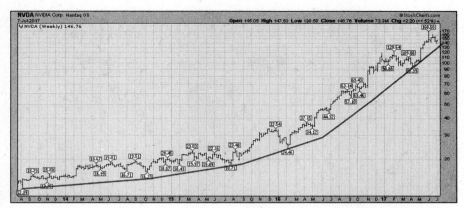

FIGURE 9-10:
A parabolic run.

Chart courtesy of StockCharts.com

FIGURE 9-11:
A parabolic run collapse.

Chart courtesy of StockCharts.com

REMEMBER

Not all parabolic runs end with a single permanent collapse. Apple Inc. has had multiple parabolic pushes, correcting significantly after each one and then surging again. That is what makes the parabolic chart behavior so difficult to manage. Attempting to maximize returns while managing risk and tax implications are all part of the investors' work. Letting huge gains slip away is also problematic, so you don't want to stay too long.

The double top

The *double top* (see Figure 9-12) is a common topping pattern in the market and a considerable hurdle for investors. Trying to find new investors who are willing to pay more for the stock is always difficult. This requires a continued improvement in the company or a newfound optimism in the industry that attracts investment. A double top is always worth watching.

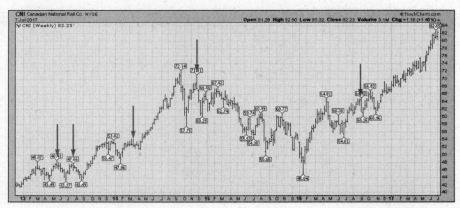

FIGURE 9-12:
Double tops.

Chart courtesy of StockCharts.com

In Figure 9-12, we see multiple places where the Canadian National Rail (CNI) stock tested a higher high and could not get through immediately. We also see a major fail in November 2014 while testing the high of September 2014.

REMEMBER

When there are new buyers for the stock at higher prices, the uptrend can continue. When the new buyers stop trying to buy the stock at higher prices, the sellers offer a lower price to try and sell the stock. This seesaw battle continues every day. When a chart builds a local high by going up to a price and then back down, this noticeable peak becomes a place of interest when price approaches it again. While it is not uncommon for price to stall briefly when reaching a previous high, close attention should be paid over the coming weeks to see whether it can continue to move higher.

The range trading top

Range trading is an extension of the double top in the preceding section as the stock continues to move up to a high, back to a low, then back up to a high, down to a low, and then retests the high. This oscillation is obvious on the charts (see Figure 9-13 for an example), but the range can be large so investors can make a significant amount of money just moving from the low to the high.

The J.P. Morgan Chase stock (JPM) in Figure 9-13 demonstrates two different types of range trade tops. One has a slight rise, while the other has a flat top. From March 2014 to March 2015, the stock made seven higher highs, but each one pulled back. The net price improvement on the highs was only 4 percent ($2.00) over a one-year period.

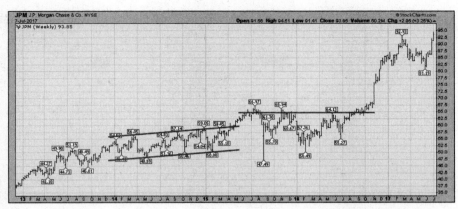

FIGURE 9-13:
A range
trading top.

Scaling for Profit: It's Only Money

Earlier in this chapter, we define an uptrend, a downtrend, a base, and a top. However, all bases and tops can be visually altered by the charting software. This is not a negative of charting software, but it is important that you understand the scaling that the computer is doing.

Charting software uses two components to scale the chart, which can create dramatic differences. The software uses these two scaling components:

» The software analyzes the range of the chart, which defines how far back in time to go.

» Then the software analyzes the high and low throughout that range on the stock and adjusts the scale.

The following sections explain different types of scaling and how to set the correct scaling on charting software.

Arithmetic scaling

Figure 9-14 has an arithmetic scale on the right on the top chart for Tesla (TSLA) and on the bottom chart for Total Fina Elf (TOT). Both charts look like they are going up at about the same rate visually.

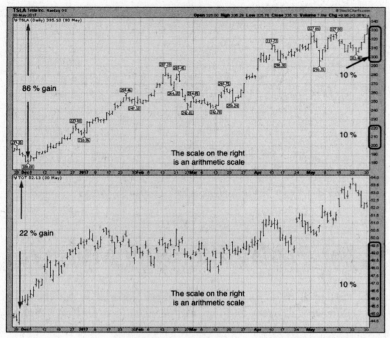

FIGURE 9-14:
Arithmetic scale.

Because each stock has its own price value, the charting software makes the price display tall enough to fully cover the height of the chart. The way to manage that is by changing the scale on the right. Tesla is moving in $10 increments while Total is moving in $0.50 increments.

Total has moved up $9.90. In percentage terms, Total has moved up 22 percent from the low to the high, while Tesla has moved up 86 percent in the same time period. Each black range on the chart is 10 percent. As Tesla goes higher, you can see that it has to move $30 rather than $20 to move 10 percent. On Total, $4.50 is a 10 percent gain at $44.50. A $4.50 gain on Tesla would be a small percentage gain.

We usually compare stocks by discussing the percentage move. When Tesla was a young company, a $4.50 move would be exciting for the stock. As the company has become a large-cap stock, the $4.50 is a small percentage move. If you want to recognize the percentage size of the move in Tesla's early days compared with the current percentage moves, you need to use a different chart scale called a logarithmic chart.

Logarithmic scaling

Figure 9-15 is a logarithmic scale showing the same stocks as in Figure 9-14, Tesla and Total Fina Elf. You can plot the scale so that as the price moves higher, the scale keeps a 10 percent move the same height starting at any price point on the chart.

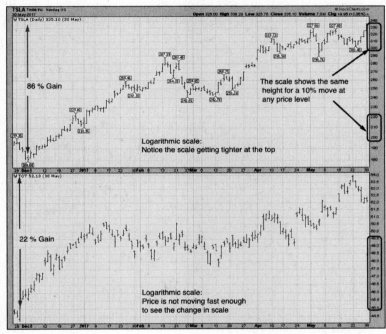

FIGURE 9-15:
Logarithmic scale.

Typically, logarithmic charts are used for long ranges of multiple years when the price is rising quickly. Apple at $2 compared to Apple at $140 can be compared when you can see the huge percentage moves that happened in the early days of the company. When you show them on the logarithmic chart, a 10 percent move back in 2000 looks the same size as a 10 percent move at $140.

Scaling guidelines

TIP

Here are some guidelines with regard to scaling:

>> Use arithmetic scales on short-term charts (under a year).

>> Use logarithmic charts for long time frames.

>> Be careful assuming one stock is going up as fast as another because both charts have the same shape. The change in scales can alter this view.

>> A parabolic move that happens over a short period of time will look more upright on an arithmetic chart than on a logarithmic chart.

TIP

You can access scaling options only when you sign up for the trial membership at StockCharts.com; these options are not available with free charts. You set your scaling option at the time you pick your trend line.

Chapter **10**

Harnessing the Power of Overlays

As stock prices wiggle up and down, you may find it hard to recognize a trend. *Overlays* — which are display formats added to stock charts that help you understand price movement — can smooth out that trend to make your reading of the charts easier. Overlays can also help you see when the big picture is getting stronger. More importantly, regardless of the news around you, the overlays can help you see when extremes in price movement are occurring.

Using overlay tools and adjusting the settings to create a method you're comfortable with make charting more valuable. The overlay tool can help you find better entries and exits by understanding the price patterns in a stock. In this chapter, you find out how to use overlays in three different tasks: tracking moving averages, trying channel investing, and noting support and resistance. (Chapter 3 introduces overlays and other chart settings.)

REMEMBER

It's critical to keep in mind that buyers for a stock are looking for a good entry. If you don't have any buyers, you can't lock in a profit when you're trying to sell. Overlays help you find areas to maximize profits and still have a solid chance of having a buyer at that level. An exit methodology is an important component of successful investing, and selling near previous highs can be beneficial.

Keeping Track of Moving Averages

Price movement is the only way to track what investors are doing. If the price is continuing to push higher, there are more buyers than sellers. If the price is falling, there are more sellers than buyers. The problem with those two sentences is that price runs up, then pulls back, then runs up, then pulls back — and the cycle continues.

Smoothing out the trend is one of the secrets to staying on the right side of the trend. Most institutional pension fund managers want to be on the right side of the longer trend. Short-term investors want to be nimble and are happy with being involved in a shorter trend.

One of the ways to smooth out the movements of anything is to use an average. Determining your average speed on the highway is one example. You can do the same thing in stock charting by creating an average trend for the stock. In the following sections, you find out how to use overlays to plot a moving average and use multiple moving averages simultaneously. We also cover the various uses and benefits of moving averages in investing.

REMEMBER

Moving averages come in many different flavors. Here are a few acronyms that may come in handy as you read the following sections and work with overlays:

>> **MA:** Moving average (such as 200 MA)

>> **DMA:** Daily moving average ("Simple" is the default)

>> **WMA:** Weekly moving average ("Simple" is the default)

>> **MMA:** Monthly moving average ("Simple" is the default)

>> **EMA:** Exponential moving average

>> **DEMA:** Daily exponential moving average

>> **WEMA:** Weekly exponential moving average

>> **MEMA:** Monthly exponential moving average

Plotting a moving average

A 40-week moving average is produced by adding the closing prices for each of the last 40 weeks together and dividing the total by 40. To get the moving average for next week, you drop the oldest information and add the latest Friday close. As you do this week after week, you create a weekly *moving average.*

Luckily, you don't have to do this calculation. Moving averages are calculated for you in stock-chart programs, and you can use them by adding this overlay to your charts. Plotting this on top of the price chart compares the moving average with the price.

You can create moving averages on any chart. They can be used by chartists on monthly, weekly, daily, hourly, and one-minute charts. For example, Figure 10-1 shows you a moving average overlay for Apple (AAPL). To plot a moving average overlay using the tools at StockCharts.com, you can type AAPL into the area on the home page where it asks you to enter the company name or symbol. Doing so will bring up a chart. Underneath the chart, there are three main areas. Using the Overlays area, click on the drop-down menu that says none and select Simple Moving Average. It will default to 50, but you can type in any moving average you want. The moving average will be calculated based on the period of the chart. If you are on a daily chart, it will be 50 days. If you are on a weekly chart, it will be 50 weeks. Be sure to click the Update button. (If you're having trouble working with overlays, review Chapter 3.)

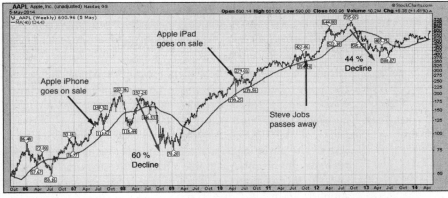

FIGURE 10-1:
40-week moving average.

Chart courtesy of StockCharts.com

Apple has had some huge price swings over the years. Figure 10-1 shows the time frame when Apple launched the iPhone and the iPad between late 2005 and early 2014. On the chart, we have annotated a few key dates around Apple. On top of the price panel, we have a 40-week moving average (WMA) plotted. The 40 WMA is a great place to look for support or resistance on most charts.

You can see that buying Apple when it moves above the 40 WMA is a good idea, and selling or protecting your stock position when price is below the 40 WMA is a simple strategy. Price was falling below the 40 WMA and rising above the 40 WMA during various periods shown in Figure 10-1.

Plotting key pieces of news flow helps explain that investors don't necessarily follow news. On one of the most visible companies in the world, there are few unknowns in terms of the products or the company for the population at large. But a few shocking ideas appear on the chart:

>> The iPhone is the greatest mass-market product ever launched, not only in terms of the number of devices sold (over a billion), but also in terms of rollout speed, customer satisfaction, and broad market awareness. With this great new product, you would expect the stock to soar. Immediately after going on sale in 2007, however, the stock dropped 25 percent in a few weeks. During two long periods in each of the two years following the amazingly successful launch of the iPhone, you could have bought stock in the company at a price at least 20 percent lower than it was on launch day.

>> The iPad, launched in 2010, was also a runaway hit. The stock did nothing for six months, and then doubled in six months.

>> When Steve Jobs passed away in 2011, the conversation in the media was that the Apple stock would probably never go higher. The stock doubled in one year.

>> There were two massive declines in the stock (60 percent in 2008 and 44 percent in 2012–2013) while earnings were improving every month.

REMEMBER

Through all the news flow, being aware of where the price was relative to the 40-week moving average would have helped you be defensive when the stock wasn't behaving well. It also would have helped you stay with the trend as price pulled back and bounced off the 40 WMA.

One of the advantages of the moving average is that a lot of people use it, so it becomes important. Much like a horizontal support/resistance line (we cover this later in this chapter) or a trend line, these moving average lines can also be support. From July 2008 to the end of the chart in Figure 10-1, price was either supported at the 40 WMA or meaningfully far away underneath it to cause anxiety for shareholders.

TIP

Some of the tools on charting websites like StockCharts.com allow you to search for companies touching their 40 WMA from above. In the Apple example, this was a very important low-risk place to add to positions. Seeing price approach the 40 WMA is one of the benefits to using charts to help you trade.

Looking at moving averages for different periods

When you change chart periods from daily to weekly (see Chapter 8 for details), you need to convert your moving averages to approximate the same information for a different period. Table 10-1 shows the approximate conversions for switching from a daily to a weekly chart. A 200-day MA on a daily chart, for example, is the equivalent of a 40-week MA on a weekly chart and a 10-month MA on a monthly chart.

TABLE 10-1

Moving Average Conversions

Daily	Weekly	Monthly
8	XX	XX
20	4	XX
40	8	XX
50	10	2
65	13	3
100	20	5
150	30	7
170	34	8
200	40	10
250	50	12
325	65	16

In the following sections, we show you how to use a variety of moving averages together in overlays.

Using two moving averages and crossovers

Plotting two moving averages on a chart allows the eye to compare two different trends. In Figure 10-2, we use two different moving averages on a chart of Apple stock. We changed the legend setting to Minimal so the actual values of the moving averages are not the focus. You can choose any two moving averages.

FIGURE 10-2:
Two moving
averages.

The short-term moving average (the lighter line) does a good job of showing the short-term trend in the stock price. If you just traded around the short-term trend, you would own the stock above the moving average and sell it when the closing price ended below the moving average. This trading strategy would kick you out of the trade often, though. The worst part is it can reverse shortly after violating the moving average, only to go higher. During the uptrend, almost every time you were to enter the trade because it was back above the moving average, your buying price would be higher than the price you'd just sold at.

If you use the long-term moving average (the darker line), the big uptrend works great. However, the strategy would have false starts (whipsaws) in November 2015 and March 2016 during the downtrend. You would be trying to buy as the price moved above the long-term average, only to fail and drop right back below the moving average. A *whipsaw* is when you get a signal to buy or sell and immediately the price action reverses right after you place the trade. Whipsaws are the hardest part of investing based on charting signals.

The moving averages crossed over in August 2015 as the short-term moving average went below the long-term moving average. This moving average crossover can be used as a signal. It appears to be a pretty good sell signal as the moving averages did not cross positively until August 2016. (Arrows point out the crossovers in Figure 10-2.)

Closer inspection of the moving average crossovers as a trading plan reveals two major issues:

>> Shortly after selling because the moving averages crossed in August 2015, you would have sold around $100. Note that you don't get to sell at the price of the moving averages; you get to sell at the price the stock is at when they cross. While you wouldn't be selling at the extreme lows in August, you would be selling after the stock dropped 25 percent from the highs.

>> The second part of the trade would have you getting back in after the short-term moving average crossed back up above the long-term moving average in August 2016. The price to get back in would have been around $107.50. This would have been $7 more than your exit price, but at least the trend had changed positively.

There are two other things to note. Immediately after you got the sell signal in August 2015, the price rallied significantly. Conversely, immediately after buying in August 2016, the price fell quickly, making it look like another whipsaw.

REMEMBER

The dates selected in Figure 10-2 show the August 2016 trade continued to the upside, but the difficulty is always dealing with price moves against you that seem to happen as soon as you put the trade on. The trading of moving average crossovers using longer-term moving averages has significant moves both ways.

Considering moving average ribbons

A moving average ribbon is visually impressive and draws attention to key points of change on a stock chart. The style does help demonstrate a significant change in trend. A stock in a normal uptrend doesn't usually collapse. It may lose buying momentum, but it usually takes time for stocks to top out and bottom out. Using moving average ribbons rather than one or two moving averages can be helpful in this regard.

To create a moving average ribbon, change the Overlays panel to have a series of simple moving averages plotted with different periods. You can re-create the ribbon effect using the settings shown in Figure 10-3. (If you're not sure how to set overlays, review Chapter 3.)

You can see in Figure 10-3 that when the moving averages spread out, the trend is strong and intact, but on the far right, when the moving averages start to compress, the stock price is falling.

A simpler derivation of the moving average ribbon concept is to use three moving averages to create the ribbons — for example, 10 DMA, 20 DMA, and 30 DMA, or 20 DMA, 30 DMA, and 50 DMA. The moving averages on Figure 10-4 demonstrate how the lines cross to create signals.

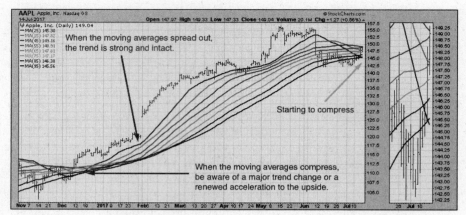

FIGURE 10-3:
Moving average
ribbons.

Chart courtesy of StockCharts.com

FIGURE 10-4:
Three moving
averages.

Chart courtesy of StockCharts.com

Analyzing the left side of the chart, you can see that the signals would be very challenging to profit from because the trends were very short. On the right side, you see two perfect signals: one signal to sell in December (when they cross to a negative alignment) and one to buy in March (when they cross to a positive alignment).

Comparing the simple moving average to the exponential moving average

Two different types of moving averages are commonly used. One is a simple moving average (SMA) that places an equal weight of importance on each bar, which is what we use in the previous sections. The second type is an exponential moving average (EMA), which places more weight on the most recent information and less weight on the oldest information.

TIP

On Figure 10-5, the exponential moving average (the dotted line) turns up sooner and down sooner. Both moving averages are smoothing out the trend. If you want to use moving averages for buy and sell signals, the EMA will give you signals earlier.

FIGURE 10-5:
Simple MA versus exponential MA.

Chart courtesy of StockCharts.com

Examining the uses and benefits of moving averages

Moving averages help clarify a trend starting and finishing. The direction of the moving average is important as it signals the trend. When a moving average starts to point down, the price has moved below the moving average. This change of direction from up to sideways or down is usually a subtle clue that the trend is changing rather than just being a pullback in an uptrend.

In the following sections, we describe the uses and advantages of tracking moving averages with overlays.

Knowing when to move in and out of a stock

Using the moving average tool to smooth the trend is a simple way to maintain a strategy for the trader who wants to move in and out of a stock and stay in a rising trend during pullbacks. Recognizing a change in the direction of the moving average is a strong clue that what has been working is starting to weaken and may be signaling the end of a trend.

Using two moving averages, as we describe earlier in this chapter, can add additional clues. A short-term moving average crossing below a long-term moving average clearly illustrates a trend change. When both short- and long-term moving averages are pointed in the same direction, the trend is strong.

Because moving averages are commonly used in technical analysis, they can be important as a place where falling stocks bounce after pulling back. When stocks are in a downtrend, the moving average can be a place where a bounce in the stock price stalls and the stock moves lower again.

You can use two moving averages to help you sell, and you can use two completely different moving averages to help you buy. You can accomplish this by having multiple chart styles that enable you to move quickly between them. There is no perfect system, so you need to find one that works for you. We discuss how to customize chart styles in Part 5.

Whatever your trading strategy is for using a single moving average, multiple moving averages, or the signals created by the moving averages crossing over, there will always be times when the trade is moving against you.

Finding entry points

Moving averages are also a major tool for finding nice entry points. When a stock goes above a moving average that you use, this can be used as a buy signal for your time frame. A stock that bounces up off a moving average can also be used as a place to buy an initial position or add to a position that is working.

When the stock fails to hold above a moving average that has supported the stock in the past, it can be a clue that major institutions are no longer buying dips in the stock.

Moving averages are used to help keep a bias toward the stock. When stocks are under a long-term moving average (200 MA), it is usually a good idea to avoid owning them. As an investor, you can choose to own only stocks above the 40 WMA or any other moving average you think prudent. For most investors new to charting, that is a radically new way to think about owning stocks.

The most common moving averages for multiple-month investing would be the 50 DMA and the 200 DMA. For shorter-term investing, the 20 DMA may be more suitable. Traders using 5 DMA and 8 DMA are trading often.

Picking the right moving average for you

If you're a new investor, look at different moving averages on a chart. If you want to place trades only occasionally, you need to find a moving average time frame that gives you those types of signals. By placing four or five moving averages on your chart, you can establish which time frame is more suitable for you.

For example, active investors who want to trade frequently would use a shorter moving average to match their trading style, such as the 20-day MA. When price moves above the 20 DMA, they buy, and when it moves below, they sell. (You can imagine someone trading on five-minute charts with a 20-period MA is going to make a lot of trades — not recommended.) If your trading style is active and you want to be buying and selling every few days, making trading decisions on a 40 WMA is not going to work for you. It won't be active enough for your desired trading style.

REMEMBER

If the price is crossing the moving average on a chart too often, you need to use longer moving averages. If the price is crossing the moving average on a chart too infrequently, you need to use shorter moving averages. Because there are many styles of investing and many different personalities in trading, you need to find a moving average time period that works for you.

Getting into the Groove with Channel Investing

Channel investing is a completely different way of thinking about the movement of a stock price. The concept of defining a channel for use in a trading strategy employs various styles. Some channels define the extremes of the price movement and use that as a trading frame. Another method for channels is to set the typical range for the stock movement so that the price will usually move outside the channel before reversing.

Channel trading can also be done on sideways consolidation rather than stocks trading higher or lower. As technical analysis has developed over time, various technicians have created different methods to automate the channel width. In channel investing, the width of the channel is the most important parameter to be used successfully. The following sections describe types of channel investing overlays with different widths.

Keltner channels

Keltner channels use the *average true range* (ATR) to set the width of the channel. The average true range is a two-step process:

>> The first step is calculated by measuring the height of each bar. Taking the High minus the Low for each day gives you the *daily range*. The average true range calculates the average daily range over ten days as a default for the Keltner settings.

>> When you have the average true range (ATR), the Keltner channel default setting measures 2 ATR above and below a moving average. For the Keltner channel, the default setting is a 20-period exponential moving average (EMA).

To summarize the default settings on StockCharts.com, do the following (and be sure to click Update after you make these changes to a basic chart):

>> Use a 20-period EMA to center the Keltner channel.

>> Calculate a ten-period average true range (ATR).

>> Draw lines 2 ATR above and below the EMA.

While that sounds complex, it's not, we promise! Figure 10-6 shows an example of the default Keltner channel on Costco (COST). Figure 10-6 also shows an expanded Keltner channel to explain how these overlay settings can be adjusted. The expanded setting is 3 ATR, shown with a dotted line marking the top and the bottom of the channel.

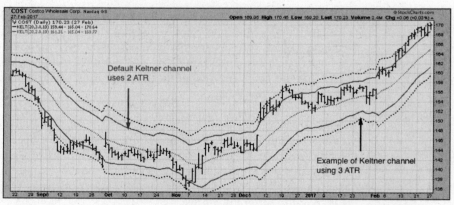

FIGURE 10-6:
Keltner channel.

Chart courtesy of StockCharts.com

With the Keltner channel defined using the default at 2 ATR, the following sections use the default setting to explore the information provided by the Keltner channel.

TIP

You don't need to play with the settings, but it is important to understand how the channel is created. Later in this chapter, we cover Bollinger Bands, which use an entirely different method to calculate the channel.

Keltner uptrends

Figure 10-7 shows a long uptrend for Caterpillar (CAT). Buying near the lower Keltner channel is a high-percentage buying opportunity. Typically, the price stays above the center line during an uptrend. Occasionally the price will drift below the center line, and this creates a potential place to buy. On Caterpillar, the lower Keltner channel has been an excellent place to expect support for the stock.

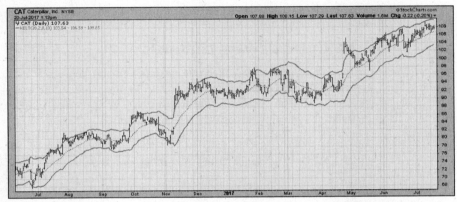

FIGURE 10-7:
Keltner uptrend.

Chart courtesy of StockCharts.com

Keltner downtrends

Keltner channels define downtrends very well. In Figure 10-8, the stock for Cenovus Energy (CVE) broke below support, and for most of the move, the stock was below the center line of the channel. With only three exceptions in six months, the stock continued under the center. You can see these points above the center at the end of February, the end of March, and the end of July in 2017.

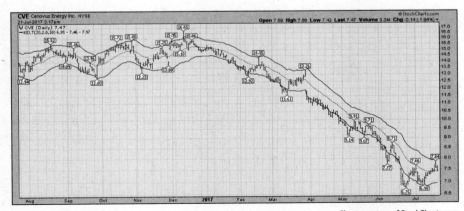

FIGURE 10-8:
Keltner
downtrend.

Chart courtesy of StockCharts.com

Each time the stock rallies back to the top of the channel is a higher-percentage shorting opportunity. If the stock starts to break back above the top of the Keltner channel, this would be a reason to close the short position. (Short selling is a very risky technique used by traders to take advantage of falling stock prices.)

After it fails at the top of the channel and pulls back to the center line, if the stock starts to stay above the center, that's also a clue that the downtrend is over. The last price bar on the chart sets up this situation. The center line is the 20 EMA, but notice how it starts to turn up for uptrends. That's another reason to watch closely.

Keltner sideways channels

In a sideways channel, the price reversals can be very quick, as Exxon Mobil (XOM) shows from March 2017 to July 2017 in Figure 10-9. While it is easy to see looking back, Canadian Natural Resources (CNQ) in the same industry trended up and down for multiple months before reversing.

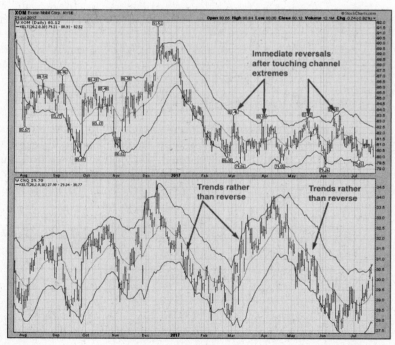

FIGURE 10-9:
Keltner sideways channels.

Chart courtesy of StockCharts.com

WARNING

The sideways channel trading strategy can be unpredictable for using Keltner channel extremes. There are other methods to trade these charts, which we discuss later in this chapter, when we talk about horizontal support and resistance.

Bollinger Bands

Bollinger Bands are named after financial analyst John Bollinger. They use a mathematical expression called *standard deviation* to calculate the upper and lower bands. To get started at the StockCharts.com website, enter a ticker symbol and click Go. Underneath the chart, from the Overlays drop-down menu, select Bollinger Bands and click Update. The lines are formed two standard deviations above and below the 20 MA (not an exponential MA). Plotting the Bollinger Bands with an area setting can help make the expansion and contraction more obvious.

The Bollinger Bands pinch significantly when price trades in small narrow moves, as you can see in Figure 10-10, showing Alphabet Inc. stock (GOOGL). As the price starts to accelerate in either direction, the bands spread out because the price is changing character. The major difference with Bollinger Bands is that they rapidly expand and shrink down compared to other types of channels.

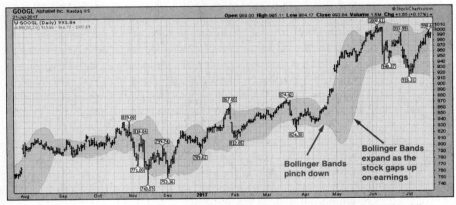

FIGURE 10-10: Bollinger Bands.

Chart courtesy of StockCharts.com

Because they are based on the deviation over the last 20 periods, as price trades sideways, they shrink down. As the price starts to break out of a sideways range, the Bollinger Bands spread apart as the price moves farther out. Two standard deviations each way will harness around 88 percent of the price moves.

It takes a big move to get to the top end of the range. When it gets there, it has already had a significant price move. Some moves are strong enough to continue, but other stocks need to pull back to the center before they start running again.

TIP

A price that trades in the lower half of the Bollinger Band and then moves to touch the top band is associated with a potential change in trend, and the stock should be evaluated for a strategy to enter a long trade. Usually the buy signal is associated with some sort of a pullback to the center of the Bollinger Bands.

Moving average envelopes

A type of channel called a moving average envelope is centered with either a 20-period SMA or a 20-period EMA. Then a percentage is used above and below the moving average that "envelopes" the price.

This method is different from the Keltner or Bollinger Band methods that we describe earlier in this chapter. With this channel method, you need to determine the percentage that captures the majority of the price moves, as the moving average channel overlay does not calculate the *volatility* of the stock.

On the StockCharts.com website, type a ticket symbol into the box at the top and click Go. When you see the chart, select SMA Envelopes or EMA Envelopes from the drop-down menu under Overlays.

On this EMA envelope style, the charting software doesn't draw in the 20 EMA center line. In Figure 10-11, Wal-Mart (WMT) and Nvidia (NVDA) are both displayed with the same default settings of 2.5 percent above and 2.5 percent below the 20-period exponential moving average. Because the software does not automatically adjust the size, it will fit on some stock prices like WMT to envelope the price, but on others, like NVDA, you have to adjust it so it fits nicely over the price information. In this example, you should adjust the percentage for NVDA to 7.0, so the price touches the lower boundary occasionally.

TIP

Two different styles for displaying the EMA channel are shown in Figure 10-11 to illustrate that style is a variable you can control by adjusting the setting in the overlay panel. While the charts are displayed with a longer time range to see the difference, investors would use a shorter time frame to see the detail of price compared to the EMA envelope on the last few price bars.

Figure 10-12 shows NVDA on both panels: the bottom with a 2.5 percent envelope and the top with a 7 percent envelope. While this seems very detailed, we have almost tripled the setting so that it works for fast-moving stocks. Fast-moving stocks make a lot of money over a short period of time, so it's worth making a quick adjustment of the default setting to help find better buying entries.

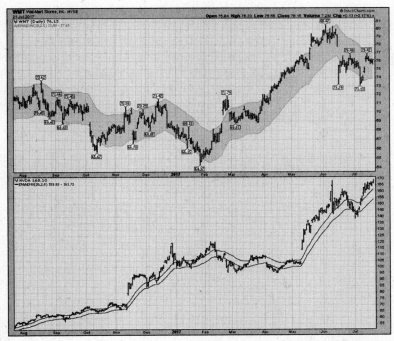

FIGURE 10-11:
EMA envelope.

Chart courtesy of StockCharts.com

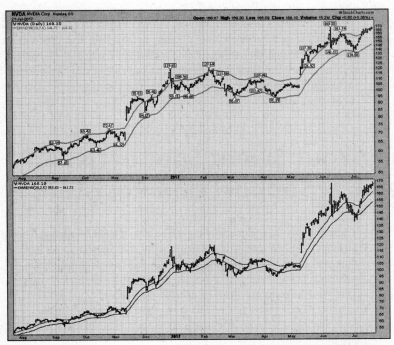

FIGURE 10-12:
Wider EMA
envelope.

Chart courtesy of StockCharts.com

TIP

There is one setting that we think is even more valuable for the channel investing methodology. Rather than setting the EMA envelope to completely wrap the price, this method, shown in Figure 10-13 for Apple stock, sets the envelope narrowly around the moving average. The envelope is a buffer zone used instead of a single line like a moving average. When the price closes above the top of the envelope, it is a buy signal for the next morning. When the price closes below the envelope, it is a sell signal the morning after.

FIGURE 10-13:
A narrow envelope around a moving average.

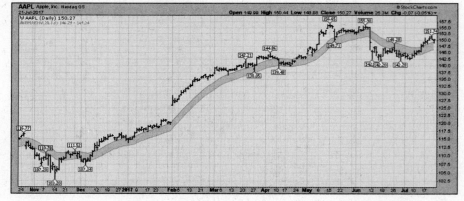

Chart courtesy of StockCharts.com

On the Overlays settings for the EMA envelope, change 2.5 to 1.0. This changes the setting from 2.5 percent to 1.0 percent. Giving the price a little room to move around the moving average creates a buffer zone that allows the price to be a little higher than the moving average for buying and a little lower than the moving average for selling. It helps keep you in strong uptrends but forces you out when they stop working.

Finding Your Sweet Spot between Horizontal Support and Resistance

Channel investing typically creates a top of the channel and a bottom of the channel. Having a strategy for channel investing can also work in sideways channels, but you need to alter a few methods. All the channel strategies relate to solving where price will run out of buying momentum on the topside and where it will run out of selling momentum on the bottom side.

While we have charted price, we have not discussed the underlying reason that these patterns or sideways channels work. When an investor makes a stock purchase, price reaches a peak and pulls back eventually. For the investor who bought just as the momentum faded, this new purchase is in a loss position right away. This investor now just wants price to get back to where he got in to minimize losses so he can sell. Investors who bought near the bottom of the channel have seen profits build in their account, only to fade away as price rolled over, and now their gains are back to zero or less. As the price reaches the maximum profit level again in the account, these investors don't want to let the gains slip away again. They are motivated to sell near the previous high as well for different reasons.

This cycle gains momentum as more and more people are selling near the upper end of the range. They also notice this stock on their watch list always seems to find lows around a certain price. The next time they buy, they want to buy down there. This behavior creates horizontal channels. Understanding the dynamics behind the price movements can help new investors find a better entry point and where they may want to sell.

Using horizontal support and resistance levels for sideways channel investing is a great way to maximize profits on stocks that have traded in a certain price range before. Figure 10-14, depicting Exxon Mobil stock (XOM), shows how drawing simple horizontal resistance lines and support lines can be a lucrative way to trade the range back and forth. Waiting for the moving average envelopes or Keltner channels may be too detailed, and using these levels of actual price points is more reliable based on investor behavior. (We talk more about how to draw these lines using the annotation tool in Chapter 17.)

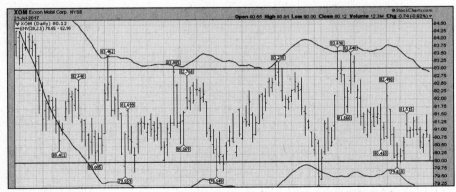

FIGURE 10-14: Horizontal support and resistance.

Chart courtesy of StockCharts.com

Figure 10-15 shows a wide range on a weekly chart. Through 2014–2016, Tesla (TSLA) had a tall sideways channel of $100 and it moved multiple times between the lows and the highs. Making $100/year on Tesla stock is welcome news to most portfolios, but you need a sideways channel strategy. Horizontal support and resistance can be drawn on the price panel using the Horizontal Line tool in the Overlays drop-down menu.

On the StockCharts.com website, click on the drop-down menu under Overlays and choose Horizontal Line. In the parameter box, enter a value. For Tesla, a price of $180 (enter only numbers, 180) is a good level. The top end of the range is $270, and a line could be added there.

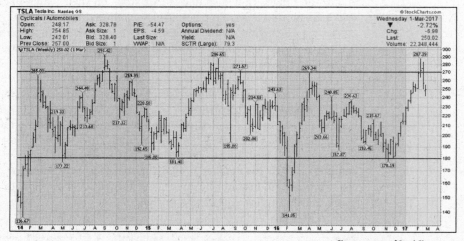

FIGURE 10-15:
Wide range for channel trading.

Chapter **11**

Using Indicators to Facilitate Chart Analysis

E arly on in the development of technical analysis, chartists tried to find methods to gauge the strength of a trend as well as find reversals. The answer
came in the form of indicators, and StockCharts.com has 50 different indicators that technicians can choose from. In this chapter, we explore some of the
key indicators for those just starting to learn the world of charting. The main
types of indicators are as follows:

» Momentum indicators

» Buying and selling pressure indicators using volume

» Leading indicators for executing trades (we discuss these types of relative
strength indicators in Chapter 12)

Beginning with Indicator Basics

REMEMBER

Indicators derived from movements in price are *lagging* when the price move has
already happened. That doesn't make them useless, though. The history of stock
moves can help you understand what happened when you see that a stock's trend
makes a base or a topping pattern (see Chapter 9 for more about bases and topping

patterns). A series of events usually happens as price changes trend. Understanding the sequence of events for a stock to start or end a trend can usually be confirmed by the use of indicators.

Keep in mind that technical analysis is a method of following investor price action, and various indicators are all designed to give you an edge. But indicators will also help you recognize price patterns. Importantly, price patterns have a success rate, much like quarterbacks throwing a football. They don't win every time.

Indicators can be used to alert you to a change in trend, which allows you to watch for a timely setup of a reversal. As price breaks support, indicators can also confirm the breakdown or give conflicting signals that suggest more analysis is needed. Specific places on a chart make chartists aware of a potential trend change, and recognizing that change can be very profitable.

REMEMBER

Simply stated, indicators can be used to show

>> Different information derived from price and/or volume, creating a divergence

>> Confirming information establishing a breakout or breakdown

>> Patterns that create high-percentage investing setups

Indicators have very different display types/scales:

>> Indicators can be *bounded* between two extremes. Depending on the indicator, it may stay at an extreme or reverse quickly from an extreme reading regularly.

>> Indicators can be *unbounded,* where they continue to climb or fall in sympathy with the price with no limit.

The following sections provide more details on divergence, bounded indicators, and unbounded indicators.

Divergence

One idea behind indicators is to have the indicator show a potential change in trend before the change in price actually happens. An example would be when the price is making a higher high, but the indicator is making a lower high. This discrepancy is called a *divergence.* Two types of divergence exist:

>> **Negative divergence:** When the price is making a higher high while the indicator is making a lower high

>> **Positive divergence:** When the price is making a lower low while the indicator is making a higher low

Not all indicators provide divergence information, but each indicator is designed to demonstrate important information about the trend in the stock.

TIP

An indicator can be used for an entry point into a stock, but the same indicator doesn't have to be used for the exit. With such a wide variety of indicators to choose from, you do have many options.

Bounded and unbounded indicators

Indicators can be divided into two types, bounded and unbounded:

>> **Bounded indicators** move between two extremes. An example would be a percentage scale where the indicator moves between 0 and 100, and the majority of the time it is between 30 and 70. The indicator design can either reverse quickly or stay at an extreme level for a long period of time, showing a strong trend. If you think about price momentum, you see that it ebbs and flows. A bounded indicator designed to reverse quickly would stall near the high end of the range and bottom when the stock is falling. Another bounded indicator might signal that a new, longer-term trend is underway and stay extreme for a while. In this chapter, the indicator is bounded unless noted otherwise.

>> **Unbounded indicators** can continue to rise higher and higher. They have no upper limit. As price rises, the indicator rises in sympathy with the price. When price finally peaks, these indicators typically start making lower highs before the price tops, so they will show a divergence (see the previous section). This variation in display style between unbounded and bounded indicators is an important distinction.

Rolling with Momentum Indicators

All indicators are plotted in a separate panel above or below the price rather than on top of the price panel. *Momentum indicators* measure the speed at which stock prices are moving. We describe the most common momentum indicators in the following sections.

Moving average convergence divergence indicator (MACD)

One of the most common indicators plotted with a stock chart is called the MACD (pronounced Mac Dee). This is the acronym for the moving average convergence divergence indicator created by investment advisor Gerald Appel. While the name sounds very confusing, the MACD usually becomes a part of every chartist's road to interpreting the market. Breaking down the name, this indicator uses two moving averages subtracted from each other and plots the result as a line. (See Chapter 10 for an introduction to moving averages.)

TIP

Here's an analogy: A basketball thrown in the air starts to slow down before it stops going up (stalls) and starts going down with gravity. Price action on a stock is similar. It continues higher, but the momentum slows before it rolls over and pulls back. This change in momentum is what the MACD shows visually in advance of the final high.

Here's an example of a MACD calculation using an exponential moving average (EMA): A short-term (12-period) moving average moves up and down, so it is quite responsive. A longer (26-period) moving average holds an uptrend longer with less wiggling. The MACD line is calculated by subtracting the two values from each other and plotting that line. The typical setting also places a second line, called a signal line, on the chart; this line helps the chartist identify turns in the price movement. The MACD histogram is another aid for reading the MACD. It is positive (above 0) when the MACD is above the signal line and negative (below 0) when it is below the signal line.

To break all of this information into parts:

>> MACD = 12 EMA minus 26 EMA

>> Signal line = 9-period EMA of the MACD line

>> MACD histogram = MACD line minus signal line

Chartists watch for divergences as the short-term moving average accelerates up and away from the long-term moving average or slows down compared to the long-term moving average. When the indicator crosses below the signal line, the uptrend in price is waning or even reversing to pull back. An indicator that crosses above the signal line is commonly referred to as a MACD buy signal.

To see a MACD visually, go to the StockCharts.com charting platform and type in a stock symbol, like MSFT for Microsoft. Click Go. A default chart should appear, and it usually has a MACD on it. Moving down below the chart to the chart settings, you can see how the MACD is selected under the Indicator area.

TIP

If you have found a chart without the MACD indicator, follow these steps. Underneath the chart, find the drop-down menu in the third section of the chart settings, under the Indicators area. Click on the Indicator drop-down menu and scroll alphabetically down to the MACD. It will autofill the default settings. Click Update.

On Figure 11-1, the MACD for Goldman Sachs (GS) hosts a wealth of information:

>> The positive divergence on the left showing the momentum is a lot better on the second low on GS. Price had made a similar low, but the MACD shows higher momentum by showing a higher low.

>> When the MACD on a daily chart goes below zero, the investor should be aware of weak momentum. Conversely, a MACD above zero and rising is very bullish for higher prices.

>> The negative divergence on the top right corner of the chart shows the price making a higher high, but the momentum (the peak of the MACD) on the second high is considerably weaker than it is on the first high.

>> At the last data point on the chart, the MACD is rolling over after barely getting back above zero. The MACD suggests the short-term momentum is very weak.

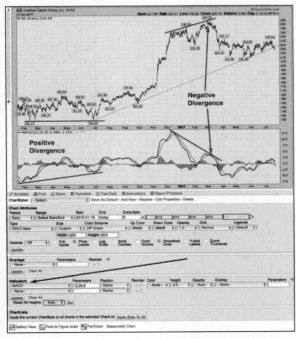

FIGURE 11-1:
MACD and
divergence.

Chart courtesy of StockCharts.com

>> There are other small divergences that can be a few days apart rather than weeks apart. Shorter-term investors may use those rather than the more obvious divergences highlighted on the chart. An example of a small divergence is in early January 2017: Price is holding up compared to the late December 2016 price, but the MACD is plummeting. The price ends up moving lower.

Momentum displays that look like the MACD

There are other momentum indicators that create similar plots to the MACD in the preceding section. Figure 11-2 shows other momentum oscillators that produce a similar pattern, but they are calculated differently.

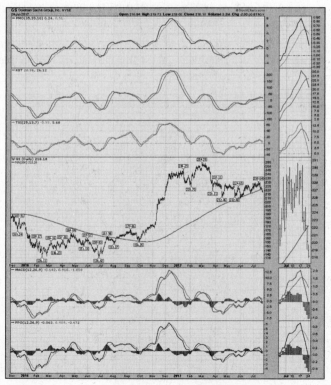

Chart courtesy of StockCharts.com

FIGURE 11-2: Momentum indicators.

You can see the following momentum indicators in Figure 11-2:

>> **Price momentum oscillator (PMO):** The price momentum oscillator (PMO) created by technical analyst Carl Swenlin uses longer moving averages and a faster signal line. The PMO is displayed in the top panel above the Goldman Sachs price plot.

>> **Know sure thing (KST):** Another good one that is smoother than the MACD is the know sure thing (KST) by technical analyst Martin Pring, which uses four different readings to identify the rate of change and derive momentum. The KST is in the second panel above the Goldman Sachs price plot.

>> **The true strength index (TSI):** The true strength index (TSI) is not as common as the PMO and the KST, but it also creates a similar line to the MACD. The TSI is in the third panel above the Goldman Sachs price plot. It was created by analyst William Blau.

>> **Percentage price oscillator (PPO):** The bottom two panels of Figure 11-2 show the MACD below the Goldman Sachs price, and underneath it is the percentage price oscillator (PPO). The PPO uses the percentage change in the price rather than the actual price movement in dollars.

On the settings panel, the default Position is to display the indicator below the price panel. In the third column, you can select one of three choices under Position using the drop-down menu. The choices are Above, Below, and Behind Price.

The following sections go into more detail on two aspects of these momentum indicators: scaling and histograms.

The scaling of indicators

Figure 11-2 shows scales on all five indicators (three above, two below) that are different because of the calculation methodology, but they all generate a similar profile for momentum. There are some subtle differences where the indicator line crossed the signal line on one of these indicators but not on another. For example, the MACD and the PPO below the chart show more defined spikes in price in December 2016, while the three indicators above the chart show smoother price movement.

Histograms for MACD and PPO

The MACD and PPO indicators have a default setting that shows a histogram in the background going above and below the center line. The histogram shows the distance between the moving average and the signal line on the MACD. The histogram tops before the MACD line turns over. When the histogram crosses the zero-line going lower, this quick, graphical look confirms the MACD line is below the signal line. When the MACD goes below zero, the price of the stock is very weak, and this negative momentum is usually causing an investor to lose money.

Because the MACD makes progressively higher peaks as the price climbs, it is an unbounded oscillator. If the stock has a high price like $1,000 per share, the MACD will have a high number compared to another stock with a price of $10 per share.

When you use percentage for momentum (the PPO indicator), it removes this effect of price pushing the momentum indicator continually higher and higher. The PPO can be used to compare longer date ranges with dramatically different levels of price for fast-moving stocks like Amazon (AMZN).

If you don't use the PPO, the early moves in a price chart will look insignificant in terms of momentum. Figure 11-3 compares the MACD and the PPO of Amazon for 15 years. The modern price move is significant, but Amazon was climbing a lot faster back in 2003 on a percentage basis. Some of the fastest moves happened in 2003 and 2007, but the MACD shows the momentum to be less than recent moves. It is the massive change in price that causes this distortion. (Note that for this chart, we chose a logarithmic scale, which works better when you're developing long-range charts. See Chapter 9 for more about scales.)

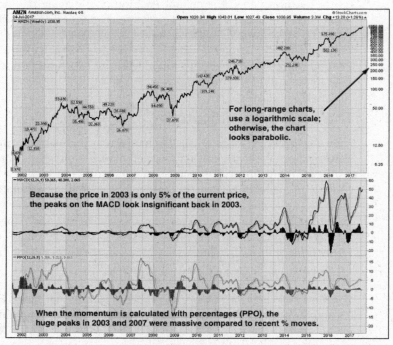

FIGURE 11-3: Long-term PPO and MACD.

Chart courtesy of StockCharts.com

TIP

Use the PPO for long-range charts on stocks with huge price changes to keep the early strength of the stock in perspective.

Relative strength index (RSI)

The relative strength index (RSI) was created by technical analyst J. Welles Wilder. According to the StockCharts.com database, the RSI is the indicator most often used. This momentum indicator measures the internal strength of the price moves. RSI is in the drop-down list in the Indicators area of the chart settings.

The design of the indicator calculates the average up days divided by the average down days to get a comparison between the two directions. A stock trending higher has more average up days than down days. The benefit of the indicator is it can tell you a lot through subtle signals in the price movement.

The first calculation is as follows:

» First average gain = sum gains for 14 periods divided by 14

» First average loss = sum losses for 14 periods divided by 14

For the second part of the analysis, use the average gain number from the previous period and multiply by 13; then add the new one and divide by 14. This ends up smoothing the data by using the average gain and doing one multiplication. Do the same for the losses.

» Average gain = ([previous average gain times 13] plus current gain) divided by 14

» Average loss = ([previous average loss times 13] plus current loss) divided by 14

Dividing the average gain by the average loss gives you the relative strength ratio, but the scale is different for every stock because of the price. Some stocks move pennies per day, and some move $10 per day, so every RS scale is unique on every stock.

Relative strength (RS) = average gain divided by average loss (a positive divided by a negative is a negative number)

To normalize this scaling issue, you turn it into a percentage between 0 and 100 so that you can compare RSI readings across stocks. The (1 plus RS) makes the number always positive:

Relative strength index (RSI) = 100 minus (100 divided by [1 plus RS])

Because you are comparing the average gain per 14 periods, the stock would have to be down every day in a row to have an RSI of zero. The typical range is between 20 and 80 for momentum stocks (any stock with a rapid change in price or earnings) and 30 and 70 for some utility stocks (like electric or gas companies). You can see that in Figure 11-4, Wal-Mart's typical RSI range was from 30 to 80. It showed that it was overbought in April and May of 2017. Then you see the price drop in June.

FIGURE 11-4:
RSI daily.

Chart courtesy of StockCharts.com

In the following sections, we explain RSI time periods and usage for a variety of charts.

Picking out time periods for the RSI

Investors looking to use charts for trading are usually uncomfortable changing the default settings on any chart. The RSI is one of those defaults that you should adapt to your trading style.

There are all kinds of different trading strategies using different RSI settings. On intraday charts, daily and weekly charts, and long-term monthly charts, the RSI is one of the most flexible indicators for helping traders find extremes for reversals that they like to use for catching profitable new positions. Some examples (specifying days) are

- ≫ RSI 2
- ≫ RSI 5
- ≫ RSI 8
- ≫ RSI 9
- ≫ RSI 10
- ≫ RSI 14
- ≫ RSI 48

The number of days you set impacts how sensitive the chart is to price change. For example, an RSI 10 is more likely to show overbought or oversold levels than a longer RSI 20. Differences are more pronounced with stocks whose prices are moving more rapidly. For example, Amazon is a more volatile stock than Duke Energy, so it will likely become more overbought or oversold at 14 days than Duke.

Using the RSI

Using the RSI formula on any time period is valuable, as the RSI has withstood the test of time and has been used by thousands of people. One of the early ways to use RSI was to assume that when the RSI was above 70, the stock was overbought, and you should wait for a pullback to get in. The same concept applied to downside moves. The stock was considered oversold below 30, so a bounce could be expected and might make a nice entry.

Advancements in the RSI study by technical analyst Constance Brown are also noteworthy. Brown noted that RSI levels may indicate changes or continuation in trend. Figure 11-5 shows trend signals on a daily chart for Wal-Mart (WMT). When the RSI is constantly staying in the lower half, usually below 60, the stock is weak. When the weak readings on the RSI move up and touch 70, it suggests there is enough strength to start moving higher and start a bullish trend that will remain in place until the next weak market signal at 30.

Continuing with that same logic, Figure 11-6 shows trend change signals on a weekly chart for HP (HPQ). When the RSI touches 30, it marks a bear market trend. The stock continues to stay below 60, and price usually declines. When the RSI touches 70, this suggests there is enough strength to start moving higher and start a bull market trend that will remain in place until the next weak market signal at 30. Coauthor Greg uses this RSI analysis every week on hundreds of charts.

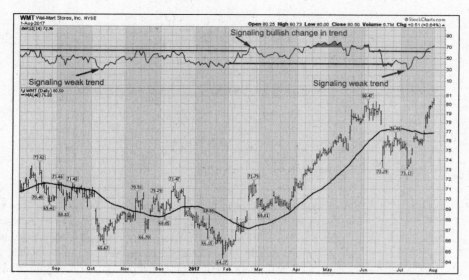

FIGURE 11-5:
RSI daily with
trend changes
marked.

Chart courtesy of StockCharts.com

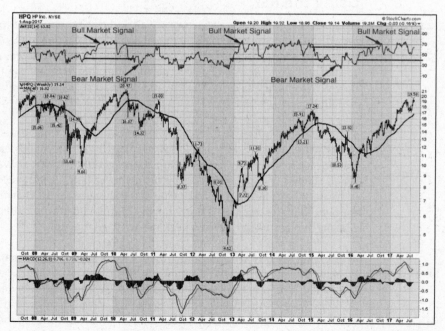

FIGURE 11-6:
RSI weekly.

Chart courtesy of StockCharts.com

The chart for HPQ in Figure 11-6 is shown over a ten-year period, so these are important trend signals. Most of the trends lasted multiple years. In October 2013 and October 2014, the stock dipped below the 40-week moving average (as you can see in the middle panel; flip to Chapter 10 for more on moving averages). This would look problematic based on how the price stays above and below the moving average. The RSI held 40 in both cases, however, and price rebounded to continue the bull market.

TIP

Knowing the RSI level helps you consider what to do and perhaps prevents you from selling the stock in a weak market. It may even alert you to a potential new position buy point or a place to add to your existing position. Being aware of the RSI as a trend indicator is very helpful. There's no guarantee that it won't immediately move to the other side of the range to change market signals, but HPQ in Figure 11-6 does a great job of demonstrating how valuable the signal can be to stay in long bull market runs.

Considering RSI on other charts

RSI can work well on commodity charts, currency charts, and bond charts as well as stock charts. The default of the RSI is 14, and that setting is a good trend-following setting. Traders use short-term RSI settings of 2, 5, 8, or 9 to get more signals.

An example of an important RSI signal occurred in July 2017 for the US Dollar ($USD). The indicator moved below 30, signaling a new bear market for the $USD after a six-year bull market run. You can see this in Figure 11-7. Three clues are here for the chartist at this point to consider that are not available to a fundamental-based investor:

>> $USD is very oversold by definition on a weekly chart, and chart watchers should expect a short-term bounce from around these levels that could last a few months.

>> The $USD primary trend is signaling a new bear market in July 2017, and any rallies should be expected to top out around 50–60 on the RSI. Placing new trades expecting the $USD to go down will be much more profitable if traders wait until the weekly RSI tops out. If the US Dollar trade doesn't work out, the stop will be a lot closer to the entry for minimal losses.

>> Even though price has not made a new low to affect casual observers, the RSI reading is changing the perception of this chart for chartists. You can see that the $USD was swinging from extreme to extreme during one period, and the RSI helped you pick that out on the chart.

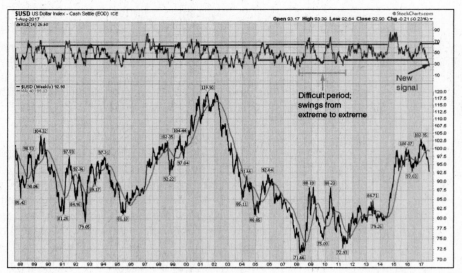

Chart courtesy of StockCharts.com

FIGURE 11-7:
RSI on currency
charts.

Chartists still watched for the $USD to stop falling and bounce in the near term. However, the bear market signal should adjust a chartist's perception that the six-year bull market in the $USD *probably* ended in July 2017. This is not a guarantee, but showing up after a long bull market run, it's highly likely to have an effect for a year or two.

A chartist may use that long-term information as a major backdrop regarding the $USD and other asset classes. With a short-term picture, the awareness that there should be a shimmering rally in the dollar from deeply oversold levels is a pretty helpful piece of information as well. The long-term picture is bearish, but the short-term position could become bullish at any time.

TIP

These RSI signals are some of the critical information gems to help chartists adapt to changing market conditions. The $USD is a significant chart that affects bonds, commodities, and equities as well as currency pairs. It is one of the cornerstones for investing worldwide. A major trend change in the dollar suggests looking around for other important clues to show up in other markets.

Stochastics

Stochastics indicators — another type of momentum indicator that you can find in the drop-down list in the Indicators area — were invented by technical analyst George Lane in the 1950s before computers. It's almost impossible to believe Mr. Lane had the discipline to calculate stochastics for multiple stocks manually.

While the manual updating of a chart is one of the best learning systems going, stochastics needed a calculation to update the chart, as we demonstrate in this section.

Thinking of stochastics as a direction-of-movement indicator

George passed away in 2004 but left the world with an interesting gem to help see a trend change as it's occurring, before the price change moves so much that it's obvious. He described the indicator as predicting the direction of movement.

TIP

Mr. Lane tried to find something that would identify a change in momentum. His style was remarkably smooth. Interviews with George showed that he used rockets as an analogy. (Nice when your stock price has rocket-ship analogies.) A rocket lifts off and soars, and the analogy worked to excite people to understand George's methods. When a rocket starts to slow, it's still climbing, but the rate is changing. When the rocket actually stops climbing, the momentum has dramatically changed and is negative. Using two different timelines for momentum, George found a reliable system that worked on three-minute charts, intraday charts, daily charts, and weekly charts.

George lived close to Chicago and developed his systems for commodities. The interesting part is they work well for indexes, exchange-traded funds (ETFs), stocks, and bonds, as well as commodities.

Measuring highs and lows with %K and %D

George went through the alphabet trying different ideas, and he found K and D formed an interesting combination. (Much like Henry Ford, who started with the Model A, went through a bunch of unsuccessful cars and finally got through the Model T. Henry Ford actually built the Model K for wealthy investors in Ford Motor Company, but it didn't sell well. Henry just kept working on new models until he hit the right one.)

TECHNICAL STUFF

You don't need to be perplexed by the acronym titles. George was simply working through a series of ideas, and the K idea and the D idea worked great as a pair.

Because the stochastic is finding where something is in a range, the calculation converts it to a percentage, so these are called %K and %D. Very simply, the %K is calculating a price range from the high in the period to the low. Then it answers the question: Is the current price closer to the top or the bottom of the range? Because price wobbles around a lot, the %D takes a three-day average.

>> %K = ([current close minus lowest low] divided by [highest high minus highest low]) multiplied by 100

- Lowest low = lowest low for the look-back period (the number of days you're measuring in the history of the stock's trades).

- Highest high = highest high for the look-back period.

- %K is multiplied by 100 to move the decimal point two places.

>> %D = Three-day simple moving average (SMA) of %K

TIP

Consider this weather analogy: If the temperature range for the last 14 days is 61–81, where is the current temperature in that range? What is the average of the last three days? An analyst can use this for the last 14 hours, 14 days, or 14 weeks. Obviously, on a 14-hour chart, you would expect the weather to warm up in the morning and cool off in the evening. On a weekly basis, 14 weeks would correlate closely to the four seasons and would help analyze seasonal temperature changes.

Back to using this formula for stocks, as the price starts to move away from the low end of the range, you want to own the stock. If the price starts to make higher highs, it stretches out the range, and the price is staying near the top of the range. When price is no longer pushing higher and starts to drift back to the middle of the range, the momentum is waning. At this point the suggestion would be to sell. Why wait until it actually starts dropping?

TIP

By changing the time period for the chart, you can change the trading style for different types of investors. While the words stochastics, %K, and %D sound very technical, the model is very simple and works well. You can use stochastics on any time frame, including 10-minute charts, 60-minute charts, daily charts, weekly charts, or monthlies.

Figure 11-8 shows a daily chart of stochastics on Citigroup (C). For some investors, it is easy to observe that these daily signals have missed significant parts of the move higher. Stochastics is about getting the move while the rocket is thrusting higher, not drifting higher. The arrows pointing down show lower lows, and the arrows pointing up show higher highs.

A weekly chart of Momo Inc. (MOMO) has a beautiful stochastics rhythm about it. Trades last a few months, and as a trader, you can catch some significant moves. Figure 11-9 shows a weekly stochastic. The rhythm shown is real, but not all the charts are this nice to the trader. Some trades will not work.

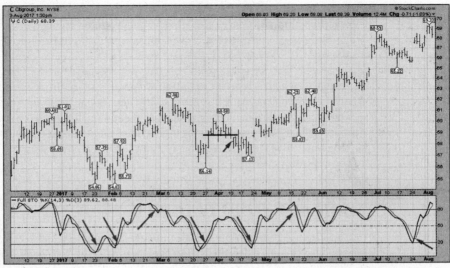

FIGURE 11-8:
Stochastics daily.

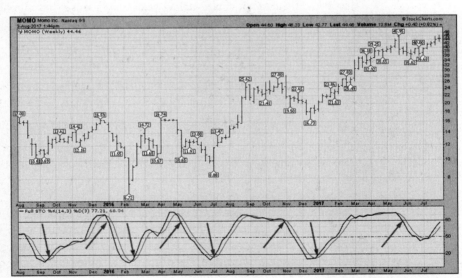

FIGURE 11-9:
Stochastics
weekly.

Using Volume with Price

Indicator values are usually derived from calculations around price. Another significant clue is volume. When price is pushing higher, you want to see the volume
expand, suggesting there are more buyers. When price is pushing lower, volume
usually expands, suggesting the selling pressure is high. If the price is dropping

but the volume is not accelerating, it suggests the stock is being held and not sold by the large institutions. These clues can be helpful for assessing a stock's strength.

Because of high-frequency trading, volume is more difficult to analyze, but there are very good indicators to help with this, as you find out in this section. Some very smart technicians have used volume and price together to create unique indicators. There are two indicators with *money flow* in the name, but they are calculated and displayed differently. You can find both of these in the drop-down list in the Indicators area on StockCharts.com.

Chaikin money flow (CMF)

The Chaikin money flow (CMF) indicator, created by stock analyst Marc Chaikin, uses the closing price relative to the open price to decide whether the money was flowing out of the stock while the market was open. It doesn't pick up gaps from the previous day's close to the current day's close. The CMF can be positive on the day even if the stock closed below yesterday's close, but climbed after opening lower.

The calculations go like this:

>> Money flow multiplier = ([close minus low] minus [high minus close]) divided by (high minus low)

>> Money flow volume = money flow multiplier multiplied by volume for the period

>> 20-period CMF = 20-period sum of money flow volume divided by 20-period sum of volume

Looking at the calculation, if the close is closer to the low than the high, this makes the first part of the calculation negative. Dividing it by the intra-period range gives it a weighting. If price closes very close to the lows on a wide range, it will have a money flow multiplier close to −1. If the close is very close to the high, it will have a money flow multiplier near 1.0.

Using the multiplier times volume gives a weighting to the multiplier in the second calculation. The third part adds up the volume-weighted multiplier and divides it by the average volume to create a CMF value.

Essentially, the CMF is about weighting the flow of money positively or negatively on volume. The scale on money flow is bounded between +1 and −1. It needs to close on the high of the day every day for the period used (default = 20) to have a 1.0 rating. Because extremes rarely happen, the StockCharts.com platform adjusts the scale to make the moves reach the top and bottom of the panel. Figure 11-10 displays the CMF indicator for a stock chart of Freeport-McMoRan (FCX).

FIGURE 11-10: Chaikin money flow (CMF).

Chart courtesy of StockCharts.com

Notice that the first divergence was a good signal that price was about to improve. The divergence in the center of the chart (the beginning of June) was suggesting price would fall, but price did not. It went on to push considerably higher. Looking for divergences compared to the price can be a useful part of the analysis of the CMF, but it shouldn't be used on its own.

TIP

The CMF indicator shows when money is flowing into the stock. Using it in combination with the RSI or MACD (covered earlier in this chapter) to help with momentum can be valuable.

Money flow index (MFI)

The money flow index (MFI) indicator uses the change from the previous day's close to the current day's close to evaluate money flow in or out. The raw calculation of one day's volume multiplied by price is money flow. Using a default 14-period calculation, this is an adaptation of the RSI calculation (described earlier in this chapter), adding volume as a weighting tool. You can see this indicator in Figure 11-11.

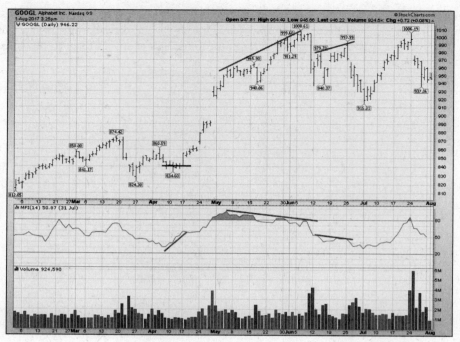

FIGURE 11-11:
Money flow
index (MFI).

Chart courtesy of StockCharts.com

The lines in this chart help identify significant up or down trends. Note how the MFI shows a downward trend when the stock moves up on a trend line.

There are four components to the calculation:

>> Price = (High + Low + Close) divided by 3

>> Raw money flow = price multiplied by volume

>> Money flow ratio = (14-period positive money flow) divided by (14-period negative money flow)

>> Money flow index = 100 minus (100 divided by [1 plus money flow ratio])

The first part of the calculation generates an average price for the period. The second part of the calculation uses volume multiplied by price to weight the importance. The third component, money flow ratio, develops a ratio of positive to negative days. The final step creates a bounded oscillator between 0 and 100. This scale is used consistently and doesn't change, unlike the CMF indicator discussed in the previous section.

On-balance volume (OBV)

The concept of money flowing into a stock is also found on the on-balance volume (OBV) indicator. One of the earliest forms of using volume was to combine the push from investors into the stock by adding or subtracting the new volume to the previous total:

>> **If closing is above the prior close:** Current OBV = previous OBV plus current volume

>> **If closing is below the prior close:** Current OBV = previous OBV minus current volume

>> **If closing is the same as the prior close:** Current OBV is unchanged

Figure 11-12 shows a chart for Exxon Mobil (XOM), with the OBV being added on up days and subtracted on down days. There is no scale on the right-hand side as this unbounded oscillator continues to rise and fall with price. In the month of July, the OBV is improving but price is declining. Investors would be watching for the price to start to accelerate higher.

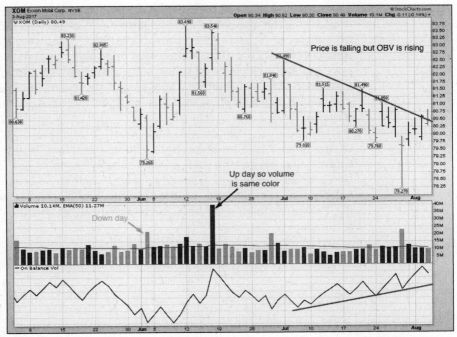

FIGURE 11-12: On-balance volume (OBV).

Chart courtesy of StockCharts.com

Accumulation distribution (ACCUM/DIST)

There are other indicators that have different calculations and display metrics to show the effect of positive volume on the stock. The last panel in Figure 11-13 has an indicator called accumulation/distribution and uses the information calculated for the Chaikin money flow (covered earlier in this chapter):

>> Money flow multiplier = ([close minus low] minus [high minus close]) divided by (high minus low)

>> Money flow volume = money flow multiplier multiplied by volume for the period

>> Accumulation distribution line (ADL) = current period money flow volume plus prior ADL

This subtle distinction may give you different signals, because the Chaikin money flow isn't calculated using the prior period close. The ACCUM/DIST indicator compares against the opening price for the period. Again, the OBV in the preceding section compares against the previous period closing price.

Recognizing the trend is the most important part of using the ACCUM/DIST or the OBV. Figure 11-13 shows OBV and ACCUM/DIST underneath the stock chart for Intel (INTC). ACCUM/DIST broke above prior highs in March 2016 even though price was still well below prior highs. The OBV didn't confirm the push to higher highs until May. Both indicators gave a signal that volume was pushing higher and price would probably follow. Sure enough, INTC roared 20 percent higher after the May signal.

On the August 2017 breakout, both volume indicators were making new highs before price, suggesting price would probably go on to new highs. There was also another subtle clue in June/July 2017, where price broke down out of the uptrend but the OBV and ACCUM/DIST maintained higher lows compared to the February/March 2017 lows. Both signals suggested that INTC was being accumulated.

FIGURE 11-13:
OBV ACCUM/
DIST.

Chart courtesy of StockCharts.com

Determining How Many Indicators to Use on One Chart

Technical analysis is about getting multiple indicators confirming a directional trade. If you use ten different indicators on one chart, you will never place a trade because by the time they all get in agreement, the best part of the trade will be behind you. If you use too many indicators, another risk is that you will reach analysis paralysis and never place a trade.

TIP

Using a combination of three to five indicators and overlays gives you the best strategies. In Chapter 21 we discuss putting it all together to give you some ideas for executing your trades based on charts.

REMEMBER

The idea behind showing all of these different indicators with different companies is that you will have different investing styles based on how often you want to trade. After seeing the weekly charts, do they intrigue you or are you more interested in three-to-five-day trades? There is no perfect strategy. The biggest challenge is to find the trading timeline you like and then pick some indicators that match the way you like to make decisions. The ChartSchool area of `StockCharts.com` explains each indicator in considerable detail with ideas for using the tool.

The world of technical analysis is always changing, and investors are constantly lured into new strategies. Try to build on something that works, and understand when your plan works and doesn't work. You will make more money investing in strong stocks with a consistent set of indicators than you will trying to find the golden egg. Even when you have the golden egg, you will be tempted to keep searching.

Ideally, you want a momentum indicator and a trigger indicator (an indicator that helps you detect a change in trend; we talk more about how to customize your charts to do this in Part 5). If you want signals to get into trades, are you looking for a low-priced, beaten-down stock that is going to be the next great stock? Perhaps you like to buy stocks breaking out to new highs; a whole world of investors agrees with that idea. You will use different indicators for those two trades. Indicators are great when used sparingly. Hopefully, you agree.

Chapter **12**

Making Sense of Relative Strength Indicators

Technical analysis (TA) has changed over the years, and one of the changes is what relative strength means. The indicators in this chapter are completely different from the relative strength index (RSI) indicator in Chapter 11 because of these changes in terminology:

» The RSI indicator in Chapter 11 compares current period closing prices to previous prices *within* a stock over the last 14 periods as a default.

» New indicators today known as *relative strength indicators* analyze how strong a stock is *compared to other stocks.*

While the chapters about overlays and indicators (Chapters 10 and 11) help you with analyzing a chart, the relative strength tools in this chapter help you compare one stock to other stocks. To outperform the market, you need to know how to compare stocks to select the one performing the best within a particular sector or industry. Relative strength indicators help you find such information.

Strong price action in a stock is obvious in the rearview mirror, but not as obvious in the real-time windshield of investing. Unfortunately, it's hard to get great investing results working with lousy, slow-moving stocks. Relative strength is one of the easiest ways to measure which stocks are advancing faster than other stocks. In this chapter, we introduce six different types of relative strength and show the strength using indicators. These techniques have created a fantastic edge for chartists to understand how their stocks are doing in the big picture:

>> Comparing a stock relative to the S&P 500

>> Comparing a stock relative to its sector

>> Comparing a stock relative to its industry group

>> Ranking a stock against peers to see the best in the market (SCTR)

>> Performance charts

>> Relative Rotation Graphs

Relative Strength Investing Basics: Seeking Better-Performing Stocks

Relative strength investing looks for stocks with better price movement so an investor can outperform the market. The idea behind *relative strength investing* is to find stocks that are outperforming the other stocks so you actually outperform the market. If the S&P 500 is up 10 percent in a year, for example, you want to use relative strength investing strategies to outperform the index. Otherwise, you can just buy the index, and that will get you diversification into various sectors.

The following sections provide some fundamentals on relative strength investing: how sectors and industries come into play, what constitutes a strong stock, and what to check on your charts when you use this investing strategy.

TECHNICAL STUFF

The word *strength* in the stock market refers to stocks that have strong price action in the up direction. When you think about a rising market, if all the stocks seem to go up, what is the issue? Well, in a rising market, an investor can just buy the SPY exchange-traded fund (ETF) or the QQQ ETF to get a basket of some of the biggest stocks out there. This would be passive investing.

Sectors and industries

The market is broken down into sectors and industries. When whole sectors or industry groups are doing well, that can be a great clue to finding new stocks. The methodology for creating these industry groups is not specific to each stock market. These sector components may be on the New York Stock Exchange (NYSE) or the NASDAQ.

In Figure 12-1, the market has 11 sectors and 157 sub-industry classifications. These are based on the Global Industry Classification System (GICS). Figure 12-1 highlights industries within the energy sector.

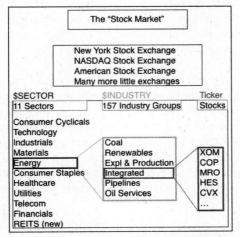

FIGURE 12-1: Sectors and industries.

When you're trying to pick stocks, your first task is to determine whether an entire sector is moving up or just a particular industry in that sector. For example, looking at Figure 12-1, you can pick any energy company, or you may want to focus your investing in integrated energy. After you decide, you can look for the strongest stocks in the sector or industry.

What makes a strong stock

The difficulty with the concept of *investing in strength* is that everyone will tell you to buy strong stocks. Defining a strong stock may be different for every stock market investor, however.

Accountants will probably default to companies with good earnings and good growth, but Tesla stock (as just one example) has doubled in under a year with losses year after year. Amazon's stock continues to rise and is around $1,000 a share, but it spends all of its profits year after year on growing the business, and the shareholders continue to look at a company with terrible bottom-line profitability because of the reinvestment. Yet the Amazon stock price action is great.

Pipeline companies have huge, consistent earnings, and the stocks are flat to down on the year. Grocery companies deliver cash flow every month, but the stock price increases are lackluster. If you look at high-margin retail stocks like Coach and Michael Kors, they have been out of favor as Amazon puts pressure on retail store strategies. They may cycle back into the fastest-growing theme.

Industrial companies do well with a receding US Dollar. Commodity companies have been poor performers from 2011 to 2016, but they have years where they are the top performers. Technology companies have been soaring for years. Biotech companies were soaring, went out of favor for two years, and then started 2017 soaring higher. It seems so confusing.

REMEMBER

What can cause this shift, and more importantly, how can you stay on top of it? Opinions don't help find strong stocks. You need to see institutional-size investors pushing the stock price higher at a rate that is faster than other stocks and faster than the broad index of good companies. (After you own the stocks, how do you know when to sell? There is never an obvious signpost saying "Exit now.") Going back to the definition: Relative strength investing looks for stocks with better price movement so an investor can outperform the market. Chartists are continually on the watch for the fastest-moving charts in the market.

Four things to know in relative strength investing

REMEMBER

For relative strength investing based on charts, you want to know four things in real-time:

>> When the stock starts outperforming (for example, new three-month highs)

>> When the stock starts rising faster than most stocks

>> When the stock starts underperforming other stocks

>> When to leave the stock

Trying to invest in top-performing stocks and accomplish great investing goals is the result of lifelong learning for investment managers. Relative strength tools enable you to find them as well.

Measuring a Stock's Relative Strength to the S&P 500, a Sector, and an Industry

When using the term "relative strength," the technician has to define relative to *what*. The commonly accepted default is the S&P 500. In the stock market, you need to compare a stock to another stock or to a stock index to decide which is performing better. You can compare the stock to anything you want.

Examples would be comparing a stock to the S&P 500 ($SPX) or the Nasdaq 100 ($NDX), or comparing the stock to an industry, a sector, or just another stock. To define what you are comparing to, an example would be to say *the strength relative to the S&P 500 ($SPX)* or the *relative strength* compared to the $SPX. We use the StockCharts.com *ratio tool* to show this comparison graphically.

The following sections explain how to create and interpret a ratio chart that pinpoints a particular stock, and how to use a ratio chart to make wider comparisons (like a sector versus an industry).

TECHNICAL STUFF

Determining relative strength using the StockCharts.com ratio tool is a great method for making comparisons and is widely used. Institutional investment managers are expected to outperform the industry index or the broad market indexes to keep their jobs. If they underperform, they probably won't have a job. Continuing to find and own stocks that are outperforming their benchmark index is a harsh reality for these institutional investors. Using the ratio tool gives chartists access to the same strength information that institutional investors would be using.

Creating a ratio chart

To use the ratio tool on the StockCharts.com charting platform, enter the ticker symbol of the stock you're interested in and click Go. A default chart should appear. Find the Indicators area of the settings panel below the chart (see Chapter 3 for more about this panel). Select Price from the Indicators drop-down list (it's alphabetical), then enter the stock ticker symbol followed by a colon, and then enter the index or ticker symbol that you would like to compare the stock to. For example, to compare Exxon Mobile (XOM) stock to the S&P 500, you type XOM:$SPX. Click the Update button.

Figure 12-2 demonstrates some setting variables and the resulting display examples using the ratio tool to show the relative strength for Procter and Gamble (PG).

>> PG:$SPX would compare Procter & Gamble (PG) to the S&P 500 Index.

>> PG:$SECTOR would compare PG to its sector, Consumer Staples.

>> PG:XLP would compare Procter & Gamble (PG) to its sector using the SPDR sector ETF, which has the symbol XLP. This would produce the same result as PG:$SECTOR.

>> PG:$INDUSTRY would compare PG to its industry group, Personal Products.

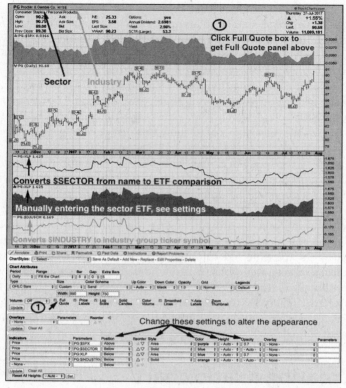

FIGURE 12-2:
Different inputs
for relative
strength.

Chart courtesy of StockCharts.com

TIP

You can find out what sector and industry group a stock is in by clicking on the Full Quote box under Chart Attributes at Point 1. Figure 12-2 shows the different inputs in the Indicators area of the chart settings panel to create these relative strength ratios. (In Chapter 3, we take a closer look at the alternatives for styles, colors, height, opacity, and overlays.)

Another important thing to note is that the scales can't be compared or used to compare one stock to another stock. Because relative strength compares one price to another price, a stock worth $100 and a stock worth $1,000 will have different scales, even though they may be performing comparably in percentage terms. As every stock, industry group, and sector has a different price, all of these scales are not relatable across different stocks. (Flip to Chapter 9 for details on scales.)

If you compare based on percentage or logarithmic scales, the start date will be used to measure the percentage change from then to now. While that is comparable, it still doesn't address other issues that are important technically. If you use a long range of one year, the stock may be down compared to the $SPX. If you use a short period of one month, the stock may be up compared to the $SPX. While this relative strength system is excellent for finding relative strength based on a specific time period, it allows only one parameter.

Interpreting a ratio chart

If the *relative strength line* is trending up, the ticker symbol is outperforming what the second symbol represents. If it is trending sideways, it is performing the same as the comparison. If it is trending down, it's underperforming.

For example, in Figure 12-2 showing PG:$SPX, the stock was underperforming the index and hit the worst level of underperformance on the time period shown during the week of June 10. At the right edge of the chart, PG was near two-month highs in relative strength to the $SPX.

TIP

Stocks making new relative strength highs are sending good messages about their performance. Watch for stocks making three-month, six-month, or one-year highs in relative strength to the S&P 500 index, as these inflection points can be helpful for seeing change in trend. Draw a horizontal line and compare how many months the current high exceeds.

You can use Procter & Gamble (PG) in Figure 12-2 to view how these various comparisons can help. First compare PG to its sector (PG:$SECTOR); the stock has been outperforming the sector for three months. The last data point, July 27 on the chart, is equivalent to the level on April 18, 2017. PG is starting to outperform its sector, but still lags in performance compared to the $SPX.

Next, look at the comparison with its sector index. For PG:XLP, this is the same information as PG:$SECTOR, but you can input the information either way. The difference is that if you change the main ticker symbol to, say, Apple (AAPL), the sector will not adjust from XLP to the index called XLK, which is the index for AAPL's sector (technology). That's the advantage of using $SECTOR rather than a specific ETF for comparison. $SECTOR automatically shifts the various sector and industry groups as you work through your stocks. It adjusts the information on the chart legend, but leaves the settings panel below unchanged. The settings panel allows the type of chart style to be changed to Area rather than Solid (line) to show the ease of adjusting the display parameters.

Finally, compare PG with its industry. For PG:$INDUSTRY, the StockCharts.com charting engine looks up the Dow Jones Industry Group and inserts that information on the chart legend when plotting it, but it does not change the setting information below. This allows you to continue to move through other charts and maintain the $INDUSTRY setting. Notice that the chart legend converted $INDUSTRY to $DJUSCM, which is the ticker symbol for the Dow Jones Personal Products industry group. PG is outperforming the industry and is at fresh, new four-month highs at the end of July in Figure 12-2.

TIP

Simply stated: If you use $SECTOR and $INDUSTRY in the settings, the StockCharts.com charting engine will match the sector and industry information with the stock, rather than you having to investigate it. Then if you change to a different stock in a different sector to look at, it will change the sector and industry group information accordingly. These shortcuts are wonderful to use.

Making broader comparisons

TIP

StockCharts allows other comparisons without changing the main chart ticker symbol or doing a lot of research. Examples include the following:

>> If you want to see how the Procter and Gamble industry group is doing compared to the sector, enter $INDUSTRY:$SECTOR.

>> To see how Procter and Gamble's sector is doing relative to the S&P 500, enter $SECTOR:$SPX. This saves a lot of work.

The chart engine quickly allows you to compare thousands of pieces of information and plot them using these tools. In the fundamental analysis of earnings, this would be an impossible task that would take weeks of spreadsheet analysis. Charting can make comparing a stock to its industry or sector very simple. Your best chance of picking the strongest stock is to find the one that is performing the strongest in its industry or sector.

Ranking Stocks with SCTR

Another method for demonstrating relative strength is the StockCharts technical ranking (SCTR) system. This is a relatively new indicator created at StockCharts. com, having been around for ten years.

Introducing technical ranking

Technical ranking sounds complex. Sports aficionados will recognize a ranking system in a sport league table found in the sports pages that used to be in the newspaper. Now these ranking tables are online under each league's website, usually under *Standings* or *Ranking*. They are published after every game played and keep track of which team is winning more often. The standings/ranking tables are a technical ranking for sports.

In the stock market, you want to do the same thing. The StockCharts.com ranking system creates some rules for comparing the price movement of a stock against other stocks. By using more than one indicator to create the ranking, you can deal with stocks of varying prices and industry groups. You can also use varying time ranges to help find stocks with improving price action. The StockCharts technical ranking system (SCTR) is based on a group of technical overlays and indicators. It is a personal favorite of ours for finding great stocks.

The SCTR indicator can be plotted on a chart. The SCTR is the only indicator that graphically shows how a company's stock price has been doing compared to its peers. Rather than just comparing to an average stock or index, the SCTR helps demonstrate great outperformance by giving you a usable scale for relative performance that can work over a wide variety of prices. The scale is very helpful, using a 0 to 100 range for maximum clarity.

Figure 12-3 shows eight stocks with the strongest SCTR in the top left (91.2) and the weakest SCTR in the bottom right (0.6). The stocks with high SCTRs are going to be much more profitable than those with low SCTRs. Notice the difference in the trends of the stocks. Stocks with SCTRs in the middle are not generating big gains.

FIGURE 12-3:
A view of SCTR rankings.

Chart courtesy of StockCharts.com

Staying focused on very strong stocks with an SCTR above 75, or weak stocks moving out of a very low SCTR, moving above 25 and improving, will help you find better profit opportunities. The SCTR number is on the Full Quote panel (Figure 12-2 shows how to access this panel), in the summary tables, and listed throughout the website. When you look at a list of stocks with the SCTR column, you'll immediately know which charts look better before you open the chart.

Plotting and interpreting the SCTR indicator

In the Indicators area of the chart attributes box, you find SCTR Line as one of the options in the drop-down menu. Figure 12-4 has the SCTR indicator plotted in the top panel on the chart of CSX Corp. The chart illustrates a lot of common traits for the indicator. First of all, on the left side of the chart, you see the stock moving higher, but the SCTR indicates the stock is still weak as it is below the 200 daily moving average (DMA; see Chapter 10). From March to June 2016, the stock moves sideways and the SCTR is just in the middle of the range, suggesting average performance compared to peers.

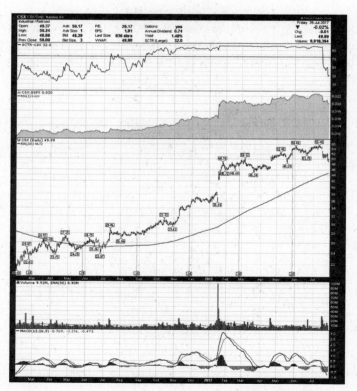

FIGURE 12-4: SCTR introduction.

Chart courtesy of StockCharts.com

In July 2016, the stock starts to move to higher highs. The SCTR pushes above 75 and then pulls back into August. September arrives, the stock price starts to trend higher, and the SCTR moves and stays above 75. This shows the stock price is moving faster than 75 percent of the large-cap stocks, and the SCTR is rising. The Full Quote panel at the top shows the SCTR peer group (Large-cap) and the current SCTR level.

The SCTR stayed above 75 for ten months. The stock price doubled from $28 to $56. In July 2017, the SCTR suddenly dropped under 75 and moved down to the last data point on the chart at 32.

Three things confirm the breakdown:

>> The SCTR moved into the bottom third of the large-cap stocks.

>> The $SPX relative strength made three-month lows shown using an area chart.

>> The moving average convergence divergence indicator (MACD; see Chapter 11) moved noticeably below zero.

An investor could ponder taking profits when the price drop occurred, but the low performance relative to peers confirms that it's a good time to lock in profits.

REMEMBER

The logic used to create the SCTR indicator has very simple thinking behind it. For you as an investor, why not try to own stocks that are outperforming and sell them when they stop outperforming? Staying with the SCTR indicator makes you focus on working with strong stocks.

Looking at the components of the SCTR indicator

TECHNICAL STUFF

StockCharts.com uses six different indicators on each stock to evaluate the strength of price movement. Some of the indicators are more important than others, so StockCharts.com adds a weighting so that a short-term move doesn't have as much importance as a long-term move. These are the components of the SCTR in order of most important to least important. The last two are accelerants that spur some quick changes for fast-moving prices:

>> Percentage above or below the 200 exponential moving average (EMA; see Chapter 10)

>> 125-day rate of change (the rate at which the stock price is going up or down)

>> Percentage above or below the 50 EMA

>> 20-day rate of change

>> 14-period relative strength index (RSI; see Chapter 11)

>> Three-day percent change in the percentage price oscillator (PPO) histogram (see Chapter 11)

TOP QUARTILE PERFORMANCE

Coauthor Greg's personal style is to have a horizontal line on the SCTR indicator at 75. The way Greg established 75 as an important level was through observation as well as logic. A large percentage of charts seem to break out to new highs around the SCTR 75 level as the stock starts to outperform others in its sector or industry.

The concept of *top quartile performance* is an important perspective to understand. A business analogy may convey why 75 percent is important. For a company to have best-in-class assets, a board of directors wants them to perform in the top 25 percent of the industry. An important part of shareholder communications is how strong the company assets are.

An example might be refineries. All of the refineries worldwide are benchmarked for performance by an independent ranking company. If Company A owns top quartile refineries, that means its refineries are performing in the top quartile (top 25 percent). If you own refineries that are not top quartile, you are leaving profits behind by not upgrading to new technologies.

If it doesn't make economic sense to upgrade the refinery due to location, market size, competition, and so on, you'll probably want to sell the refinery as it doesn't meet your corporate strategy of having the best assets in the industry. If a top refining company suggests this refinery is not worth reinvesting in, there are other companies that will buy an average profitable performer. As an investor, if all the company's refineries are average at best, how can they outperform their peers? How will they attract investors who can choose to buy the best company instead?

This analogy holds true in investing as well. If your goal is to be a top-performing investor, you have to find a method that helps you outperform the market. The SCTR is a great indicator for finding outperforming companies to consider. While just being in the top 25 percent doesn't sound that hard to achieve, a large part of the price move is while the stock is climbing up the ranking.

The concept of outperformance is great. The question for analytical-type investors is what makes this indicator work so well and how can you calculate it? Investors should not subscribe to black box ideas for investing wisdom. It is important to understand how the SCTR is calculated because these inputs should be valuable for investors generally.

Breaking down peer groups for technical ranking

For each stock, StockCharts.com calculates the weighted value of technical strength and then ranks that value against a peer group rather than the entire market. Plotting the closing SCTR rank for each stock, day after day, creates a line chart that shows how the stock is performing and has been performing compared to its peers.

By breaking the market down into different SCTR peer groups, the calculation dramatically changes the responsiveness of the indicator. Each peer group is large enough to be meaningful and small enough so the indicator moves relatively quickly. You don't want an above-average stock to just waddle in the ranking table. You want to find outperformers, and when they stop outperforming, you want to exit. For the U.S. market, StockCharts.com uses four SCTR peer groups:

» Large-cap (companies with a value of more than $10 billion)

» Mid-cap (companies with a value between $2 and $10 billion)

» Small-cap (companies with a value between $300 million and $2 billion)

» ETFs

TECHNICAL STUFF

Three other world markets currently have SCTR tables:

» On the Canadian $TSX market, all stocks and ETFs are in one peer group.

» For the London, England, $FTSE market, all stocks and ETFs are in one peer group.

» On India's Bombay stock market, all stocks and ETFs are in one peer group.

The SCTR scoring system can help the newest investor using stock charts as a method of investing to find the strongest stocks. The most experienced investor also appreciates this fast methodology for continually finding winners.

Understanding market movement in the rankings

Because stocks are in industry groups, the stock market rotates between sectors and industries based somewhat on the business cycle. The SCTR indicator shows that winning stocks keep winning for a while, and lousy stocks can stay lousy for a long time. Using the SCTR to keep track of the relative strength of a stock compared to its peers is very important. In sports, would you expect the worst team in the league to perform the best all of a sudden? The same question could be asked for stock market investments.

The SCTR indicator quickly forgets poor performance, and stocks that move fast from the bottom can move up in the rankings quickly. When stocks are moving so fast as to become top performers, they may not be breaking out to new highs, but they may be making new three-month or six-month highs. They have to start performing to move up the table.

REMEMBER

The secret to big investing gains in the stock market is to find strong stocks moving higher. A prominent industry phrase: The best way to own a winner is to buy one.

It takes institutional buying to push stock prices higher. Understanding that most institutional investment strategies look for some level of relative strength outperformance is helpful. Big investing gains in the stock market happen when there are more buyers than sellers, sending a stock price higher.

Another strategy that has big rewards is waiting patiently for a stock to stop going down and bottom out, and then watching the change as the stock starts improving. While institutions may buy enough at a low price to change the trajectory of a stock, the price action of a weak stock can be very choppy as investors slowly change their minds about whether it's going to become a strong stock. Examining how a stock changes trend is enlightening.

The first half of 2016 was a good example of a choppy period for CSX in Figure 12-4. When the SCTR starts to meaningfully improve, these can be great stocks to own. But buying them in the choppy phase is difficult. It is arguably a more volatile, difficult route to investing.

Great stocks don't stay great forever. They have a great phase, an average phase, and an underperforming phase. The best traders own the stocks only for the great growth stages. A look at the SCTR ranking for Apple Inc. (AAPL) in Figure 12-5 shows how transient the traders have been at different times. Although the general investing public is unaware of how far the stock moves against the shareholders in one of the best companies in the world, the SCTR points out the periods of strength and weakness pretty well.

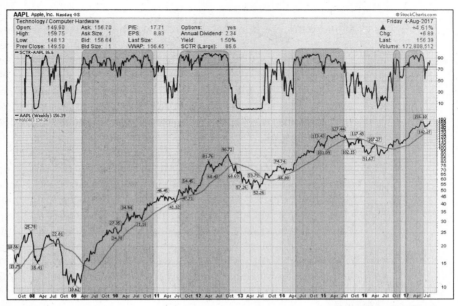

FIGURE 12-5:
SCTR patterns.

Chart courtesy of StockCharts.com

Pay particular attention to the periods where the SCTR dipped below 75 and then charged back up shortly after. All of those are places where deciding whether to hold or sell is a hard choice for investors. In general, the chart shows that about 60 percent of the time over the last ten years, it would have been great to be in AAPL stock. The other 40 percent of the time had very large pullbacks, which might have caused shareholders to sell at significantly lower levels.

Simply, when Apple was outperforming its large-cap peer group, the stock moved up considerably. When Apple was not outperforming its peers, it was a troublesome time to own the stock.

Protecting your capital with SCTR

REMEMBER

Using a strong SCTR does one very important thing for investors, and that is to protect their capital. When you invest with charts, you will find that most of your biggest losers have low SCTR levels. Avoiding declining SCTR levels can be very important. There is never a sign at the top saying a stock is about to fall, but there are indicators suggesting something is changing. The SCTR should always be respected as an important indicator, even if the current price move does not seem extreme. It's best to use multiple indicators.

While there are hundreds of great examples of stocks topping out, Blackberry (BB.TO) is a classic. In early 2009, government officials like congresspeople, senators, presidents, prime ministers, and members of Parliament as well as CEOs and managing directors around the world were using the Blackberry device because they loved the secure communication channels. President Barack Obama was the first president to use a Blackberry while in the White House, and he loved it. Worldwide, the Blackberry network was widely acknowledged for security of communication.

StockCharts.com created the SCTR in 2007, so there was no history for the indicator before that time. Figure 12-6 shows Blackberry was one of the top-performing stocks with an SCTR above 90. Focusing in on 2008, the rest of the stock market was in a severe decline, but Blackberry held up into July 2008. Famous TV stock pickers were praising the Blackberry security system and discussing that typing on Apple's new iPhone screen was too cumbersome. President Obama was voted into office in November 2008 at the depths of the financial crisis and insisted on being a Blackberry-wielding president. If you are an investor, a president's unwavering support can't sound more promising.

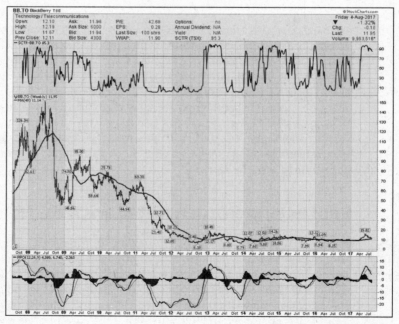

FIGURE 12-6:
SCTR protecting capital.

Chart courtesy of StockCharts.com

The price and the SCTR for the stock dropped as the financial crisis plummeted everything. The SCTR surged as everything bounced in March 2009, but Blackberry's SCTR broke down in the second quarter of 2009, suggesting Blackberry was not becoming a leader in price action.

Blackberry's SCTR never got back above the 75 level for three years after it fell behind. The stock fell from $92 to $4. There were many buyers at a new bargain price for Blackberry as it fell, but the SCTR suggested avoiding it and finding another stock to own. Any of those investors with a multi-month horizon suffered losses.

REMEMBER

Defending your capital is important, so having rules for selling stocks where the SCTR is below 75 or below 50 can be important for longer-term investors. A one-day dip below the level may be too tight for big gainers, but two weekly closes below one of those levels can be a great warning. If the stock does a rare 180 and starts to make new highs, write it off to a dreaded whipsaw, but at least you have a reason for protecting capital. A weak SCTR should be a signal that something is changing, especially on a very strong stock.

Using SCTR for base breakouts

Another method of using the SCTR is for value investors. When the stock is beaten down and starts to rally, investors who like to buy low-priced stocks can use the SCTR to find potential trend changes.

When stocks sell off, there is no outperformance. Stocks that are performing poorly with an SCTR in the bottom 25 percent of the market are very weak. Because of the way the indicator is calculated, stocks moving out of this zone or off the base and starting to improve can be good candidates for upward price moves of significance. (You can find more information about bases in Chapter 9.)

Figure 12-7 shows the stock for Validus Holding (VR), where the SCTR is moving back above 30. Because you can use more than one indicator on a chart, it may be helpful to compare a few other indicators. For example, in Figure 12-7, both the full stochastic and the MACD are improving (see Chapter 11 for more about these indicators).

TIP

Because the stock had a big uptrend for years and recently pulled back, it may return to its former trend. Although that doesn't always work out, one observation from looking at thousands of charts suggests than even great stocks give you excellent opportunities to buy at big percentage discounts from previous highs. An SCTR moving above 25 from the bottom can be an important signal of a new trend emerging. This strategy can work to help find nice buy points in long-term, uptrending stocks that suffered a short period of weakness.

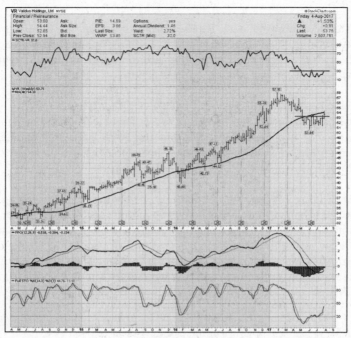

FIGURE 12-7:
SCTR improving
from a low level.

Checking Out Performance Charts

Performance charts are used to compare multiple stocks on one chart. Performance charts use the *first date* on the chart as the reference point. This is extremely valuable for finding out which stocks are starting to outperform in a new uptrend. Setting the chart to 65 days, you can see which stock has moved up more in the last three months.

The performance chart tool on StockCharts.com allows you to compare up to ten stocks at the same time to see which one is rising faster. Having the lines on the chart, you can look back to see whether the trend is changing. Figure 12-8 is an example of a performance chart in line mode. It compares FB (Facebook), AAPL (Apple), NFLX (Netflix), and AMZN (Amazon). You can create a chart comparing specific stocks by typing in the symbols under Create a PerfChart at www.stock charts.com/freecharts/ and then clicking Go.

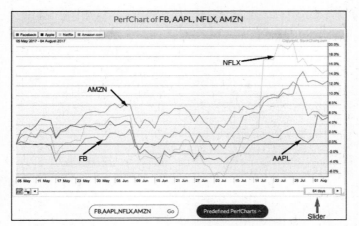

FIGURE 12-8: Performance chart in line mode.

You can also compare performance by major sectors. From the Free Charts tab on StockCharts.com, scroll down to the tool titled PerfCharts. Click on the pre-defined PerfCharts drop-down and select the major sectors you want to compare. This brings up the chart in line mode. (If it comes up in another mode, click the icon of a line chart at the bottom left.) With ten lines, the chart looks a little too much like spaghetti. Sliding the slider in the bottom right corner changes the number of days on the chart, or you can right-click to see a menu of time-period choices. While the chart may be anchored to the first data point for percentage gains, the last one to two months on the chart may identify new trends that are starting to emerge.

The second way to display PerfCharts is in Histogram mode (see Figure 12-9). This is done by selecting the Histogram icon in the bottom left corner. You can toggle back and forth between line mode and histogram mode using these icons.

In Figure 12-9, you can compare an index or sector or industry group as well. This is a nice way to look at your portfolio of stocks and compare them to the index to see whether they are outperforming over the same time frame. Click on the slider and move it through time. You can also align the start date with a recent low for the overall market and compare your current stocks to the index.

TIP

Bookmarking the chart page within your browser makes it easy to refer back to your performance charts with the same settings.

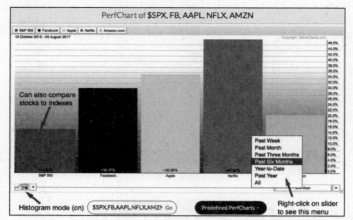

FIGURE 12-9:
Performance
chart histogram
display.

Chart courtesy of StockCharts.com

Using Relative Rotation Graphs (RRG)

In the stock market, there is a lot of discussion about sector rotation. Although it's usually softly discussed on the business news channels, they do not present charts to allow you to see this rotation. One of the most important changes in recent years is the visualization of sector rotation using relative strength. The other relative strength methods presented in this chapter make a considerable difference in comparing how a stock is doing. Even experienced chartists can be excited by having all of these innovative tools to keep up with some of the most advanced asset managers.

On the chart in Figure 12-10, the $SPX is in the center where the crosshairs meet. The sector ETFs are plotted around this point. Because the $SPX is an average of the stock market, there are always some groups pulling the $SPX higher and some groups that are underperforming the average, pulling it lower. The vertical scale is momentum. The horizontal scale is relative strength.

REMEMBER

When these sector ETFs appear in the top half — and more importantly, the top right corner — they are outperforming. That's a powerful visual clue. Sometimes, the clue is more valuable as you watch it move into different quadrants.

Julius de Kempenaer developed a dynamic, visual model of watching the sector rotation relative to a common reference point. By using two axes to measure a stock, the model shows how a sector ETF can change in momentum and in relative strength compared to a central point.

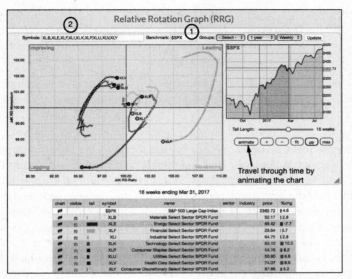

FIGURE 12-10:
RRG sector static.

Figure 12-10 shows tails on each ETF. These tails are formed by connecting the dots for the previous locations for each week of the ETF on the chart. Using the mini chart in the top right corner, you can slide through time to see the sectors move on the StockCharts.com website.

By creating this model, the investor can see all the sectors at once. You can quickly see which sectors are ahead in momentum by looking at the top half of the chart. You can see which sectors are gaining strength to start leading, or notice which sectors are losing momentum and starting to trail the $SPX. You can extend the tails to 16 weeks, which is a little longer, to show the circular rotation. This picture is a still screenshot showing the circular motion around the $SPX. In Figure 12-10:

>> Point 1 allows you to change what you are comparing to.

>> Point 2 is where you add the ticker symbols you are watching.

>> In the top right corner, you can select daily or weekly. This is how you control the third dimension of time.

>> The tails' colors are based on where the last data point is.

>> You can extend the tails from 0 to 30 weeks on the slider below the mini chart.

>> The lines headed toward the top right of the chart are moving toward becoming leaders. They can start in any quadrant, but the direction heading toward the top right is desirable.

>> Lines heading toward the bottom left are losing relative strength and momentum. The farther away from the center the last data point is, the worse the sector performance.

To use this tool on StockCharts.com, click on the Free Charts tab. Scroll down to locate one of the main charting panels called Relative Rotation Graphs (RRG) and click Launch RRG Chart. Choose one of the predefined groups in the list at the bottom and click on Animate. Watching the components spin as the slider in the mini chart on the top right moves through time is quite fascinating. If you stop the animation, the current date of the last endpoint is shown below the main chart.

REMEMBER

Why is this charting style so important? It quickly allows you to find the next sector that is gaining strength. A directional line pointing to the top right corner is improving in momentum and relative strength.

4

Getting Organized and Managing Stock Trends

Explore industry groups and sectors using charts.

Track trends with scans, lists, and alerts.

Conduct breadth analysis to find out how many stocks are involved in a bull market.

Review the week's action by counting up and down days, responding to one-off days, and more.

Chapter **13**

Organizing Charts into Industry or Sector Groups

StockCharts.com has over 60,000 ticker symbols in its database. Some of these are stocks, while others are currencies, commodities, bonds, indexes, exchange-traded funds (ETFs), and indicators. If you're not prepared, recognizing a nice chart setup for a high percentage trade would come down to luck. Being organized ahead of time in order to find attractive setups in the market is critical to systematically outperforming the market.

This chapter shows you how to create a ChartList, add charts to a list, and control its sort order, among other tasks. The tools presented here save days of manual work and are extremely important to improve your workflow.

Recognizing the Importance of Sectors and Industry Groups

A sector is a segment within the economy, such as energy or consumer goods. An industry includes a smaller defined group of companies within a sector; for example, the oil industry is part of the energy sector.

REMEMBER

Usually, when an industry group does well, almost all companies within it do well. As an example, if semiconductor stocks are having a good run, most of the stocks of semiconductor companies will participate. Some will be strong and lead the group, but on average the group will move up in sympathy. Often the industry lift will be responsible for 50 percent of a stock's movement; the individual stock's characteristics are responsible for the other 50 percent. What that really means is that you want to have your stocks organized by industry, so if one particular industry starts to do well, you can focus part of your portfolio on that industry group.

In 2017, for example, the semiconductor group took off. Because of the high margins in the business and the excellent growth characteristics, this industry group usually adds fuel to a big bull market. Micron (MU), Advanced Micro Devices (AMD), and Nvidia (NVDA), to name a few, all soared. Seeing this outperformance can help you invest.

TECHNICAL STUFF

Apple was an example of one stock in an industry group that dominated so much that all the other competitors, like HP and Dell, were being crushed. That is the exception.

If you're interested in commodities, the same challenges exist. Gold miners, oil exploration, agriculture stocks, copper stocks, and industrial metals can all be industry groups within which the stocks move together. Some move faster than others, but in general the whole group rises. Part of this is due to the industry ETFs that buy shares of companies within the group as the ETF gets capital inflows. The same is true for selling when the industry is being sold off.

REMEMBER

To be ready for investing, you need to identify industry groups that match your investing style. For example, if you want banks and real estate investment trusts (REITs) rather than lithium and gold companies, you should set up the industry groups you like in your StockCharts.com account. Then you identify which chart styles and settings you prefer to use (Part 2 can help). You want to have your indicators stored as a default setting. In addition, technical analysts recommend analyzing the trend on different periods, like weekly, daily, and 60-minute charts (see Chapter 8 for details).

Creating and Populating ChartLists

To get started with grouping stocks, you need to create ChartLists. ChartLists are a storage method on StockCharts.com. In one ChartList, you save multiple charts. ChartLists are the equivalent of folders on computers. Setting up different types of charts in each ChartList is very helpful.

Note: You need to sign up for a free trial to set up lists at StockCharts.com. On the home page, click "Free 1-Month Trial."

Creating a list with a name and a number

Your first move is to create a new list. Under the Members tab, scroll down to the ChartList banner and click the icon button with the plus sign (+) for New List. Figure 13-1 shows the banner with the new list icon.

FIGURE 13-1:
The ChartList
banner.

Chart courtesy of StockCharts.com

Now it's time to name your list. The StockCharts.com website defaults to alphabetical order when it sorts lists, but that structure doesn't work very well if you use lots of ChartLists. You'll constantly be changing the contents of the lists at the top, whereas you'll just be observing the contents of the ones farther down when you need to.

TIP

Because the naming convention alone doesn't really help keep the lists organized, you can use a numerical system to help control the sort order. A numbering sequence for ChartLists is important to help keep your work in an order you like. Table 13-1 is a suggestion for sorting (find out more about these list categories in the later section "Organizing Your ChartLists"). Four digits work best for ChartList names. Because you may create a lot under industry listings, the group is numbered 3000. This is a unique group that you actually want to sort alphabetically to facilitate finding a name within the list of industries. For example, you may have insurance brokers, reinsurance, property insurers, and the like, so using the letter "I" in front allows them all to be together, and then sorted by their group under the industry numeric.

TABLE 13-1 ## A Sample Numbering Sequence

Number	Name
1000	Interesting charts
1500	Scan list 1
1510	Scan list 2
1750	SCTR large-cap
1760	SCTR mid-cap
1770	SCTR small-cap
1780	SCTR ETF
2000	Watch list
2100	Current
2200	Closed
3000	Industry listings
3500	B – Biotech
3500	I – Insurance brokers
3500	I – Property insurers
3500	I – Reinsurance
3500	O – Oil and gas
3500	O – Oil and gas services
4000	ETF listings
4500	SP 500
4510	NASDAQ 100
4520	Dow 30
5000	Market overview

TIP

You aren't going to type in all of these names at once. But having a structure allows you to add to the list in an organized, structured way. For your first list, you can use the name 5000 – Market overview.

Populating a list with one or more charts

After you create a list, you can start adding charts to it. To add a single chart (for example, a chart of the S&P 500), use the Add Charts to List tool that should be showing on the bottom of the list's main page (in this example, the 5000 – Market overview page). At the top in the View List As drop-down, it should say Edit. If not, click on the drop-down arrow and select Edit. You can add one chart at a time, or you can add many at a time by finding an industry group/sector or uploading an Excel list. Figure 13-2 shows the panel for adding charts to a list.

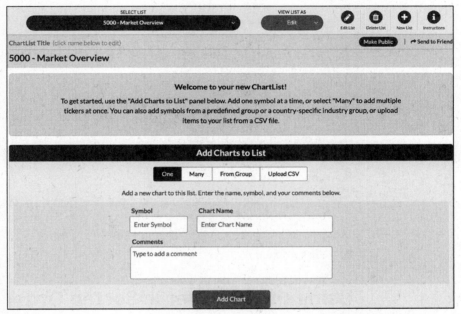

FIGURE 13-2:
Adding charts to a list.

Chart courtesy of StockCharts.com

If you want to add one chart at a time, follow these steps on the list's main page:

1. **Click One under Add Charts to List.**

2. **Type a ticker symbol in the Symbol box.**

   For example, type $SPX in the Symbol box.

3. **Type a name into the Chart Name box.**

   For example, for $SPX, you can type S&P 500 in the name box.

4. **Click the Add Chart button below the panel.**

The charts will sort alphabetically by ticker symbol. This gets you started with putting charts in a list, one at a time. If you want to add multiple charts at once, click Many at the top under Add Charts to List, type the ticker symbols you want (for example, $NDX, $INDU, $COMPQ, and $RUT), and then click the Add Chart button below the panel.

Building lists with industry groups or sectors

To populate a whole list with the stocks of an existing industry group or sector, create another new ChartList. Follow these steps:

1. **Go up to the top of the page and click the button with the plus sign (+) where it says New List.**

2. **Give your list a name.**

   For example, you can use the ChartList name 3500 – T – Toys, and then click OK.

3. **In the Add Charts to List area, click on the From Group tab as shown in Figure 13-3.**

4. **Choose your group.**

   You choose from a predefined sector group or an industry group. Scroll down the list. For example, the industry group menu is sorted first by sector and then alphabetically. Scroll under Consumer Staples Sector, and select Toys.

5. **Click Add Chart.**

Using the Number in Sorted Order button

You can save stocks within a list in a particular order if you like. For this step, go to Summary View, which you can select from the top of the page under the View List As drop-down menu (you can see this menu in Figure 13-3). In this example, we use the 3500 – T – Toys ChartList. If you aren't in the list you want, select it at the top of the page using the drop-down menu. Then go to Summary View.

From Summary View, as shown in Figure 13-4, you can sort the list on SCTR (StockCharts technical ranking; see Chapter 12) or any other column heading, or click on the Show/Hide Columns button for more choices. Putting the strongest SCTR first (as in Figure 13-4) allows you to look at the strongest stocks first when you change from Summary View to Ten per page viewing.

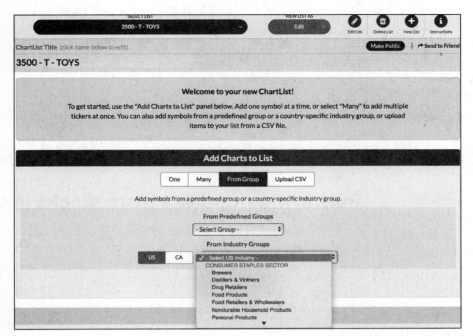

FIGURE 13-3:
Adding
predefined
groups to your
ChartList.

Chart courtesy of StockCharts.com

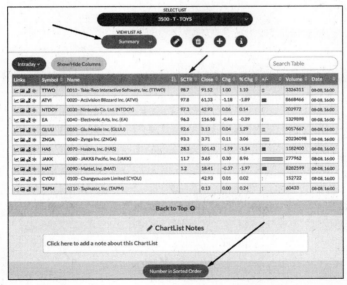

FIGURE 13-4:
Summary View
for ChartLists.

Chart courtesy of StockCharts.com

When you have the correct column and the list is sorted in ascending or descending order based on your preference, click the Number in Sorted Order button at the bottom of the page. This adds numbers in front of the names so the stocks will be saved in this order.

When you are in Summary View, you can sort on any column. Looking at stocks from strongest to weakest helps focus your investing on the best-performing stocks. Summary View gives you details about the stocks, but it doesn't allow you to remove them from the ChartList. To make changes within the list, use Edit View.

Removing numbers from stocks inside a list

Each time you look at some stocks in a ChartList, look at the stocks from strongest to weakest to stay focused on the best setups. Using the SCTR column to gauge chart strength, the higher the number, the stronger the stock performance on a scale from 0 to 100, with 99.9 being the best.

There are some important controls under the icons at the bottom of the list in the Edit View. Figure 13-5 shows the Edit ChartList screen. The chart names have had a four-digit number added to them to preserve the sort order from the Summary View (see the preceding section).

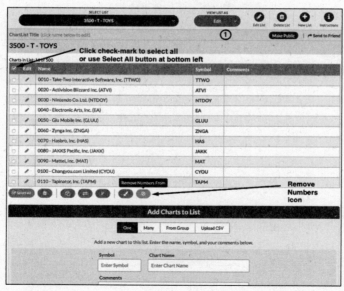

FIGURE 13-5:
Edit mode for ChartLists.

Chart courtesy of StockCharts.com

To remove the numbers so you can change the sort order, select all the stocks by using the check-mark at the top of the page or the Select All button below. You can also individually check the ones you want to modify or delete. After selecting the stocks (probably removing numbers from all, so use the Select All button), use the Remove Numbers icon highlighted in Figure 13-5 to delete the numbers. If you don't select any charts, no numbers will be removed.

There is also a delete button at the bottom that allows you to select multiple charts one at a time. Then click the garbage can icon to remove the charts you checked on the list.

If you want to re-sort the stocks within the ChartList and then add new numbers (as explained in the preceding section), click on the View List As drop-down at the top, select Summary, and select a column to sort on (Summary View is where the sorting columns are displayed).

TIP

Click on the very helpful Instructions icon in the top row of icons if you need further assistance.

Organizing Your ChartLists

You'll always have people throwing stock suggestions your way. Those one-off stocks need to accumulate in a ChartList. You also need to develop a routine to look for great stocks on a daily or weekly basis. As your charting methods become a standard routine, having lots of places to temporarily store a group of stocks to look through is critical. This section has some ideas for naming and sorting ChartLists.

Over time, you'll find that ChartLists are divided into two groups: very active ChartLists that change often, and ChartLists that are very stable with rare changes year in and year out. The top half of the following list notes active folders that you dump stuff into and out of regularly. The later charts don't change massively. They become reliable places to look for consistent information in the market.

Some folders that are always good to have are

>> Interesting charts folder

>> Ten different temporary scan folders

>> SCTR folders

>> Watch list

>> Open positions

>> Closed positions

>> Individual industry listings

>> Top volume ETFs

>> Market overview

>> NASDAQ 100

>> S&P 500

>> Dow 30

The following sections give you some ideas about what to include in each of these ChartLists.

Interesting charts

The interesting charts can be for stocks others have told you about or you heard about on TV, the radio, the StockCharts member page, or the ticker cloud. By keeping them together in a folder, you can scroll through them when you have time.

TIP

If you annotate on the chart what made each stock interesting, going back a few months later and looking at what happened subsequently can be a great lesson.

Temporary scan lists

The term *scan* refers to the StockCharts.com scan engine searching the entire market for a particular trade setup, like the moving average convergence divergence indicator (MACD; see Chapter 11) crossing up above the signal line.

When you have certain setups that you're looking for every day or week, use empty folders to copy a list of scan results into so you have the info when you're ready to do additional analysis. Scan results can be moved into a new or existing ChartList. Keeping these lists close to the top of all the ChartLists gives you the ability to access them as quickly as possible. As you work through scan results in a temporary folder, you can move the good ones into a watch list or into the current open positions list, if you decide to buy.

TIP

Some of the first ChartLists in your StockCharts.com account are the temporary scan ChartLists. The creation of static industry ChartLists for you to use are covered here before you start working with the scan ChartLists in Chapter 14, using more advanced methods.

SCTR list

Keeping track of the top-performing stocks is always helpful. SCTR (StockCharts technical ranking; see Chapter 12) alerts you to strong industry groups and individual stocks. You may be waiting for a pullback to buy into a strong stock. You should update this list regularly with the most current scan results to be able to recognize strong stocks quickly.

Watch list

Your watch list will likely be your most active as you hear about stocks from friends or news reports and want to start watching their performance. Or you may be sorting through sector or industry charts and find a stock that you want to start watching. Continually flushing charts into and out of this list makes it one of the most active ChartLists you have. There are also some charts that you'll want to watch while the market is open, so you can put them in this list.

Current open positions

Obviously, you'll want to check the list of stocks you own in one place. Any stock you currently own would be in this list.

Closed trades

TIP

Keeping a file of closed trades is important. If you look back through these stocks, you may see patterns in your good trades and patterns in trades that went against you. Reviewing these is the best way to get better at investing. At the end of the year, you can archive these to a year-end folder.

Sector or industry lists

Industries come into vogue for periods of time and then sell off. Within an industry, you want to trade in the strongest, most-liquid stocks. (Find pointers on building these types of lists earlier in this chapter.)

A good example is biotechs. They have explosive growth, but the industry has a lot of losers that investors are selling as well. Keeping a list of biotechs allows you to sort them based on SCTR rankings or volume sorts to trade in only the most-liquid biotechs. These stocks are very volatile, so only a small portion of your portfolio should be in biotechs.

ETF list

There are thousands of ETFs that you can trade, but having a good list of the most-liquid ETFs is very helpful. If individual biotech stocks are too volatile, for example, you may prefer to trade one of the biotech ETFs instead. If biotechs start to outperform, you can quickly go through to find the most-liquid ETFs and place your trade.

Market overview

This ChartList is a collage of different indicators and ticker symbols that help analyze broad market conditions.

Index lists

By being aware of the different indexes, you can quickly look into the lists to find large-cap stocks and sort them by sector. As shown earlier in this chapter, three critical ones are the NASDAQ 100, S&P 500, and Dow 30. If others are critical to your trading or investing style, they should be added as well.

Chapter **14**

Keeping Track of What's Going On

As a chartist, your charts become a large part of your work. You need to look for stocks that have setups you like, as well as buy them at an attractive entry point and then sell them when you determine a good exit point and close the trade. You can make your decisions based solely on charts or use charts with some other form of analysis.

As you find out in this chapter, managing your stock trading becomes much easier when you create watch lists. Using a watch list, you begin to collect information on stocks you want to monitor. Starting with predefined scans is a good way to look for key stock trends, such as stocks hitting new 52-week highs. You can place the scans of the indicators you check regularly into your watch list. When you decide to buy a stock, you place it into your list of stocks you own; you can also create a list of stocks you sold. No rule says that you have to use these steps, but they can help you get organized and comfortable with your charting process.

TIP

For an introduction to the ChartLists described in this chapter, check out Chapter 13. To use ChartLists, you need to become a member of StockCharts.com; to do so, click "Free 1-Month Trial" on the home page.

Making a Watch List

Creating profits starts by having a main watch list that you continually move good setups into. Chartists have looked at a healthy list of ideas over the years. You can take advantage of this experience at StockCharts.com, where there is a scan engine that allows you to sift through thousands of stocks in order to spot opportunities you may have been missing. This capability makes the engine one of the most powerful tools available to you on StockCharts.com. Analysts and users have created over 75 scans and sorted the results for investors all on one page called Predefined Scans. You pick from these predefined scans to create a ChartList dedicated to scans, and then populate it with the ones you like best. (If you need more information on how to develop ChartLists, see Chapter 13.)

Surveying predefined scans

You can use the predefined scans to find the stocks you like and want to watch. This is a great place to start. Populating your watch list with stocks that have good setups is an important part of using StockCharts.com to make your charting experience great.

After you log in to the site, click on the Gears icon beside the ChartLists button in the bottom right-hand corner of the Members page, as shown in Figure 14-1. Make sure the Scan Center option is turned on. Close the window.

FIGURE 14-1:
The Gears icon.

Chart courtesy of StockCharts.com

Scroll down the Members page until you are just above the ChartLists banner and click on the Predefined Scans button. Figure 14-2 shows the Predefined Scans link.

Clicking this link displays a window with the Predefined Scan Results summary table shown in Figure 14-3. There are hyperlinks all over this page so you can click on one of the links and see the list of stocks that was found by a particular scan.

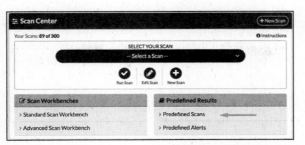

FIGURE 14-2: The Predefined Scans link.

Chart courtesy of StockCharts.com

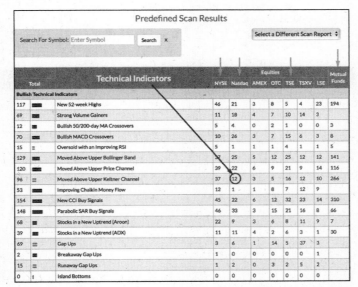

FIGURE 14-3: The Predefined Scan Results summary table.

Chart courtesy of StockCharts.com

Predefined Scan Results

| Total | Technical Indicators | Equities | | | | | | | Mutual Funds |
		NYSE	Nasdaq	AMEX	OTC	TSE	TSXV	LSE	
Bullish Technical Indicators									
117	New 52-week Highs	46	21	3	8	5	4	23	194
69	Strong Volume Gainers	11	18	4	7	10	14	3	
12	Bullish 50/200-day MA Crossovers	5	4	0	2	1	0	0	3
70	Bullish MACD Crossovers	10	26	3	7	15	6	3	8
15	Oversold with an Improving RSI	5	1	1	1	4	1	1	5
129	Moved Above Upper Bollinger Band	37	25	5	12	25	12	12	141
120	Moved Above Upper Price Channel	39	22	6	9	21	9	14	116
96	Moved Above Upper Keltner Channel	37	12	3	5	16	12	10	266
53	Improving Chaikin Money Flow	12	1	1	8	7	12	9	
154	New CCI Buy Signals	45	22	6	12	32	23	14	310
148	Parabolic SAR Buy Signals	46	33	3	15	21	16	8	66
68	Stocks in a New Uptrend (Aroon)	22	9	3	6	8	11	9	7
39	Stocks in a New Uptrend (ADX)	11	11	4	2	6	3	1	30
69	Gap Ups	3	6	1	14	5	37	3	
2	Breakaway Gap Ups	1	0	0	0	0	0	1	
15	Runaway Gap Ups	1	2	0	3	2	5	2	
0	Island Bottoms	0	0	0	0	0	0	0	

Many predefined scans are all set up for you. The following is just a sampling:

>> Seventeen bullish technical indicators (see Chapter 11)

>> Seventeen bearish technical indicators (see Chapter 11)

>> Five candlestick bullish reversal patterns (positive change in the direction of the price trend)

>> Five candlestick bearish reversal patterns (negative change in the direction of the price trend)

>> Two candlestick continuation patterns (the price trend continues at the same level)

>> Five single candlestick patterns (see Chapter 4)

This list is a veritable gold mine with so many interesting scans that demonstrate different ways to look at the market. For example, consider Keltner channels (see Chapter 10 for more information). Scroll down the list of technical indicators until you find the Keltner channel scan. If you click the link in the column of numbers on the far left (in Figure 14-3, the number with the link is 96 and the name of the scan is Moved Above Upper Keltner Channel), it opens the scan results across every exchange. For this example, zoom in and click on the link for the NASDAQ. This provides a list of companies that you can look through (see Figure 14-4).

Predefined Scan Results - Moved Above Upper Keltner Channel (NASDAQ)

Available Action - Choose -
- Store these results in a new ChartList
- Merge these results with an existing ChartList
- Replace an existing ChartList with these results
- Download In CSV Format

Click here to edit this scan
11 Aug 2017, 5:30 PM

Search Table

	Symbol	Name	Exchange	Sector	Industry	SCTR	U	Close	Volume	Yesterday's Daily Upper Kelt Chan(20,2,0,10)
	BIS	ProShares UltraShort NASDAQ Biotechnology	NASD					24.610	74602	24.809
	CHEF	Chefs' Warehouse, Inc.	NASD	Consumer Staples	Food Retailers	92.4	sml	17.600	503453	16.225
	CROX	Crocs, Inc.	NASD	Cyclicals	Footwear	94.3	sml	9.210	3414626	8.699
	GOLD	Randgold Resources Ltd.	NASD	Materials	Gold Mining	77.1	mid	97.940	580371	96.676
	HBIO	Harvard Bioscience, Inc.	NASD	Health Care	Biotechnology			3.050	45724	3.133
	PNNT	PennantPark Investment Corp.	NASD					7.710	307738	7.758
	RICK	RCI Hospitality, Holdings	NASD	Cyclicals	Recreational Services	95.8	sml	25.230	105692	25.317
	TVIX	VelocityShares Daily 2x VIX Short Term ETN	NASD					23.440	29571417	20.655
	TVIZ	VelocityShares Daily 2x VIX Medium Term ETN	NASD					16.140	76854	15.113
	UGLD	VelocityShares 3x Long Gold ETN	NASD					11.180	752311	10.891
	USLV	VelocityShares 3x Long Silver ETN	NASD					12.660	1996611	12.584
	VIIX	VelocityShares Daily Long VIX Short Term ETN	NASD			1.3	etf	23.100	327694	21.382

FIGURE 14-4: Keltner channel scan results.

Chart courtesy of StockCharts.com

Saving scans to ChartLists

After you've taken the time to pick the scans you want to view regularly, you can save these scans to temporary scan lists until you decide how you want to use them. Here are the steps to do that:

1. **Click on the column headers to change the sort order of the companies.**

2. **Click on the SCTR last and put the largest SCTR number at the top.**

   The stocks that populate the list will be current on the day you click, not the same as the stocks in this figure. (By the way, SCTR stands for StockCharts technical ranking; see Chapter 12 for an introduction.)

3. **Click the drop-down menu for Available Actions at the top.**

   It may extend above or below the drop-down, so scroll up if you don't see it at first. This gives you an opportunity to save these predefined scan results into a ChartList without typing each company into every list.

4. **Select Store these results in a new ChartList from the drop-down menu.**

A pop-up box should appear similar to Figure 14-5. Fill in the information for the ChartList name. An example of the ChartList title is shown in Figure 14-5 as a temporary scan file, 1500 – Scan list 1.

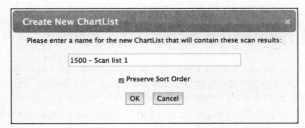

FIGURE 14-5:
Create a new
ChartList.

Chart courtesy of StockCharts.com

TIP

Click the Preserve Sort Order toggle if you want to save the current order of the SCTR ranking. This was the last column you adjusted, so that will be the sort order preserved. If you click the toggle, when it saves the stocks into the ChartList, it will add a number to control the sort order to show the stocks with the strongest charts first. The SCTR allows you to quickly see which charts are better. Chapter 13 discusses controlling the sort order of charts in a list.

Creating and Using Your Three Main ChartLists

Before you can do anything with the scan results (covered earlier in this chapter), you need to create ChartLists for the watch list, current stocks you own, and closed trades. These lists are your three most important lists.

On the top right of your screen, click the New List icon and create three new ChartLists, one after the other (flip to Chapter 13 for details on how to complete this task):

>> 2000 – Watch list

>> 2100 – Current

>> 2200 – Closed

The following sections provide tips on reviewing scans and moving them to your three main lists.

Deciding which stocks to move

After you have created your three main ChartLists, you can start to move stocks between your temporary scan results and your watch list. Using the drop-down tool with ChartList names on the top (see the top of Figure 14-6), click to select and go back to your ChartList titled 1500 – Scan list 1. This will enable you to look through the scan results, and if you find a chart you like, you can move it to your Watch list ChartList.

TIP

As you can see at the bottom of Figure 14-6, an arrow is pointing to Apply Style To All. The Apply Style To All button allows you to set up one chart in your temporary scan ChartList and apply this style to the other charts. You need to set up all the indicators and overlays that you want to be displayed (see Parts 2 and 3 for details), and then apply the settings to all the charts in this list. Click the Apply Style To All, read the warning pop-ups, and click OK. That saves so much work!

To continue the example we start earlier in this chapter: Because the default chart does not have the Keltner channel overlay on it, it is hard to see what the Keltner scan is finding. Scroll down to the Overlays area below the chart and select Keltner Channel from the drop-down list. Remove the two moving averages and click Update.

Figure 14-6 shows the updated chart. *Note:* We have removed the indicators MACD and RSI to fit the Apply Style To All button on the screenshot, which is at the very bottom of the screen. You can keep the RSI and MACD on your screen.

REMEMBER

Because you're working inside the temporary scan list 1500 – Scan list 1, you won't accidentally change other saved charts using the Apply Style To All. You wouldn't want to use the Apply Style To All in your Watch list, Current stocks, or Closed stocks ChartLists. This Apply Style To All setting only affects the current ChartList you are inside. Using it in temporary ChartLists works great.

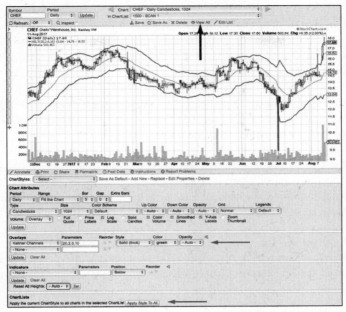

FIGURE 14-6:
Keltner channel on default.

At the top, in the center of the screen, click on View All. This allows you to scroll through ten stocks per page. If you don't like a chart, hover in the top right-hand corner of the chart and a little garbage can should appear. You can quickly delete the chart and keep scrolling. Examples of charts you might discard for a trade expecting higher prices are stocks in big downtrends that have bounced to the top of the Keltner channel, low-volume stocks, stocks with prices stuck in a sideways range, and so on.

Stocks you would like to put in your watch list might be stocks that have just made new three-month or six-month highs. But because the price is already extended, you would want to wait until the stock pulled back to the center of the Keltner channel. This would be a stock to move to your watch list so you could wait for the pullback without forgetting about it. Click on the chart to move out of View All mode into SharpChart mode.

Moving stocks into your three lists

In the center of the chart beside the View All button at the top is a Save As button (refer to Figure 14-6). This allows you to save the chart into your Watch list ChartList instead of the temporary ChartList you are currently in. You can save the chart as the ticker symbol and the date — for example, CHEF 20170811 — in the 2000 – Watch list ChartList. Chefs' Warehouse (CHEF) is the chart used in the example. This will sort the stocks alphabetically by ticker and tell you the date you put it in the watch list.

This same process is repeated to move stocks from your 2000 – Watch list ChartList to 2100 – Current ChartList when you buy the stock. Change the date to the date you moved it into the current list.

When you close the trade, you should move the stock from 2100 – Current to 2200 – Closed. For your closed trades, you can alter the saved chart name with a W for a winning trade or an L for a losing trade. You can look through your closed trades to see whether there are patterns in your losing trades or winning trades.

At the end of the year, using the Edit ChartList View, change the 2200 – Closed ChartList name to 2300 – Closed trades [year]. Then create a new ChartList for closed trades (2200 – Closed) again.

Setting Alerts

One of the advanced features for chartists on the StockCharts.com website is the customized alert. StockCharts members who are Extra or Pro members can create custom alerts. You can try these features with your 30-day free trial when you first sign up on the site. You find the alert feature in the Technical Alert Workbench, which can be found in the Extra Control Center on your membership page. These alerts pop up when you log in and help you quickly find stocks with key changes you want to see.

Staying with CHEF as an example from the previous section, suppose you want to be alerted when the stock crosses below the 20-period exponential moving average (EMA; see Chapter 10), which is the center of the Keltner channel. That would be a good place to look for an entry to buy the stock for the first time. Figure 14-7 shows the Alert Center.

The Alert Center allows you to specify the name of the ticker symbol and what it needs to do for you to be alerted. For CHEF, you want it to pull back below the 20 EMA.

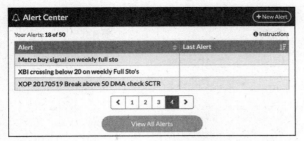

FIGURE 14-7:
The Alert Center.

Chart courtesy of StockCharts.com

TIP

In the world of stocks, the typical scan or alert signal is one thing crossing another. An example is price crossing a moving average by either crossing up or crossing down. StockCharts.com has simplified how to scan for that condition. The "x" represents *crossing above*. Whatever is listed first is crossing above the second part. For example, [Close x EMA(20)] means the close is crossing up above the 20 EMA. [EMA(20) x Close] means the 20 EMA is crossing above the close. In regular English, the price has fallen below the 20 EMA.

When you click on New Alert in the Alert Center, a new page appears. Figure 14-8 shows the User-Defined Alerts page. From here, you can do a number of things:

TIP

>> Click into the main panel and edit the conditions for the alert.

>> In the bottom right is a button for checking syntax to make sure the phrase is understood by the scan engine.

You can type the word "Syntax" into the StockCharts.com search box if you need assistance writing the alert. Lots of examples are shown.

>> Click on the notification drop-down where it defaults to email to change the notification method. The other choices are text message or on-screen pop-up.

>> Lastly, click Save As and name the alert descriptively so it means something when it pops up in an email. An example might be CHEF Pulling Back Below 20 EMA For Buy Signal.

Figure 14-9 shows the Alert Status page. To reach this page, use the Control Center on the Members tab or scroll down to the bottom of the User-Defined Alerts page and Click the Your Alerts link on the View Alert Status line.

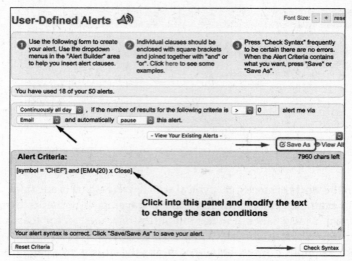

FIGURE 14-8:
User-Defined
Alerts page.

Chart courtesy of StockCharts.com

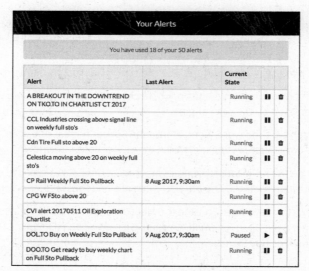

FIGURE 14-9:
Alert Status page.

Chart courtesy of StockCharts.com

Chapter **15**

Conducting Breadth Analysis

The term *breadth* is used to describe how many stocks are involved in a bull market. Bull markets are the strongest when lots of sectors and stocks are trending higher together. To help understand how strong a bull market is, you can use breadth indicators.

When breadth charts are showing lots of breadth, the likelihood of an immediate long-term plunge in the market is low. While it's still possible for a significant market decline to occur suddenly (such as after 9/11), the major breakdowns in the markets of 2000 and 2008 had all the classic signs of trouble. They were not random or out of the blue. The classic signals of markets under stress were in place before the markets crumbled.

Rather than focusing on the news events to taint your perceptions of the market, you want to use the price action of investors toward stocks. If they are buying almost every sector of the market and lots of the stocks are doing well, you are in a big bull market. When fewer stocks are leading the charge, it becomes concerning, but there will always be a few stocks moving up regardless of market condition.

THE END OF THE WORLD

After watching the markets go through massive moves down in 2000 and 2008, a lot of investors expect some sort of terminal event that will wipe out their portfolios for the third and final time. But the market continues higher, and those investors on the sidelines have really had the worst of both worlds. They got hurt when the market fell, and they got hurt by not being invested during bull markets.

Ben Bernanke's book *The Courage to Act* discusses the pressures of being a Fed Chairman during the 2008 global financial crisis. It's fair to say that when the markets are under duress, there are groups of people who work to stabilize the situation. Art Cashin, UBS Director of Floor Operations at the New York Stock Exchange, has a great saying. Paraphrased, it's this: "If you're betting on the end of the world, remember that it comes only once."

You want to identify when the breadth is so weak or *thin* that the market is more likely to struggle. That becomes the time to lighten your portfolio. Secondly, when the market is really down and out, the reversals from those lows can be very profitable. Every time the market is pulling back, you want to identify that as a potential buying opportunity.

Without question, trading in the markets is hard emotional work. The breadth charts that we describe in this chapter can help normalize those pressures.

REMEMBER

Breadth charts are one of the easiest ways to evaluate the strength of a bull market. When the indicators get very close to breakdown levels, be aware that the market has lost a lot of strength and there may be a larger correction.

Investigating Bullish Percent Indexes

Bullish percent indexes start with a chart style called point and figure (PnF) charting. Simply, the bullish percent index keeps track of how many stocks are making higher highs within a group of stocks. In the following sections, we show you charts for single stocks and groups of stocks.

Understanding how a buy or sell signal for a single stock is recorded

REMEMBER

In PnF charting, columns of X's are rising prices for a stock, while columns of O's are falling prices. When a stock makes a higher high, it moves to a buy signal in PnF charting. It will not move to a sell signal until it makes a lower low. Figure 15-1 shows where new buy signals were initiated as the column of X's made a higher high after a sell signal had been recorded. In the bottom left, there was a buy signal, and the market continued to make higher highs and higher lows until the third column of O's made a lower low. When the chart is on a buy signal and a column of O's goes lower than the previous column of O's, a new sell signal is generated.

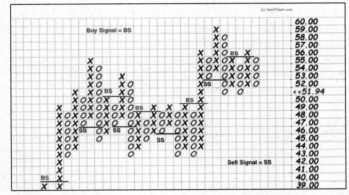

FIGURE 15-1: PnF buy/sell signals.

Chart courtesy of StockCharts.com

The good thing about bullish percent indexes is that they allow the market to move with pullbacks in price. They don't switch quickly between buy and sell signals. Looking in the top right corner, the most recent signal is a buy signal as the price touched $56. Now, until the price falls to $50, which would make a lower column of O's, the stock is on a buy signal. Therefore, Figure 15-1 currently has a $6 range between signals.

Interpreting the results for groups of stocks

The PnF chart shown in Figure 15-1 shows how one company PnF chart makes a new buy or sell signal. However, bullish percent indexes are about groups of charts. For the NASDAQ 100, for example, the bullish percent index keeps track of how many stocks are on a buy signal out of 100 stocks. When 73 percent of the stocks are on a buy signal, 27 percent are on a sell signal. Eventually, the percentage of stocks making higher highs slows, and more stocks start making lower lows. When this change occurs, you can monitor it with bullish percent indexes.

REMEMBER

No exact percentage of breadth (stocks moving higher in the rally) is the right level to start a market correction. Every market top is different. Just using basic math, you do have an idea of when these markets start becoming sensitive to bigger pullbacks. If 75 percent of the stocks are on buy signals, for example, the market is pushing higher as three-fourths are going up and one-fourth are not. If 65 percent are pushing higher, it is still possible to make higher highs, but 35 percent are on sell signals, pulling the market average down. The bullish momentum is clearly less but still positive. If it flips so only 40 percent are on a buy signal, the market will be in a correction of some sort as the majority of stocks are going down. The bullish percent index charts give you the opportunity to try to find the sensitive levels.

Figure 15-2 shows an analysis of a one-year period of the bullish percent index (BPI) for the S&P 500 large-cap index ($BPSPX). Notice that the BPI is around 67 percent for the 500 largest companies. Remember that the $SPX is the largest broad group of huge companies in the world. This is an aircraft carrier in comparative size to other indexes, and it turns around slowly. At 66 percent, you can see the market was in a small correction in October 2016. The bullish percent index dropped quickly after it went below 61 percent.

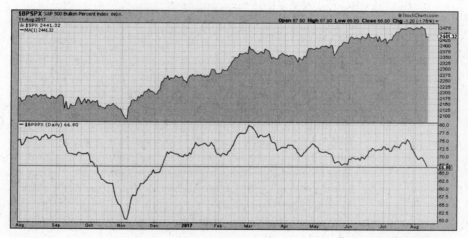

FIGURE 15-2:
A bullish percent index for the S&P 500 ($BPSPX).

Chart courtesy of StockCharts.com

Analyzing a three-year period with the daily chart in Figure 15-3, the $SPX looks very strong above 70 percent. A line at that level shows a strong market. You want to stay invested. The lower line is the level in mid-August 2017. When the breadth for the $SPX drops below 65 percent, the correction is larger. Two other useful points to note are that 50 percent held quite a few of the little lows and deep corrections were in the 25 percent range. Even in the huge bear markets, not all charts were on sell signals.

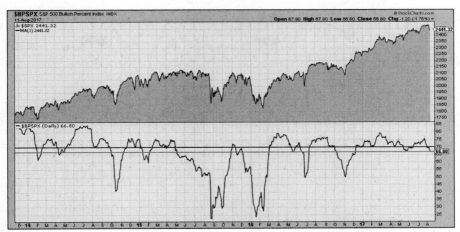

FIGURE 15-3:
A bullish percent index ($SPX) for three years.

Chart courtesy of StockCharts.com

The final chart for the $BPSPX in Figure 15-4 expands the chart out to 20 years. The levels first shown in Figure 15-2 seem to work very well over the 20-year horizon as well. Notice that during the big downturns, the market never got back above 70 percent on the bounces. During the roaring 1999–2000 period, the $BPSPX was very low, but the market was still able to push to higher highs. Big names like Microsoft were involved in the rally, and there were lots of concerns about computers failing because of the century change. While the market went higher, only a few stocks pulled it up with only 40 percent to 60 percent of the stocks on a buy signal. Rare conditions indeed.

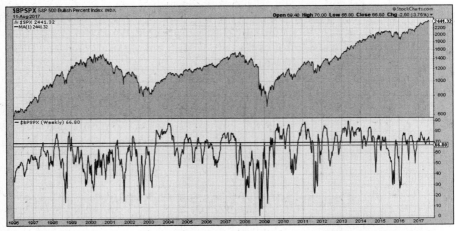

FIGURE 15-4:
$BPSPX for 20 years.

Chart courtesy of StockCharts.com

Studying the Percentage of Stocks above the 200 DMA

The percentage of stocks above the 200 daily moving average (DMA) is also a gauge of market breadth. As the stock market starts to go up from a major low, a lot of stocks clear the 200 DMA. As long as the uptrend continues, the stocks stay above the long-term average. As more and more stocks stop rising, the 200 DMA catches up with the price. When stocks start to go below the 200 DMA, this can be a meaningful sign that the uptrend is losing strength.

In the following sections, we examine a simple chart showing the percentage of stocks above the 200 DMA, and then we compare it to other types of charts.

Looking at the basic chart

Much like the bullish percent index covered earlier in this chapter, this indicator never gets to 100 percent of the stocks. However, unlike the bullish percent index, which has lots of room between a buy signal and a sell signal, the 200 DMA is a single line. If it crosses down below one day and turns around the next day and starts to go higher, it can flip immediately. The bullish percent index has to go all the way past the previous high on the last column of X's to change from a sell signal to a buy signal.

Figure 15-5 shows the percentage of stocks above the 200 DMA as a histogram chart. You can see big, wide black areas where breadth was plentiful and the market roared forward. There is only one line on this chart as the current level is within 2 percent of the 70 percent line. When the market pulls back early in the uptrend, most of the stocks don't pull down to their 200 DMA, so this black histogram stays nice and high.

The histograms start to diminish in height as the rally goes on, having fewer stocks above the 200 DMA. When only 70 percent of the stocks on the $SPX are above the 200 DMA, this can be a meaningful inflection level. With the chart sitting at 68 percent, any further weakness should be evaluated as potentially more than just a pullback after a few down days.

Comparing breadth information

A long-term comparison is helpful for perspective. Once the market gets weak, looking for typical levels when investors start to hit the buy button becomes important.

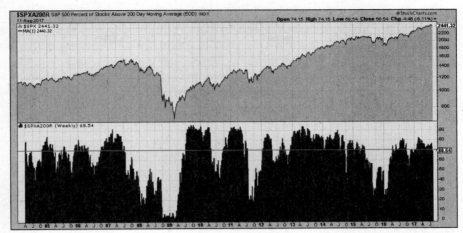

FIGURE 15-5:
Percentage of
stocks above 200
DMA for $SPX.

In Figure 15-6, three different styles are used on the same chart. The S&P 500 index ($SPX) has an area chart, the bullish percent index for the S&P 500 ($BPSPX) has a line chart, and the percentage of stocks above the 200 DMA ($SPXA200R) has a histogram plot.

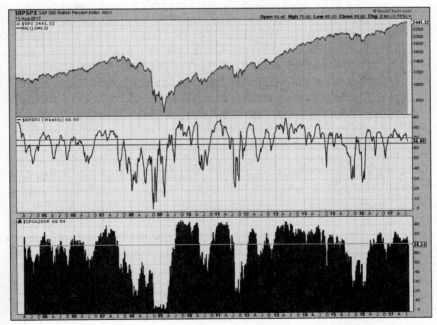

FIGURE 15-6:
Combining
breadth
indicators.

One of the advantages to plotting three different styles on one chart is the instant awareness of what each chart represents. If they are all the same, you need to keep referring to the legend. The second major advantage to plotting the information on the same chart is to look for correlation, which is normal, or one of the indicators showing a dramatic discrepancy.

Using this chart as a template for breadth makes it easy to set up multiple copies of the chart. Because the $SPX is typically the last index to break down, it is important to watch breadth on different indexes.

Reviewing the Breadth of Different Exchanges

The following sections discuss the breadth of three different exchanges: the NASDAQ Stock Exchange, the New York Stock Exchange (NYSE), and the Toronto Stock Exchange (TSE).

The NASDAQ composite breadth

The NASDAQ composite ($COMPQ) is the name for all of the NASDAQ listed stocks compiled together. The NASDAQ Stock Exchange has a lot of small tech companies that struggle as well as some exceptionally huge, successful tech companies. The index behaves different from the S&P 500 ($SPX) and can be helpful in monitoring breadth as an early warning. The threshold levels never get as strong, and the charts can show weakness early.

Figure 15-7 shows the NASDAQ composite ($COMPQ) with a bullish percent index ($BPCOMPQ) below the level the market usually breaks down from (60 percent). It also shows that the percentage of NASDAQ stocks above the 200 DMA ($NAA200R) is only at 50 percent. It will be difficult to make higher highs if only 50 percent of the stocks are above the 200 DMA.

The settings on the chart to make the display can be confusing at first. Figure 15-8 shows the settings used to create the NASDAQ composite chart shown in Figure 15-7. The chart style for the percentage of stocks above the 200 DMA is a histogram type. Use the overlay tool to add reference lines on the chart.

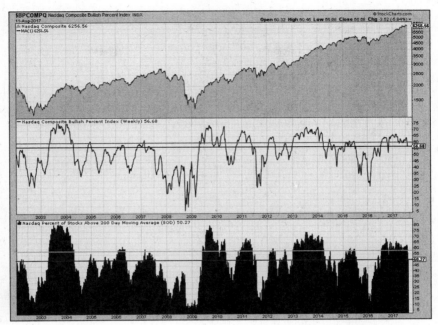

FIGURE 15-7:
NASDAQ
composite
breadth.

Chart courtesy of StockCharts.com

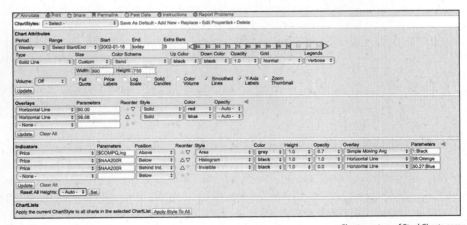

FIGURE 15-8:
NASDAQ breadth
settings.

Chart courtesy of StockCharts.com

The NASDAQ 100 Index ($NDX) is typically the fastest-moving index because of the high-growth-rate companies that are listed there. The NASDAQ 100 list includes all the giant tech companies. Because of the size of these large companies, as long as this index continues to do well, the NASDAQ 100 market can continue to outperform. Almost all of these companies are also in the S&P 500. When the NASDAQ 100 chart holds up, usually that is supportive of the S&P 500. If the

NASDAQ 100 breadth starts to weaken, that can be a much better clue that the overall market is probably going to pull back deeper than most people expect when the correction starts.

Figure 15-9 shows that the bullish percent index is very weak, with only 52 percent of the stocks on a buy signal, but the percentage of stocks above the 200 DMA shows 69 percent, well above 65 percent.

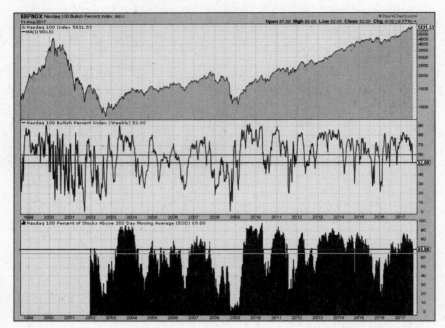

Chart courtesy of StockCharts.com

FIGURE 15-9:
NASDAQ 100
breadth.

REMEMBER

Which chart is right? If the percentage of stocks above the 200 DMA is still holding up well, the market will probably try to rally before a more serious break. If a lot of stocks are well above the 200 DMA, a significant move will be required to get below the 200 DMA.

Lastly, while it looks like the crash of the tech stocks in 2000 was obvious in the top panel, the bullish percent index was whipping wildly in extremes for multiple years. These huge percentage swings made it difficult to be on either side of the market. Unfortunately, the data for the percentage of stocks above the 200 DMA was not calculated at the time.

The New York Stock Exchange composite breadth

While the NASDAQ Stock Exchange has more high fliers (see the previous section), the NYSE has a lot of the great stable U.S. companies that investors can trust to deliver dividends and growth of capital. With so many banks, utilities, and pipeline companies listed on the exchange, the breadth charts are different as well.

A significant majority of financial, insurance, and real estate stocks are listed on the NYSE. These stocks don't have a growth rate that compares to the NASDAQ 100, but the shareholders of these stocks are focused on dividends and consistent growth. This type of investor is a longer-term investor and does not typically chase momentum stocks.

Figure 15-10 shows both indicators for the New York Stock Exchange composite right at the levels where it usually holds. The levels are so close, there was not room to post the lines with the market levels.

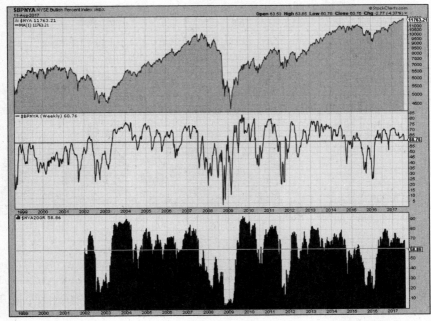

Chart courtesy of StockCharts.com

FIGURE 15-10: New York Stock Exchange composite breadth.

The Toronto Stock Exchange breadth

Canada exports a lot of products to the United States, but its stock markets can be very different. The chart shape in August 2017 (see Figure 15-11) makes the Canadian market breadth an interesting contrast to U.S. market breadth to see how the charts break down. The BPI is well below the 70 percent level, and the percentage of stocks above the 200 DMA is below 46. The market has moved 1,000 points away from the high while the U.S. markets hit all-time highs. Using the breadth indicators would help Canadian investors see the weakness in their market before their trading account becomes damaged, while U.S. stocks continued higher almost every week.

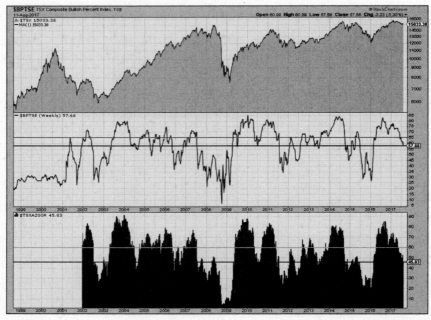

FIGURE 15-11:
Toronto Stock
Exchange
breadth.

Chart courtesy of StockCharts.com

The Canadian market has a significant weighting in oil and gas, financials, and mining. These three groups make up two-thirds of the market in Canada. While the developments in other sectors of the market can add thrust, at least two of the major sectors have to be doing well for the market to go higher.

Chapter **16**

A Quick Check of the Week's Action

Sometimes we study the individual charts so closely that we fail to see the big picture and get caught wrapped up in the day to day. Sometimes you need to step back and take a weekly look so you don't risk selling your winning trades just before another breakout. The news media commentary won't affect your perspective as much when you step back and periodically take a longer view.

In this chapter, we describe a few handy tasks for taking stock of weekly action in the market (no pun intended!): counting up versus down days, responding to unusual price action, keeping track of certain key events, and noting a break of support on indexes.

Counting the Days

It is not uncommon for one day a week to be down and the rest of the week to be up. Commonly, Monday can be a down day, which taints the opinion of the week. One suggestion you may hear is to try to avoid selling on Mondays. There are some other methods for evaluating the market, as you find out in the following sections: You can count up days, down days, inside days, and outside days.

Up days

In a big bull market, there will be more up days than down days. Keeping track of the strength of the market can help you stay focused on the positive trend.

WARNING

Keep in mind that television financial reporters are trying to make news, so they tend to focus on things that could disrupt the market to keep you tuning in.

TIP

A good rule of thumb is three to four up days per week in a bull market, with one to two down days. A down day in which the volume is lighter than the day before suggests more people are interested in buying than selling. Calculating the general direction is a simple thing to do. In Figure 16-1, which shows the NASDAQ 100 Index, the market went almost straight up with three to four positive days every week for about three months. If each week is giving you more up days than down ones, you're probably in a big uptrend. In general, as long as the market is three days up for every two down, try to ride the trend.

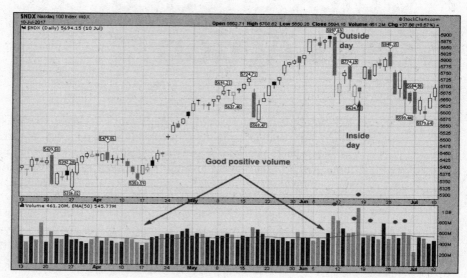

FIGURE 16-1: Counting the days.

Chart courtesy of StockCharts.com

Down days

Stockbroker Bill O'Neil taught most investors to count down days. Specifically, if the volume bar was higher than the day before and the market was down over 0.25 percent, that would be a *distribution* day. If you start to get too many in a three- to four-week period, be more careful. Five or six higher-volume days can be a harder hit to the market than five or six slightly lower close days.

In Figure 16-1 you can see a collection of big candles on high-volume days that are on down days in June. This is the upper limit of how many down days you want to see clustered together. The days with a higher volume on a down day are marked with little ellipses. This selling over numerous days suggests broader market weakness showing up. It doesn't say sell everything, but it does suggest some caution for the next few weeks. (If you're having a hard time reading the chart, review candlestick chart basics in Chapter 4.)

Inside and outside days

REMEMBER

The largest volume on Figure 16-1 happened on a Friday. The huge volume shows up on a candle that was inside the previous day. An *inside day* is when the low is higher than the low of the previous day, and the high is lower than the previous day. The whole candle is within the previous day. Typically, inside days show indecision, but they seem to show up near turning points or reversals in the market.

An *outside day* is when the candlestick extends above and below the previous day. Candlestick pattern analysis is only a guide to the next five or ten candles, but they can be important clues to watch for. The June 9 outside candle happened on a Friday. After pushing to a new high in the morning, it closed the day lower after starting the day above the previous highs. The price action from that one candle marked the highs for at least the next month, and the market moved lower. The second-largest volume was an outside day and a huge down day after a stellar run-up for most of May. These are also called *outside reversal days*.

REMEMBER

Notice the change in the candlesticks after the outside reversal. The June 9 outside reversal kicks off a period where the candles on the right-hand side of this bar are longer than the ones on the left side of the candle. When the candles are starting to get longer, the *average true range* is increasing. The average true range measures the candle heights and averages them over 14 days. Seeing them expand means the volatility is increasing, which usually happens as a top is being formed (see Chapter 9 for more about topping patterns). Calm markets don't usually top out. Eventually one candle is the final high, but the market usually tries to go back and test the most recent high. Sometimes the test is slightly higher, the same height, or lower. The best tests of a previous high come one to two months later. If the tests of the previous high can't hold above the highs, more caution is warranted.

Figure 16-1 also had outside days on March 21 and April 5. Both of those days marked highs for the next week. The taller the outside day, the more respect it should be given. In candlestick charting, these are considered important days.

Volume and volatility can help you see the change in price action. Figure 16-1 does a great job of demonstrating the three different periods of the market in the chart:

>> The left-hand side has a flat sideways consolidation.

>> The center has a huge run-up.

>> The right-hand side shows increased volume, increased volatility, and downward price movement.

Responding to Weird Price Action

What is weird price action? There's no singular definition for weird price action, but subtle changes in the market can serve as nice clues. Here are some examples:

>> Large outsized candles either up or down become reference candles for future bars to compare against.

>> Tiny candles called *dojis,* where the market opens and closes at almost the same level, with very little range between the high and the low, show indecision. Is it a sleepy market or indecisive? Dojis are usually found near reversals, but occasionally the market will power on in the same direction.

>> Extremely low or high volume suggests something is changing. When the price has been moving in one of three directions — up, down, or sideways — a change in the candles/volume usually shows up to mark a change in trend.

In the following sections, we describe some types of unusual price action that you may see during a quick check and provide pointers on what to do.

Volume and price bar extremes

Visually keep track of the following points, which can clue you in on how to respond to weird price action:

>> Inside days and outside days (we cover these earlier in this chapter)

>> Highest- and lowest-volume days

>> Largest and smallest candles, including wicks

>> Largest and smallest candle bodies

Staying with Figure 16-1 of the NASDAQ 100 Index (which appears earlier in this chapter), the lowest volume occurred on the final low point (April 17) before the market accelerated higher. The highest-volume candle up to that time marked the top. The lows made with the high volume on May 17 continue to be the lows later on in the chart. The market goes down to that level again to see whether more buyers will step in.

The large price candle on May 17 with big volume was the first such shock in months. Paying attention to where those high-volume bars occur is very valuable (the volume bars are below the price chart). High-volume days that occur with an outside day are especially worth noting. While they may not mean anything, they usually mean something. The odds are that something is changing. Outside days are an important signal — as the market moves forward after one of those days, compare the market behavior after with the market behavior before the high-volume day. Does it resume its previous trend?

Compare where high-volume days are. Are the high-volume candles starting to change the character of the market? Are more than just the occasional candle getting really long? On the right-hand side of Figure 16-1, there are eight filled sizable candles over a few weeks. On the left side, there are two, maybe three, in three months.

REMEMBER

Volume can help signal reversals. If the price starts to fall meaningfully on higher volume for multiple days in a row, this is usually a bigger clue of a trend change. Stay alert on a high-volume day, but don't overreact and get out of a good stock too soon. If the high-volume day is making you concerned, research further using other tools in your chart toolkit for time periods shorter than a week to see whether there are other buy or sell signals.

Outside reversal dates on weekly charts

An outside day is when the price bar extends above and below the previous day. An *outside week* is when the same thing happens on a weekly chart where the price made a higher high and a lower low.

While one outside week may come and go, when multiple weeks start to cluster, the market is struggling to make higher highs. Weekly outside reversals are important clues. In Figure 16-2, the June 9 (2017) candle you saw on the daily chart in Figure 16-1 happened on a Friday, creating an outside week. After pushing to a new high in the morning of June 9, it closed the day and the week lower. The price action from that one candle marked the highs for the next month, and the market moved lower. It becomes a reference candle to keep referring back to.

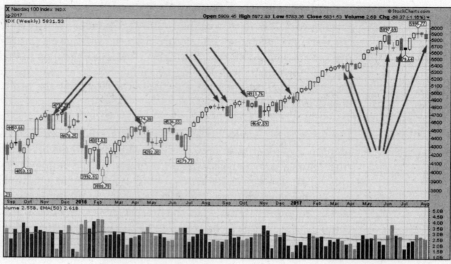

FIGURE 16-2:
Weekly
information

Chart courtesy of StockCharts.com

Weekly charts summarize the market quite cleanly. In Figure 16-2, the uptrend continues with almost every week providing a higher high. The arrows point to outside weeks. Almost every one of them is a bearish candle. The last week of March 2017 is a bullish outside candle. These clusters of outside weeks are significant in marking congestion zones that the market has to work through. Staying in tune with outside weeks can be a simple way to monitor the progress of the market.

REMEMBER

Generally, a normal week is a week with higher highs and higher lows. Three conditions suggest watching the market a little more closely:

>> A lower low

>> A close near the lows of the week after pushing to a higher high

>> Outside weeks

None of those are sell signals; they just suggest paying a little more attention to the price action. The last section of this chapter deals with support breaks that may influence selling.

Tracking Key Events

One of the things to keep in mind when you check the week's action is that certain events can always produce higher-volume days. Specifically keeping charts in your Market overview ChartList (see Chapter 13 for an introduction to these lists) can help you stay tuned in to those events.

In the following sections, we talk about two types of key events: options expiration days and Federal Reserve (Fed) meetings.

Options expiration days

Options contracts expire on the third Friday of the month, so you typically get increased volumes on that day. Because it is the third Friday, it is not the same calendar date every month. Figure 16-3 shows the options expiration days marked on the S&P 500 Large Cap Index ($SPX). The solid lines are options expiration days, and the dotted lines show quarterly options expiration days.

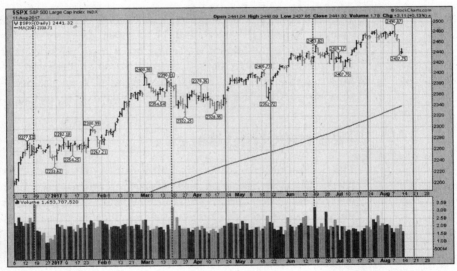

FIGURE 16-3:
Options
expiration days.

Chart courtesy of StockCharts.com

REMEMBER

There are three different series of options expiration (OE) dates. While these dates come and go regularly, the volume associated with them can make them important turn dates for the market, as mentioned earlier in this chapter:

>> **Options expiration:** Regular options expiration occurs in February, May, August, and November. There is still a volume effect, but it's not as important as the other two cycles. This date may prove insignificant for volume or trend change in the market.

>> **Options expiration through earnings season:** Options expiration during earnings season occurs in January, April, July, and October. The highest volume into the month shows up close to OE. The options expiration that occurs during earning announcements usually marks an increase in volume from earlier in the month. This increased volume can continue into the week following. Looking at Figure 16-3, the volume in January, April, and July starts to pick up just before options expiration. Notice how the volume stays somewhat elevated for the next week.

>> **Quarterly options expiration:** The highest-volume days of each quarter are usually the quarterly options expiration days. They occur in March, June, September, and December. *Quadruple witching*, which is another name for the quarterly options expiration day, always generates high-volume days — usually the highest volume of the quarter. Even in December, as people are focused around holidays, the volume will be significant.

While there are no tradeable facts around these dates, they will skew your volume analysis. Some of the dates on the chart shown in Figure 16-3 also mark change in trend dates. If the market was going up, it may stall and move sideways. As an example, the OE date marks numerous turns on the chart. December, January, March, April, May, June, and July all have trend changes within one day: from up to sideways, from sideways to down, from down to sideways, or from down to up.

Fed meeting dates

The Federal Reserve (the central bank of the United States) has become a huge part of the stock exchange, and massive attention is paid to the Fed chairman's every word. The statement after each meeting is scrutinized for the subtlest phrase changes from meeting to meeting. Plotting those meetings also produces meaningful dates on the chart that are associated with higher volume. Figure 16-4 shows the Fed meeting dates plotted on the chart of the S&P 500 Large Cap Index ($SPX).

The Fed meets roughly every six weeks. There are also a few other Federal Reserve events that are widely followed, like the Fed chair testifying to Congress. This chart just keeps track of the Fed meetings. Notice that some of the market tops and bottoms occur on a meeting date.

By nature of the calendar, the Fed always seems to meet within a few days of options expiration (see the preceding section) when it meets mid-month. These meetings occur in the same months the quadruple witching occurs: March, June, September, and December. Between the Federal Reserve meeting and the quadruple witching, these months have extra weightings.

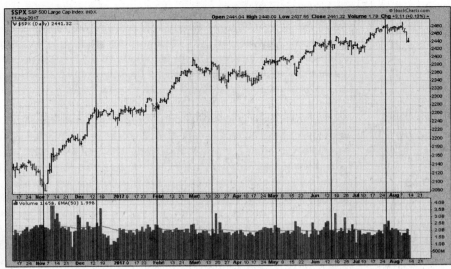

FIGURE 16-4:
Fed meeting
dates.

Lastly, be careful about the accuracy of the news media. The November 2016 stock exchange bottom shown in Figure 16-4 occurred in concert with the Federal Reserve meeting, and the rally was well underway after the presidential election. Was it the election or the Federal Reserve that caused a bump in the financial exchange-traded fund Energy Select Sector SPDR Fund (XLE) of 17 percent in the six weeks following? The XLE started rising November 2 and topped on December 14, bookmarked by the Federal Reserve meeting dates.

Spotting a Break of Support on Indexes

REMEMBER

In Chapter 10, we cover horizontal support and resistance on individual stocks. The guidelines also hold true for indexes, but the reason is somewhat different. As long as the charts are making higher lows, the uptrend is intact. If the market pulls back, traders will often look at prior support and expect it to hold.

On Figure 16-1, the lows of late June broke below the lows of mid-June. This is considered a break of support. The daily chart of the NASDAQ 100 Index ($NDX) now has a series of lower lows and lower highs. The next place lower that the market bounced from was the May 17 drop. The early July low came within points of this level as traders piled in on the buy buttons. Whether you consider the close of May 17 or the early morning bounce on May 18, the traders *shoot* against this level. *Shooting against a level* is when traders try to buy as close to that level as they can, stopping as close as possible to minimize losses.

One of the biggest changes that has come from the computerization of the market seems to be that support gets broken more often, only to reverse and surge the other way. When a support level is broken, many traders are stopped out of their trades. Almost immediately following the break of some level of support, the market finds an inner strength and comes roaring back.

TIP

One suggestion for watching support breaks is to watch how growth stocks behave as the level is breached. Watch growth stocks as the market is falling on the support break. If they are holding up well, the market may suddenly reverse. The easiest way to see this is to note that the NASDAQ 100 (QQQ) will not drop nearly as much as the other markets, like the S&P 500 Large Cap Index. Specifically go to the top 10 in the NASDAQ 100 and see whether they are performing way better on the lows. If the market is down 1 percent on the lows and the top NASDAQ stocks are barely down, the market is trying to reverse the downtrend. Since 2009, there have been numerous support breaks on the indexes that reverse and go higher. One good place to get a quick glance at top NASDAQ 100 gainers is Markets Insider: `http://markets.businessinsider.com/index/market-movers/nasdaq_100`.

5

Personalizing Your Stock Charts with Styles

IN THIS PART . . .

Customize your candlestick charts with indicators and more.

Tune up your bar charts with daily and weekly styles.

Get creative with weekly and monthly line and area charts.

Chapter **17**

Customizing Candlestick Charts

U sing stock charts comes down to two key variables. One is matching the chart settings to your personality. The second is finding indicators that help you understand the performance of stocks in your portfolio and watch list. Investors new to charts may find both of those variables overwhelming with so many choices.

Chartists use a wide range of options, and all have different ways to look at the market and use the information they find. There is a rhythm for chartists. Some like to do the analysis while the market is open. They execute open and close orders throughout the day or just before the close. Lots of investors like to analyze the market in the evening after their regular job is finished. Your choices need to match how you like to trade or invest.

In Parts 2, 3, and 4, you explore the components of a stock chart along with different styles and techniques. Now you can take what you've discovered and develop your own chart style with indicators you like. Then you can save this as your default chart. Finding out how to save and access multiple personal styles quickly and easily takes charting to a whole new level of information gathering.

In this chapter, we show how to begin developing your style with the help of candlestick charts, introduced in Chapter 4. Among other tasks, you discover how to draw trend lines and add commentary right on your saved charts by using the annotation tool. This can be very valuable and save you time. Sharing your work with friends and colleagues is simple if you know where to look, so we also outline the fastest ways to share your custom charts.

Picking Your Personal Candlestick Indicators

While candlesticks are a great price display tool on their own, using candlestick charts with multiple indicators can improve their value. In the following sections, we focus on setting up indicators for the two most commonly used candlestick chart types: daily charts and weekly charts.

REMEMBER

Understanding what you want the indicators to tell you is important. We show a variety of indictors in this chapter; you can pick and choose the ones you think will mean the most for your style of investing. You can always change your style, so don't get caught up in trying to pick the perfect style right away.

Daily candlestick charts

REMEMBER

The main reasons for using a customized daily candlestick chart are as follows:

>> Clarity on viewing each candle is important.

>> Each candle has an extreme level of detail.

>> It has a near-term view.

>> Typically, you get a view for trading in and out.

>> It highlights major long or short reference price movements.

>> It shows five to ten period references.

Figure 17-1 shows the main characteristics of a daily candlestick chart with some common indicators; this chart focuses on the stock of Louisiana Pacific (LPX). *Note:* As you become more familiar with other indicators, you can add them to your personal style. You may find that some of the common ones in the following list are not helpful to you personally, so you can drop those and add others as you become more comfortable with charting.

» The moving average convergence divergence indicator (MACD; see Chapter 11) is used to show momentum, which is better when above zero, and best when rising and the lines are spread apart.

» The full stochastics oscillator (see Chapter 11) is a tool for swing traders, who can use a rising stochastic indicator and consider selling on moves back below 80.

» You can use candlestick patterns with six months of history on the chart. Three moving averages (20, 50, and 200; see Chapter 11) illustrate a short-term trend, a medium-term trend, and a long-term trend. Try to trade in the direction of the long-term trend.

» Color volume (see Chapter 3) helps you spot exceptional volume days, either low volume or high volume. You should consider stocks with a minimum volume of 100,000 shares per day. Never own a significant percentage of the daily volume as a trader.

» The ratio tool (see Chapter 12) helps you compare the stock to the industry group (in this case, building materials and fixtures) or the S&P 500 ($SPX). Try to invest when this trend is rising.

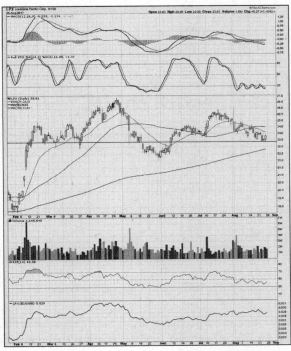

FIGURE 17-1:
A daily
candlestick chart.

Chart courtesy of StockCharts.com

Figure 17-2 shows the chart settings to create Figure 17-1. In the Chart Attributes area, we set the period as daily for seven months with five extra bars to add some white space; the type as candlestick with the size 1024, which fits best on the laptop we have; and the color scheme as yellow with blue for the up color and orange for the down color. We also added three types of moving average overlays and set colors for each, and we included a black horizontal line at a price point of 23.4. The indicators we added include MACD, full stochastics, RSI, and price.

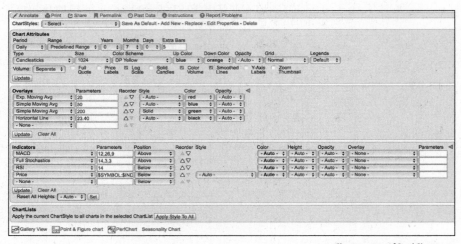

FIGURE 17-2:
Settings for
the daily
candlestick chart.

Weekly candlestick charts

REMEMBER

The main reasons for using a customized weekly candlestick chart are as follows:

>> You are not as concerned with daily candles.

>> You are looking for longer trends.

>> You want to try to ride the trend as much as possible.

>> You want to try to outperform the indexes year after year.

Figure 17-3 shows the main characteristics of a weekly candlestick chart with some common indicators. The stock shown is for Career Education (CECO).

>> The StockCharts technical ranking (SCTR; see Chapter 12) compares the stock to a peer group. Try to make sure the stock is in the top quartile for performance.

>> The ratio tool shows relative strength to the S&P 500 ($SPX). The ratio may start to show weakness before the SCTR for exiting the trade.

>> Colored candles are in this price panel. Use colored candlesticks on a three-year chart. Watch for weekly outside candles (see Chapter 16) or more candles that are filled in. Look for change in candle character. Use three moving averages to help define the trend.

>> Color-coded volume shows volume extremes. Use a 20-period moving average to compare the volume bars against.

>> The MACD shows momentum trend.

>> Full stochastics helps you identify entries and exits in conjunction with other indicators.

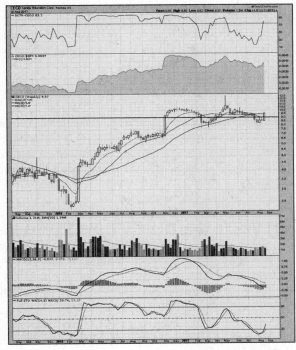

Chart courtesy of StockCharts.com

FIGURE 17-3:
A weekly candlestick chart.

Figure 17-4 shows the chart settings to create Figure 17-3. As you can see in the Chart Attributes area, the period is weekly with five extra bars for some white space. The type chosen is candlestick, which is best for getting full detail of the price movement during the day. We chose sand for the color scheme, blue for the up color, and orange for the down color. We also chose three moving averages for overlays and the following indicators: SCTR line, price, volume, MACD, and full stochastics.

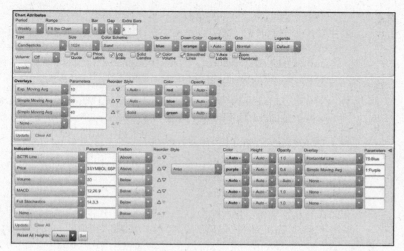

FIGURE 17-4: Settings for the weekly candlestick chart.

Chart courtesy of StockCharts.com

Saving Your Personal Style

Multiple views for the same ticker symbol can be helpful. You may like using the weekly candlestick chart with certain settings and the daily candlestick chart with different settings. Having quick access to switch between different ChartStyles (used on StockCharts.com) helps you work quickly and enables you to enjoy the charting experience.

Creating your default ChartStyle setting

Each chartist has a particular style for looking at the market. One of the big benefits of having an account on a charting website is the ability to save all your favorite styles and access them quickly without having to reset the indicators and overlays each time you go to the charting software.

To create your default ChartStyle setting on the StockCharts.com website, you use the area called ChartStyles at the top of the settings panel above the Chart Attributes area. Figure 17-5 shows the ChartStyles settings area that you see after you sign in.

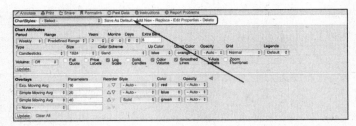

FIGURE 17-5:
Saving
ChartStyles.

The drop-down menu shows a default ChartStyle. Make changes to the chart you are looking at by altering the Chart Attributes, Overlays, and Indicators to get the group of settings you like. (If you want to review these options before working on your ChartStyle, review Parts 2 and 3.) Click the Update button to make sure that all of the settings are showing on the chart. To change the default ChartStyle settings to the one you have finished preparing, click the Save As Default link. It will prompt you with a warning; click OK. You can always get back to the StockCharts default chart at any time. The settings that are in the panel are now part of your default ChartStyle.

Saving multiple ChartStyles

Continuing with the ChartStyles tool, you can save additional ChartStyles rather than just one default. Click the *Add New* link on the ChartStyles line shown in Figure 17-5 and create an exclusive, relatively short name for the new ChartStyle. You are allowed to have up to 50 different ChartStyles as a pro user, so a unique name is important.

TIP

When you click Add New, one of the options in the box that pops up is the Button drop-down menu with 1–9 available. These buttons can be seen on the side of the chart in Figure 17-6. If you add a button number, another rectangular button will show up on the left of the chart where the circle is. Hovering over the button will show the name you associated with that button. You can quickly click on these buttons to change from one ChartStyle to another to look at one stock with different settings.

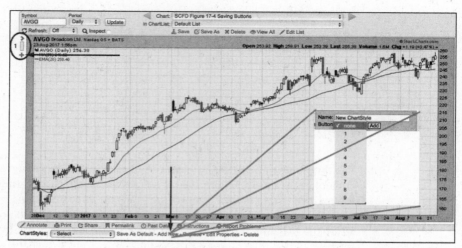

Chart courtesy of StockCharts.com

FIGURE 17-6:
Adding ChartStyle
buttons.

Lastly, use the drop-down menu on the ChartStyle line in Figure 17-6 to select from some of the StockCharts contributors' ChartStyles. You can use this drop-down at any time or save it as one of your own preferred styles. You can also revert back to the `StockCharts.com` default style.

Trading Using a Candlestick Chart with Your Settings

After lining up all the tools for investing on the basis of stock charts, the next step is to start to test your ideas. It usually works best to write down when you would have bought the stock, and when you would sell the stock. You will find that many times a sudden move will make you want to sell the stock, especially if you have a profit. If you have a loss, you resist selling. You'll want to at least get back to even and then sell. This dynamic creates support and resistance lines where people sell near where they bought (see Chapter 10).

We use indicators to help you stay in the trade. In the following sections, we discuss trading with your personalized daily and weekly candlestick charts.

Trading a daily candlestick chart with annotations

Looking at the daily candlestick chart in Figure 17-7 (showing the stock of Louisiana Pacific, or LPX), you see that notes have been added for each indicator.

Notes can help you remember what you want to focus on for each indicator. These notes are called *annotations*, and there is a tool that lets you create them.

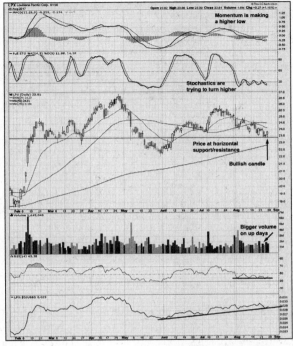

FIGURE 17-7:
Trading a daily candlestick chart.

Annotations can be placed by clicking the Annotate tool immediately above the ChartStyles drop-down menu. Figure 17-8 shows the link for accessing the Annotate tool.

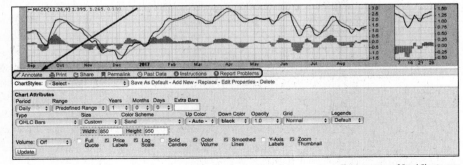

FIGURE 17-8:
The Annotate tool.

Figure 17-9 shows the annotation tool icons in the top left corner. Click on the line tool on the left, and then select the type of line, the thickness of line, and whether you would like an arrow on the end from the choices across the top. Click the color palette to select the color of the line. This tool is very easy to use. The question mark icon near the bottom left is very helpful. It also changes the keystroke information based on Mac or PC for copying lines or other tasks.

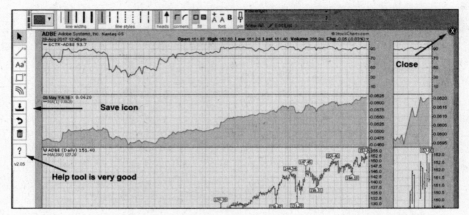

FIGURE 17-9:
Annotation
tool icons.

Chart courtesy of StockCharts.com

You can go in and play with the annotation tool to gain experience using it. The garbage can icon deletes all your annotations. After 15 minutes working with the tool, you will be able to draw lines and add text. The download icon, two boxes above the garbage can, saves the annotations. Click X in the top right corner to close the annotation tool.

Now that you know how to set those annotations, here are some explanations about how to use them (refer to Figure 17-7 for examples):

>> For the MACD (see Chapter 11), which is falling and is just below zero, the note says, "Momentum is making a higher low." If it were to turn up now, that would be great. As the price may turn up quickly, you want to be ready to put on the trade as it moves higher. If it turned up now, it would be a significantly higher low than the last major low (May 2017) on the chart, which is excellent. The histogram has been improving (getting less negative) for three weeks, suggesting the MACD could start turning up. You're using an individual candle to generate your trades, so you want the MACD to be near zero so it has room to accelerate up. You don't want it extended up near the top of the range.

>> The stochastics note says, "Stochastics are trying to turn higher." You can see they have been oscillating back and forth around the 20 range. The stochastics indicator is in a good low position, waiting for a turn back up. If it starts to turn up, you'll want to buy. It will turn up only if the price goes up. This would be a decision trigger to actually place the order at a certain price. (Flip to Chapter 11 for more about stochastics.)

>> The price panel has multiple good things going for it. Price is in a short-term downtrend. The third to last bar is a big down bar. The second to last bar is called a *bullish harami,* which is a small positive bar within the range of the previous big down candle. This signifies the short-term selling momentum has stalled. The final candle confirms the selling exhaustion by testing lower and closing higher. The price is at a horizontal support/resistance level. A black line has been drawn at $23.40 to show this support area.

   The long-term moving average (MA) is trending up to support the trade. The 50-period MA is above the 200-period MA, which is a good sign of a strong trend. The 20-period MA is below the 50, so short-term momentum is down. If price continues to improve, you would put on the trade quickly to capture the price gain for a move higher over the next five to ten periods. (Check out Chapter 11 for more on moving averages.)

TIP

   The predefined scans at StockCharts.com have bullish harami scans. Look through the scan results to find setups, and then watch how candlestick patterns play out after the signal over the next few days or weeks. Notice you can move back through scans from a few days before in the top right corner. Access the predefined scans from the members page after you sign in.

>> The volume is improving on up days because the volume panel shows taller price bars on up days. (Chapter 3 introduces volume.)

>> The RSI (see Chapter 12) is trying to base around 40 (where the black line is), which is a great place to look for stocks turning back up.

>> Lastly, in the panel using the ratio tool (see Chapter 12), the stock is outperforming its industry group because the line is trending up.

In Figure 17-7, if the price of LPX were to drop below $23.40 — the horizontal support/resistance line — you would likely choose to sell because selling momentum is not exhausted, so you would close the trade with a small loss.

REMEMBER

This is an example of how to use indicators to support a candlestick-based trade. The goal is to have just a few indicators to help make the trade decisions. Too many will lead to a common syndrome called *analysis paralysis.* Looking at too many indicators means you'll never put on a trade. So as you become more familiar with the key indicators that enable you to make the best decisions for your trading style, you may start to drop indicators that you find are not as helpful.

Trading a weekly candlestick chart

Weekly candlestick charts are used by longer-term swing traders. These traders are looking for a multi-week trend that takes the price higher. With less focus on the intraday price movements, weekly candles usually require wider initial stops. If the stock is going to rally significantly, it helps if the early weeks of the rally start outperforming other stocks to attract new investors.

In Figure 17-10, annotations and lines point out the following:

>> The StockCharts technical ranking (SCTR; see Chapter 12) has pushed up quickly to show a stock moving quickly.

>> The relative strength area chart has also broken the downtrend. This indicator and the SCTR suggest early outperformance for a good start.

>> On the price panel, the stock had run up from $2.20 to $12.50 with a giant exhaustion move ending the run after breaking to a new high. An *exhaustion move* is where price makes a big move higher, and then immediately reverses and loses all of the gains. These are typically seen at price highs. The stock consolidated for three months and found its low around the midpoint of the November 2016 reference candle. *Reference candles* are large candles that move to a new price range for the stock. (You can see the second reference candle at March 2016.) Usually, a stock will hold at the top or the midpoint of the reference candle.

The most recent week shows a *marubozu* candle. *Marubozu candles* are tall white candles with no shadows above or below. That candle pushed the stock back above the flat 40-week moving average. With the stock consolidating since the early November burst, this looks set up to continue to run after consolidating. The price made new one-month highs and also pushed above horizontal support and resistance.

>> The volume has been expanding over the last five weeks, but was a little soft with this big weekly candle. That is a slight negative.

>> The MACD momentum is pointing lower but is very close to breaking the downtrend. The MACD is also near the zero line, which suggests lots of room to move higher.

>> The full stochastics have broken back above 20, so there is lots of room to the upside for the indicator.

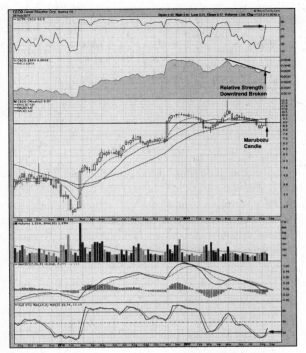

FIGURE 17-10:
Trading a weekly
candlestick chart.

Chart courtesy of StockCharts.com

If you owned this stock, you would want to preserve your gains by putting on a stop to indicate the price at which the stock should be sold if it continues to decline. A close stop would be halfway down this week's big white candle at $9, and a wider stop would be just below the bottom of this candle at $8.50.

There is a strong potential for this stock to trade up to the previous highs around $10.75, and based on the acceleration in 2016, the stock could potentially fire up for another big run.

Sharing Your Customized Charts

After you create custom charts, you can share your charts with friends and fellow investors by social media or email. Figure 17-11 shows the line where the sharing link is found, right above the ChartStyles menu.

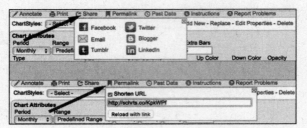

Chart courtesy of StockCharts.com

FIGURE 17-11:
Sharing your
charts with
friends.

TIP

Figure 17-11 shows the dialog box that appears when you click on the Share link. A box opens up, and you can select the method of delivery. If you want to shorten the link, use the Permalink link to get the actual URL address of the chart. The chart can be sent to a friend, or you can use the short link on Twitter as an example. Both of these options are shown in Figure 17-11. If you want to print your chart, you click Print rather than Permalink.

Chapter **18**

Fine-Tuning Your Bar Charts

B ar charts — the topic of this chapter — give you the same information as candlestick charts (see Chapters 4 and 17), but the information provided is a little more discreet. The extreme tails seem to be emphasized more than the candle bodies.

Bar charts, which we introduce in Chapter 5, are used to recognize longer stock patterns, so you will find that different indicators are more helpful when you plan to hold an asset for a longer period of time. On a bar chart, you tend to look for consolidations rather than the information on a single candle, as you would on a candlestick chart.

On bar charts, your eyes are drawn to areas of consolidation rather than individual price bars. You're more likely to use larger patterns, like new 52-week highs, prices around Keltner channels, or moving average crossover strategies with bar charts (Chapter 10 has more about these patterns). You can still use candlesticks with these types of patterns, but the candlestick information is based on one-, two-, or three-candle patterns, not larger patterns.

By using Keltner channels with a bar chart, you are less likely to be concerned with the individual bar information. There are also color-coding opportunities using one, two, or three colors with bar charts, if you choose to use one of these tools. In this chapter, we review some of the more popular tools you may want to add to your bar chart styles. (For more information on specific tools, please review Parts 2 and 3.)

Adjusting Bar Chart Settings to Your Liking

In this section, we discuss custom settings you can use for daily bar charts; we also talk about a few settings for weekly bar charts. If you want to review basic information about the settings panel for bar charts, check out Chapter 5.

REMEMBER

Saving your bar chart style is the same as saving styles for candlestick charts; we review the process in Chapter 17. There, we also show you how to personalize your charts with annotations.

Colors

If you don't want to highlight the difference between up and down days, the bars can all be the same color. In the Chart Attributes area, set the up and down colors the same. Using the color volume toggle to get the difference between up days and down days is usually helpful in any case. This setup would have been the newspaper version in the old days.

A typical chart with two colors and volume up and down colors to match enables the ability to match the volume with each bar. This setup is more common now with color screens rather than printed charts.

TIP

You can also use a color-coding system by trader and author Dr. Alexander Elder. The coding uses three colors — red, blue, and green — to denote trends that speed up or slow down. For more information, the Elder Impulse System is discussed at http://stockcharts.com/school/doku.php?id=chart_school:chart_analysis:elder_impulse_system.

Overlays

The importance of the bar chart is more about the setup relative to larger price patterns. The overlays you choose depend on the type of trader you are:

» If you like pullbacks within an uptrend, you might like to use Keltner channels or EMA envelopes (see Chapter 10 for details).

» If you like to buy breakouts to new three-month, six-month, or 52-week highs, you'll buy as the stock breaks out and will want to use moving averages or horizontal support/resistance areas for support zones. (Chapter 10 covers moving averages and support/resistance areas.)

Indicators

You have a variety of indicators to choose from when you work with daily bar charts. Figure 18-1, which shows the stock of Adobe Systems (ADBE), has a few examples:

» The chart shows the SCTR ranking indicator on the top. Here, the SCTR is 93.5 and very strong. (SCTR stands for StockCharts technical ranking; see Chapter 12 for details.)

» The relative strength (see Chapter 12) compared to the S&P 500 is shown as a shaded area chart and will react sooner than the SCTR for potential selling information.

» The price chart is clean with a 200-day moving average.

» The volume indicator is color coded and has a moving average for the volume. (Chapter 3 introduces volume indicators.)

» The moving average convergence divergence indicator (MACD; see Chapter 11) shows the momentum of the stock. This setup is for trading breakouts above previous resistance.

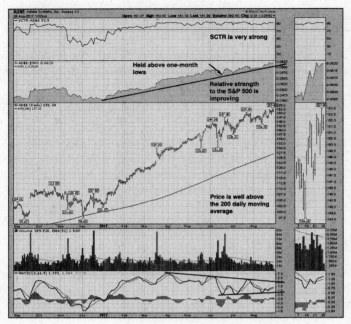

FIGURE 18-1:
Daily bar chart
indicators.

Special settings for weekly bar charts

As chartists gain experience, they use weekly charts a lot more for guidance in their trading. With 50 indicators to choose from, you can keep trying new indicators for a long time. Settle on a few core indicators and then try some of the others to see whether they help you with some new signal. Consider the following custom settings for weekly bar charts:

>> Strong trending stocks are usually moving up and away from horizontal support/resistance, so moving averages or price channels can help manage your trade. A 20-week moving average is a great place for strong uptrends to find support.

>> One of the best parts about weekly charts is the ability to watch the momentum through the percentage price oscillator indicator (PPO; see Chapter 11) or the MACD. These can give you important information about a trend ending or starting. Especially for high-flying stocks or commodity-related stocks, momentum indicators can really improve your timing.

>> Using other tools like relative strength is very helpful. Stocks that have weak relative strength are probably being sold. Improving relative strength is critical to outperforming the market average. On a weekly chart, comparing the stock to the S&P 500 ($SPX) shows the percentage gain for a week between a stock and the percentage gain of the $SPX. The ability to see whether your stock is

outperforming the index week after week is a critical part of the advantage of charting your stocks.

>> Annotating trend lines on weekly charts can help you understand the reason to continue to own the stock or sell it. Trend lines connect price lows on the stock price. The stock price creates the trend; chartists use lines to help identify it. The longer the trend, the more profitable the stock. When these trends break, it can be important to watch. (Chapter 17 explains how to use the annotation tool on StockCharts.com.)

>> Weekly volume is very helpful because small volume weeks or large volume weeks can help identify points near major changes in trend.

>> You may also want to use the on-balance volume (OBV) indictor, the Chaikin money flow (CMF) indicator, or the accumulation/distribution indicator (see Chapter 11 for details). Each of these works really well on weekly charts.

TIP

If you want a few line charts, some weekly candlestick charts, and some daily bar charts, you can save each of these as a unique ChartStyle and create a button for each one (check out Chapter 17 for details). If you end up having more ChartStyles than buttons, use the ChartStyle drop-down menu in the settings panel to access the other styles.

Trading Using a Daily Bar Chart with Your Settings

Figure 18-1 (shown earlier in this chapter) is a chart for someone who wants to trade breakouts using relative strength. Breakouts occur when the price moves above previous highs. That can be a breakout above one-month, three-month, six-month, or annual highs. It depends on your trading strategy. A common place to look for breakouts is to watch stocks that move above 75 on the SCTR. When that also coincides with a breakout to new highs, it can be an indication of a good trading opportunity.

Here are some explanations of how to trade with the help of custom daily bar charts, using Figure 18-1 as an example (the stock shown is Adobe, or ADBE):

>> The SCTR (StockCharts technical ranking; see Chapter 12), the indicator at the top, shows ADBE's ranking against other stocks in its peer group. Adobe is a large-cap stock, and the price action is behaving better than 93 percent of the stocks. The move above 75 in January was a timely signal as the stock was also breaking out to new highs around $110.

>> The relative Strength indicator (see Chapter 12) below SCTR shows a comparison to the S&P 500 ($SPX). You can see that ADBE was starting to improve and was not quite at three-month highs. The S&P 500 was moving up quickly from the November 2016 lows, and Adobe was lagging until January 2017. In January, it started to improve and was almost at new three-month highs.

If Adobe starts to make new two-month lows in relative strength, it is a good time to add protection with options or sell some of the position to lock in some gains. When a big uptrend stops, it usually needs time to consolidate the existing gains. That change in the relative strength trend can be a great indicator.

>> Looking at the price section next, you can see that price action is smooth until June; then it starts to get choppy. This usually happens around a final high in the price.

TECHNICAL STUFF

Large institutions start to sell part of their position to lock in gains, which eventually caps the stock move for a period of time. Institutional investors won't allow one stock to dominate a portfolio. The investor might start a position in a stock at 2 percent. If the stock price improves, the investor may add to the position. Some funds may allow a 5 percent weighting. If the stock starts to dominate the portfolio, the institutional investors sell to lock in gains and limit the size of the stock value within the portfolio. This becomes resistance as sellers lock in gains and the stock move stalls.

Strong long-term stocks commonly find support around the 200 daily moving average. As long as the 200 daily moving average is trending up, the big trend is higher.

>> The volume section shows the number of shares traded each day.

>> The moving average convergence divergence indicator (MACD; see Chapter 11) is a momentum indicator. When it is above zero, the stock is behaving well.

TIP

You never want to sell a winner too early, so using stock options when strong technical conditions weaken can help protect your portfolio. June is a good example on the ADBE chart. If in a few months down the road the price resumes its uptrend, you still own the stock. Conversely, if price has broken down hard, you're protected by your options and you can sell the stock. At that point, you want to look for a new stock to buy and start the cycle again.

For an exit on the stock position shown in Figure 18-1, initially you would likely set a stop for downside protection at $110. Keep moving your stop up. The August lows of $142.50 look like the most recent place for a stop. As long as that holds, look for breakdowns in relative strength and a breakdown in momentum, which are good reasons to exit from a long uptrend. Nobody ever went broke taking profits.

Figure 18-2 shows the settings to re-create the daily bar chart. In the Chart Attributes area, we chose a daily period for a range of one year. The type of chart is OHLC Bars with black as the down color and auto as the up color. The overlays chosen were simple moving average and events, such as dividends, stock splits, and the like. The indicators chosen were SCTR line, price, volume, and MACD.

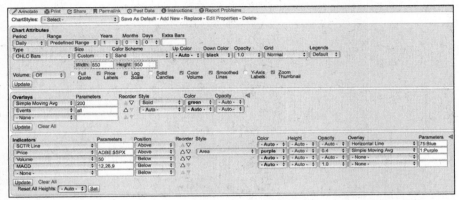

FIGURE 18-2:
Settings for the
daily bar chart.

TIP

The most important part of trading is continuous learning, and some people like to print out their charts for review. Figure 18-2 shows a Print link beside the Annotate tool on the top line (you need to sign in to StockCharts.com to see this link). This works very well and will scale the chart to fit on the paper in landscape or page view. You'll find it is much better than working through the scaling tools on your computer. By keeping all of your completed trades in a ChartList (introduced in Chapter 13), you can access the same chart long after you sell and compare it with the paper version.

Trading Using a Weekly Bar Chart with Your Settings

When trading using a weekly bar chart, you want to look at different indicators. Two helpful indicators are the SCTR line and the Chaikin money flow (CMF). Figure 18-3, showing the stock of Newmont Mining (NEM), has an SCTR line on it to keep you focused on stocks with improving performance. The SCTR (see Chapter 12) has just moved above the 75 level, indicating the stock is starting to outperform a large majority of its peers. On the same chart, you can see that the CMF (see Chapter 11) has recently moved into positive territory. Looking left on the chart, positive CMF is usually bullish.

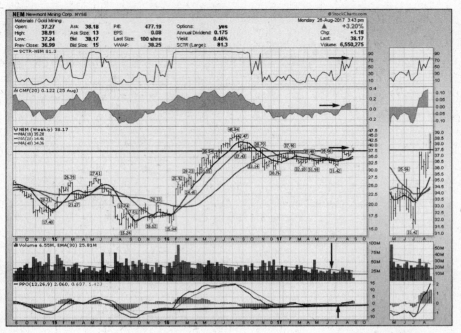

FIGURE 18-3:
A weekly
bar chart.

The price panel shows the stock pushing above resistance. This particular chart is shown on a Monday, so the price bar has the rest of the week to continue or reverse the breakout. Traders will buy this on the breakout and then sell right away if the breakout does not hold up. The three moving averages (introduced in Chapter 10) can be used as a strategy with price bars as well. The moving average crossovers actually align with the short-, medium-, and long-term moving averages in the proper sort order on the right side of the chart. The zoom panel on the right shows the moving averages from a close-up viewpoint.

If the last price bar has a green shading, the market is open and the price is real-time from the main exchange for members of StockCharts.com. If the last price bar is shaded yellow, the price is delayed 15 minutes for non-members. Members seeing a yellow shaded bar are seeing BATS (Better Alternative Trading System) data, so the price is similar but may not be identical to the NYSE/NASDAQ real-time data. If there is no shading, the market is closed. These variances can be seen on the StockCharts.com website.

TECHNICAL STUFF

Non-members see prices delayed 15 minutes. StockCharts.com members get BATS real-time data for the United States and delayed data for all other markets. BATS is an electronic exchange based in Kansas City and offers its trading data for free. Members also have the option of adding official real-time data for the United States, Canada, the United Kingdom, and India for an additional monthly cost.

The volume panel shows that the lowest volume on the chart happened just a few weeks before the final low. The highest volume on the chart was associated with a big breakout. This may happen again as price breaks above resistance, but it is still early in the week. The straight line is to compare the volume setup with historical levels.

Lastly, the PPO is improving with a slight uptrend. It has recently moved into positive territory. These conditions all align to suggest that price may be starting a strong advance. From a trading perspective, it's very helpful when all the signals align.

Figure 18-4 shows the settings for the weekly bar chart. In the Chart Attributes area, we chose a weekly period and a three-year range. We chose three types of moving averages (10, 20, and 40) and designated a different color for each. We also chose a horizontal line at 37.5. Indicators chosen were the SCTR line, the Chaikin money flow (CMF), volume, and the percentage price oscillator (PPO).

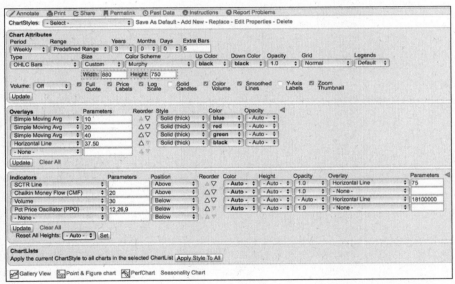

FIGURE 18-4:
Settings for the weekly bar chart.

Chart courtesy of StockCharts.com

Chapter **19**

Adjusting Your Line and Area Charts

L ine and area charts (introduced in Chapters 6 and 7) remove all the detail around trading ranges and just show the closing price for each week. The line just connects the closing prices. Investors use these charts to find breakouts above/below previous areas of resistance/support without all the other details found in candlestick or bar charts (covered in Chapters 4 and 5). Trend lines are very clean, using closing prices.

In this chapter, we show you how to customize line and area charts for your needs:

» Line charts work great for longer-term trading. The two examples in this chapter use weekly and monthly charts. For 401(k) buy and hold investors, this is going to get you in near the beginning and out near the end.

» Area charts are the types of charts you see most frequently on TV financial shows because they provide the easiest visual for seeing price movement. They essentially show the same information as line charts but in a more dramatic way.

Creating a Custom Weekly Line Chart

Figure 19-1 (depicting the stock of Valero Energy, or VLO) shows an initial setup of your ChartStyle for line charts. (We introduce ChartStyles, which you can find on StockCharts.com, in Chapter 17.) These are the choices you need to consider:

» Relative strength indicators against the rest of the market can be helpful on a weekly line chart. You want your chart to outperform other markets. The SCTR and a ratio chart of the stock compared to the S&P 500 ($SPX), the industry group, or the sector is one such example of an indicator you may want to use. The SCTR (which stands for StockCharts technical ranking) refines the information down to a number rather than just a trend. (See Chapter 12 for more about relative strength investing.)

» Using the Chaikin money flow (CMF; see Chapter 11) helps identify whether the underlying price action is improving. On-balance volume (OBV) or accumulation/distribution can also help.

» The price panel is very clean with only a single line on it. Adding some moving average(s) or a price channel would be helpful information so you can more easily see when the price moves above or below the average. In this chart, we use the 40-day moving average; a 200-day moving average could also be useful. (For more information on moving averages, see Chapter 10.)
The horizontal line at the top shows the highest stock price or resistance level, which in this chart appears to be the point at which the stock price resists going higher.

» Volume is always valuable in case some clues are hiding there. For example, on high-volume days there likely was some type of news that drove stock sales. If you see a high-volume day, be sure to check the news about the stock before making any trading decisions. The price change you're seeing may be a very short-term reaction to the news of the day.

» The percentage price oscillator (PPO) shows momentum. Choices also include the know sure thing (KST), moving average convergence divergence indicator (MACD), or price momentum oscillator (PMO). Check out Chapter 11 for more about these indicators.

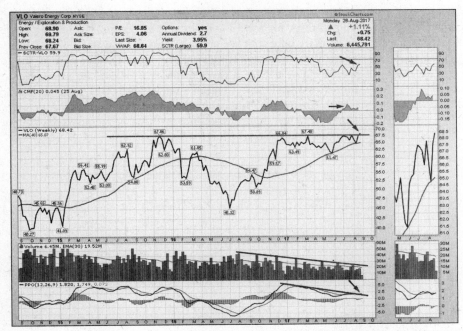

FIGURE 19-1: A weekly line chart.

So what are you looking for when you trade with a custom weekly line chart? In the case of Figure 19-1, each indicator is giving you positive signals as the price is breaking out. Breakout traders would buy this breakout and sell if it moved back below the breakout level. Here are the details on each panel:

>> You can see the SCTR is moving above 60. It is not great, but it is still outperforming 60 percent of the peer group. If it continues to move above 75, that would reinforce the bullish case.

>> The CMF recently turned positive.

>> The price is breaking out to new highs. That is how new bull moves start. The price is making higher highs, leaving the consolidation behind. The 40-week moving average is trending higher.

>> The volume is drying up, suggesting an explosive move if volume starts to expand. Notice that the two previous summers had significantly higher volumes. Six of the last eight weeks had lower volumes similar to Christmas or Thanksgiving short weeks.

>> The PPO just broke above a downtrend in momentum while above zero, which is very bullish.

TIP

The settings for a weekly line chart in Figure 19-1 are shown in Figure 19-2. In particular, note that we set the chart for a weekly period over a range of three years. We used a simple moving average of 40 days and set the color to green so it would stand out from the black line used for the price. We also added several indicators: SCTR Line, Chaikin Money Flow (CHF), Volume, and Pct Price Oscillator (PPO). Change the indicators and overlays to create your own optimized chart (Chapter 3 has an introduction to these settings). Save your weekly line chart ChartStyle by using the instructions in Chapter 17.

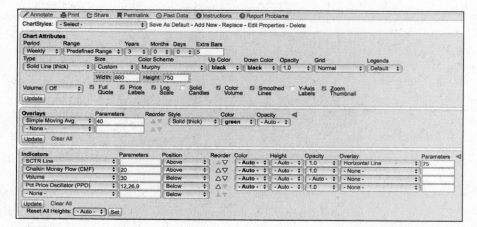

FIGURE 19-2: Settings for a weekly line chart.

Chart courtesy of StockCharts.com

Developing Your Own Monthly Line Chart

We get so caught up in the day to day that monthly charts seem to be too long for the fast world we live in. Actually, the monthly line chart helps you stay with difficult trades that you may have found on the weekly line chart.

Monthly charts change only 12 times a year, so looking through a ChartList of monthly charts during a pregame show can be interesting and rewarding (see Chapter 13 for the scoop on ChartLists, found at StockCharts.com). Understanding where all the long-term charts are helps with directional trades and major market turning points that daily charts would never pick up.

In the following sections, we provide pointers on how to customize a monthly line chart.

REMEMBER

Monthly closes don't end on Fridays necessarily, so a monthly chart may look slightly different than a weekly chart of the same ticker symbol. If you use price labels, the previous highs and lows won't match between weekly and monthly charts because a monthly close takes only the last closing price of the month and plots it.

Selecting your indicators

Figure 19-3, showing gold stock ($GOLD), is an example of a setup for a long-term monthly line chart. You want long indicators that show you major trends:

>> The RSI indicator usually stays above 50 on a monthly chart in a bull market. The relative strength to the S&P 500 ($SPX) is a very good indicator to use for keeping track of outperforming industries (see Chapter 12 for information).

>> You can see in the Chaikin money flow (CMF) panel that the price of gold turned up at the two arrows. This is how CMF helps you identify price changes.

>> A clean price chart uses the monthly close.

>> Gold stayed above the moving average line for most of the 18-year period. It took a dive below the line in 2013. When that happens, you should take a closer look at other indicators to see whether it is better to hold or sell. A short-term investor would likely sell, while a long-term investor would likely hold initially. But you can see that the downward trend continued into 2017, so taking profits when the price moved below the moving average at the end of 2012 would have been the right decision.

>> Volume is a worthwhile indicator for a monthly line chart because you can quickly see how active trading was on the stock during the month and pick out the most active and least active days.

>> The percentage price oscillator (PPO) is a good momentum indicator for long-term charts. By using percentages rather than the price to calculate momentum, the waves of the PPO are similar in size at any price, whereas the moving average convergence divergence (MACD) indicator will have higher waves as price rises up. (Flip to Chapter 11 for more about momentum.)

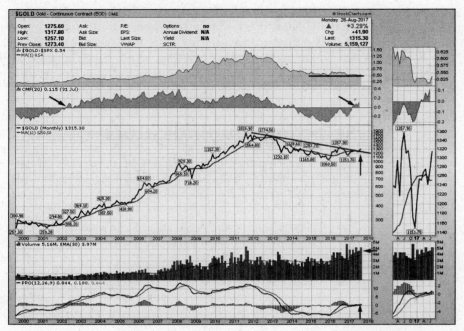

FIGURE 19-3:
A monthly
line chart.

Chart courtesy of StockCharts.com

Saving your monthly line chart

Figure 19-4 shows the settings for the monthly line chart in Figure 19-3. In particular, note that we set the chart for a monthly period over a range of 18 years. We used a simple moving average and the following indicators: Price, Chaikin Money Flow (CMF), Volume, and Pct Price Oscillator (PPO) (see Chapter 3 for basics on settings). Save your monthly line chart ChartStyle by using the instructions discussed in Chapter 17.

FIGURE 19-4:
Settings for a
monthly
line chart.

Chart courtesy of StockCharts.com

Trading a monthly line chart

A monthly line chart is especially helpful when you want to look at a longer-term trading history and determine how that history either supports or denies your assumption for trading with more-detailed daily or weekly charts.

How important is the big picture on gold if you want to buy Newmont Mining, a gold stock shown in Chapter 18? When the weekly bar chart of Newmont Mining (NEM) is just breaking above resistance, you want to see a supportive picture for gold.

REMEMBER

You can see a longer-term view using a monthly line chart (refer to Figure 19-3). Is the price in the top right corner or the bottom right corner? Has price just broken a long trend line? What about major horizontal support and resistance levels? Those three questions give you more understanding than almost any other frames of reference. When you have an idea of where the price is in the big picture, you can start to add information by reading the indicators.

Price has been consolidating sideways for five years and is in the top one-third of the chart. It has just broken a downtrend, but there is horizontal resistance around $1,350. Because you have only closing data, weekly or daily charts may help define the resistance level a little better. That is a pretty interesting place on the chart for a chartist. Moving above a six-year downtrend is meaningful, as something must be changing.

Looking at the indicators, you find the following:

>> The relative strength in the top panel has not started to improve yet, but it is not getting worse, so that's okay. As price consolidated, the relative strength stayed the same. If it's going to start to outperform, this is where you can look to see the big change start.

>> The CMF indicator couldn't be any more bullish. Looking left shows the last time CMF went bullish, and it was a worthy ride that lasted ten years.

>> The volume is expanding, and the most recent month will be one of the highest-volume months ever. That is very supportive.

>> The PPO just broke above zero, but there's really no great place to draw any trend lines. However, the PPO also coincided with the CMF breakout back in 2002.

All of that adds up to a very supportive long-term look for gold based on the information you have available. Using long-term charts like the ones in this chapter helps you quickly assemble some historical information and analyze the current market based on similar conditions.

For example, you could use the historical information in the long-term line chart in Figure 19-3 to start some long-term positions in gold or gold miners and try to ride the major trend until conditions change. A chartist would move to a weekly chart and maybe a daily chart to get more information. The next step would be to look for the strongest gold miners in the industry to invest in. With a strong long-term backdrop, more analysis of the industry is worth doing to build some portfolio positioning in gold.

Nothing assures you that this time will be the same as the last time. However, seeing the same setup with lots of volume suggests this could be a good opportunity. Technical analysis is about lining up the odds in your favor. This chart does that.

Setting Up a Specialized Monthly Area Chart

Area charts are just another way of displaying a line chart. They are commonly used on TV to help the viewer distinguish the price line more clearly. Area charts also offer a unique style that is different from a daily chart with candlesticks. One of the nice parts about charting is creating attractive, colorful charts that you enjoy looking at to review. Monthly charts are not reviewed that often, so contrasting this ChartStyle to a daily candlestick chart can be refreshing and generate new perspectives.

The indicators you choose will have similar perspectives to the monthly line chart that we describe earlier in this chapter. Once you have chosen your indicators, you can review them by looking back on the chart to see whether they help you find important trend changes in advance or at least in a timely manner. We encourage you to try using the RSI indicator (see Chapter 12 for details) and notice the support/resistance levels in bull and bear markets.

Large institutional investors may use monthly charts for their guiding principles in the current portfolio. For individual investors, monthly charts are a great support tool for buying stocks and building confidence based on longer-term indicators.

Figure 19-5 shows a monthly area chart for copper stock ($COPPER). Once again, the three questions we used on the monthly line chart are valuable. Where is the price on the right-hand side? Have any trends been broken? Where are the horizontal support/resistance levels?

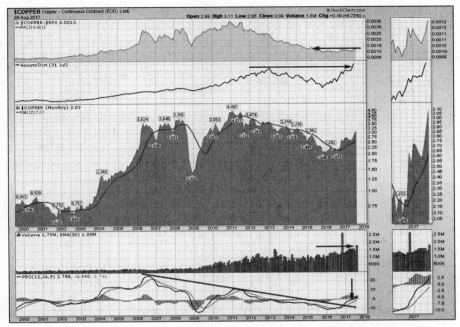

FIGURE 19-5:
A monthly
area chart.

Chart courtesy of StockCharts.com

Copper has moved from the 50 percent level on the scale to about three-fourths of the way up. It has also broken a five-year downtrend. The 12-month moving average does a great job of highlighting bull and bear markets.

Copper was used to show that you can view industrial metals and other commodities on the StockCharts.com website. Here are some details to pick up from Figure 19-5:

» The relative strength of copper compared to the S&P 500 ($SPX) is above two-year highs, so this chart is outperforming the $SPX. That is a strong first signal (see Chapter 12 for more about relative strength).

» The accumulation/distribution line (see Chapter 11) is at new highs, so that is very bullish.

» The volume (introduced in Chapter 3) is very, very strong and supportive.

» The percentage price oscillator (PPO; see Chapter 11) is above zero, and a major momentum downtrend has been broken. This is clearly a bullish tone for the metal.

With this very positive monthly perspective, investing in copper-related mining stocks or construction equipment used in mining has a strong supportive backdrop. If the relative strength started to underperform or the price moved below the 12-month moving average, that would give you different signals that you could use for your portfolio management.

Figure 19-6 shows the settings for the monthly area chart. In particular, note that we set the chart to a monthly period over a range of 18 years. We used a simple moving average and set the color to green so you can easily see it against the black price line. We also added the following indicators: Price, Accum/Distribution line, Volume, and Pct Price Oscillator (PPO) (see Chapter 3 for basics on settings). Save your monthly line chart ChartStyle by using the instructions discussed in Chapter 17.

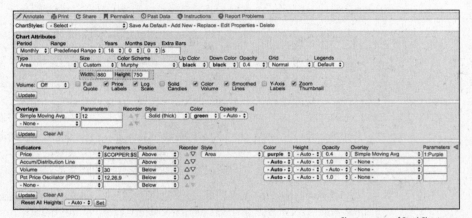

FIGURE 19-6: Settings for the monthly area chart.

Chart courtesy of StockCharts.com

TIP

You may prefer the line chart to the area chart or vice versa. You may find you want to do more with area charts because you find them easier to use. Try using daily or weekly settings on area charts to see whether doing so helps you get around the detail of candlestick and bar charts.

6

Putting Your Stock Charting Expertise to Work

Chapter 20

Using Your Charts to Inform Your Buy, Hold, and Sell Decisions

You will never hear a CEO announce to shareholders that it's time to sell the company's stock. That role is specifically left to investors and traders. Deciding when to buy a stock and when to sell a stock is *your* decision. Nobody in the markets thinks it is easy to actively work the markets. It takes time, commitment, and patience. Buying the stock of great companies with beaten-down prices takes a lot of courage. Buying the stock of great companies hitting new highs takes just as much courage. In this chapter, we take a look at how to use charts to help improve your decision making on buying, holding, and selling stocks.

Separating the Strong from the Weak

Focusing on strong stocks is one of the most important themes of the market. Usually those strong stocks are part of a strong sector. We have multiple methods of finding strong stocks and sectors with technical analysis. Three of these are covered in depth in Chapter 12 on relative strength:

>> StockCharts technical ranking (SCTR)

>> Performance chart using sector exchange-traded funds (ETFs)

>> Relative Rotation Graph (RRG) tool

All three of these tools are available if you're a member of StockCharts.com. (On the home page, you see a green button that says "Free 1-Month Trial.") From the Members page, you want to focus your tasks on finding strong areas of the market. Understanding how to identify strong sectors and industries quickly is very important; the following sections can help. Click along with the following instructions to develop your skill level using the site.

Sector summary

Chapter 12 has an infographic explaining the stock market and showing you the sectors, industries within each sector, and stocks within each industry. You will need to drill down into these sectors very quickly. Combining the various StockCharts.com relative strength tools helps you see strength in the market based on your investment timeline. All of these tools are accessed from the Pro Control Center on the Members Page.

In the Pro Control Center (see Figure 20-1), scroll down to Reports & Analysis Tools. Notice the top five buttons in this Reports & Analysis area are all designed to help you see what is going on in relative strength and popularity. Working with the Sector Summary and the Industry Summary, you can find the strong sectors and strong industry groups quickly. Start with the Sector Summary button and use this link to drill down into the industries and stocks.

Drilling down into sectors

Click "Sector Summary (Drill down into the major market sectors)" to open a screen sorting Sector ETFs. (See Figure 20-2.)

On this Sector screen, adjust the sort order by clicking on the column headers. Click on SCTR to see the top overall sectors first. On the top left, you can click on different time periods. The default setting is Intraday, but we have adjusted it to show the change over three months. Other time frames are one week, one month, six months, and a year. Three months is a sweet spot. This period is long enough that you can see a meaningful trend start but not too short.

FIGURE 20-1:
Pro Control
Center.

Chart courtesy of StockCharts.com

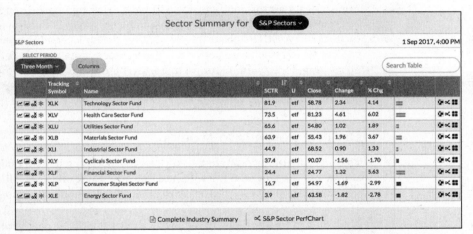

FIGURE 20-2:
Sector ETFs.

Chart courtesy of StockCharts.com

Drilling down into industries

Click on any sector name and it will take you to the industry lists within that sector. In Figure 20-3, technology is shown. Because you can't actually buy an industry group, there is no SCTR for each one. Change the time period on the top left to see the industry performance over different time intervals. The screenshot in Figure 20-3 has one month selected from the drop-down menu. For industries, one-month changes can identify new trends early. You can use three months as well for swing trading. Longer periods tend to be too long for practical use in identifying new trends. Shorter periods like one week can just be normal market oscillations.

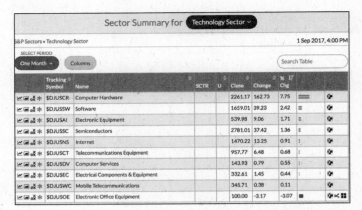

FIGURE 20-3: Industries.

Chart courtesy of StockCharts.com

TIP

Almost every sector and industry will have some top-performing stocks, but the best moves take place when the whole industry group is moving and the majority of stocks have SCTRs above 75. By clicking through each of these industries, you can see which stocks are performing well. When large portions of an industry are all surging, focus your attention there. That industry group will probably have one of the largest % Change bars. In Figure 20-3, the computer hardware industry is surging, followed by software.

Drilling down into stocks

To continue drilling down to the stock level, click on an industry name. Figure 20-4 shows you the stocks in the software industry. Click on the SCTR column to bring the strongest stocks to the top, with an SCTR in the 90s at the top of the list.

The column to the right of the SCTR shows the SCTR peer group. Click on the U column to sort on market cap size. The stocks with no SCTR may be at the top, but scroll down to the market cap–size stocks you like to work with (for example, perhaps you are only a large-cap investor). Then alter the time using the drop-down menu in the top left corner to one week, one month, or three months. When stocks start to show up on these lists, something is going on that is making investors show interest in them. Stocks that are performing well usually have a reason. Investigate the chart pattern to see whether a stock is changing trend from down to up for a possible entry. *Note:* Not all stocks have SCTRs due to a small market cap or a low stock price, or they may be foreign small- or mid-cap stocks.

With this quick technique, combining the Sector/Industry/Stock drill-down with the SCTRs and the % Change bars, you can find strong stocks fast.

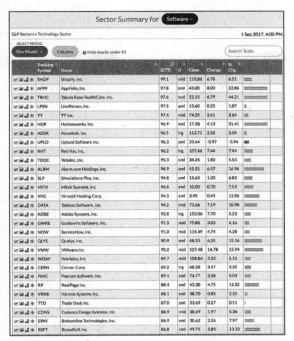

Sector Summary for Software

Tracking Symbol	Name	SCTR	U	Close	Change	% Chg
SHOP	Shopify, Inc.	99.1	mid	110.86	6.78	6.51
APPF	AppFolio, Inc.	97.8	sml	43.00	8.00	22.86
TRHC	Tabula Rasa HealthCare, Inc.	97.6	sml	22.15	6.79	44.21
LPSN	LivePerson, Inc.	97.5	sml	13.60	0.25	1.87
YY	YY Inc.	97.4	mid	74.35	2.61	3.64
HDP	Hortonworks, Inc.	96.9	sml	17.28	4.13	31.41
ADSK	Autodesk, Inc.	96.5	lrg	113.71	2.33	2.09
UPLD	Upland Software Inc.	96.3	sml	23.64	-0.97	-3.94
RHT	Red Hat, Inc.	96.2	lrg	107.46	7.44	7.44
TDOC	Teladoc, Inc.	95.3	sml	34.35	1.80	5.53
ALRM	Alarm.com Holdings, Inc.	94.9	sml	45.31	6.57	16.96
SLP	Simulations Plus, Inc.	94.8	sml	15.65	1.00	6.83
MITK	Mitek Systems, Inc.	94.6	sml	10.00	0.70	7.53
VHC	VirnetX Holding Corp.	94.3	sml	3.95	0.45	12.86
DATA	Tableau Software, Inc.	94.2	mid	72.66	7.19	10.98
ADBE	Adobe Systems, Inc.	92.8	lrg	155.06	7.70	5.23
GWRE	Guidewire Software, Inc.	91.3	mid	75.80	3.03	4.16
NOW	ServiceNow, Inc.	91.0	mid	115.49	4.74	4.28
QLYS	Qualys, Inc.	90.9	sml	48.25	6.35	15.16
VMW	VMware Inc.	90.2	mid	107.48	14.78	15.94
WDAY	Workday, Inc.	89.7	mid	108.84	5.33	5.15
CERN	Cerner Corp.	89.2	lrg	68.28	3.47	5.35
PAYC	Paycom Software, Inc.	89.1	sml	74.77	3.58	5.03
RP	RealPage Inc.	88.4	sml	43.30	4.75	12.32
VRNS	Varonis Systems Inc.	88.1	sml	38.70	0.85	2.25
TTD	Trade Desk Inc.	87.0	sml	53.69	0.27	0.51
CDNS	Cadence Design Systems, Inc.	86.9	mid	38.69	1.97	5.36
EPAY	Bottomline Technologies, Inc.	86.9	sml	30.62	2.26	7.97
BSFT	BroadSoft Inc.	86.8	sml	49.75	5.85	13.33

FIGURE 20-4:
A stock list.

Chart courtesy of StockCharts.com

Industry summary

Under the Pro Control Center, scroll down to Reports & Analysis Tools. The Industry Summary button brings up all the industries on one page and allows you to change the look-back period in the center at the top of the page. Change from intraday to one-week, one-month, and three-months to find emerging areas of strength.

When you know which industries you're interested in, you can use the Sector Summary to drill down and find stocks you like based on your chart settings.

Knowing When to Hold 'Em and When to Fold 'Em

You may have actually bought a strong stock using some of the tools on StockCharts.com, or you may have used this technique to start watching how some stocks perform. Technical trading gets emotional because you see the price moves relative to history and you want to hold your gains. When the markets have a bad day, it makes you want to sell every stock going down to preserve your profits. That's not a great idea. Instead, use the guidance in the following sections to help you decide how long to hold a stock.

Checking the speed of movement

Some stocks, such as biotech stocks, can have sudden shocks that wipe out profits and become huge losers very quickly. They also go up very fast. It's a double-edged sword. This volatility is helpful if you are in strong stocks across multiple sectors, but you never want a significant portion of your portfolio in any one stock.

You may want fast-moving stocks, but you want to sell with profits. Slow-moving stocks have trouble outperforming the market averages, so typically you want some faster movement. The relative strength indicator will be rising if the stock is rising faster than the S&P 500. The SCTR (see Chapter 12) should be well above 75 for identifying stocks going up faster.

Looking at typical support levels

REMEMBER

Most stocks in fast uptrends hold above the 20-day moving average. On a significant pullback, they may drop down to the 20-week moving average. You can use those pullbacks to add to positions, but the preference is not to sell strong stocks when they are pulling back in a normal rhythm of the market. If the overall market is receding from the highs, a pullback is normal. Every few months the market will make higher highs and higher lows in an uptrend and hold above the 40-week moving average. That scenario is supportive for your stocks.

TIP

A shorter-term trader will sell stocks falling below the 20-day moving average. Longer-term traders will want to hold until they fall below the 50-day moving average or longer. For commodity-related stocks, the 50-day moving average or the 10-week moving average (about the same) are good for trading an upsurge in momentum. Very long-term traders may use the 250-day moving average (about one year).

For information on moving averages and horizontal support and resistance, go to Chapter 10.

Gauging gains

Unfortunately, there is no magic percentage gain for selling because different market conditions lead to faster or slower markets. Identifying the strength of the stock can help with the management of the trade. Determining when to lock in gains is also a somewhat emotional decision to make; some people are risk takers and some are not. Risk takers may ride a gain for a longer period of time than non–risk takers.

Regular gains from regular stocks

Many investors look to lock in profits above a 25 percent gain by selling the shares as the momentum rolls over (indicated by the moving average convergence divergence indicator, or MACD; see Chapter 11), or they use options to protect their profits and continue to hold the stock. This gives the investor some time to see whether the stock can regain the momentum.

TIP

If the stock moves up into a profitable position and then rolls over without giving a big gain, the indicators you are using will start to show weakness. Always keep a stop above your buy point in a profitable trade so it does not turn to a loss (see the later section "Selling Stocks Before They Head South"). As the stock moves up in price, you can adjust that stop upward to protect even more of your gain.

Gains from strong stocks

Stocks that have moved up rapidly (25 percent within a couple of months) have some terrific momentum. Usually they will have more upside available, but the stock price may need to wobble sideways and consolidate the gains. If the whole industry is running fast, that adds to the likelihood that there are more gains to come.

TECHNICAL
STUFF

It is hard to find institutional investors that will continue to add to positions on the top of a 25 percent move without some consolidation. Without the institutional investor buying stocks in large volumes, the stock will probably drift sideways for a period of time. One clue is the MACD on a weekly chart staying above zero during this consolidation.

Following technical clues to help manage your trades

REMEMBER

After a stock has drifted sideways to down, a few key technical events happen:

>> The stock touches an important moving average. Some of those are the 10-week moving average, 20-week moving average, and 40-week moving average (see Chapter 10). Expect bounces off some support.

>> The stock goes low enough to get oversold readings on technical indicators, such as the relative strength index or RSI (30 or 40) or stochastics below 20. These are typical buy areas. (Chapter 11 has more info on the RSI and stochastics.)

>> Trend lines are broken. Look for ways to hold strong stocks that may be consolidating. Selling some on a break can lock in profits. (See Chapter 9 for more about trends and consolidation.)

>> Price breaks below where the price has bounced up from before. After multiple attempts to hold above the previous lows, a lower low can be a clue that the support is fading. Rising stocks don't make lower lows. One low might be an exception for a few weeks, but uptrends have a series of rising lows.

>> The stock starts to make new 52-week lows.

Figure 20-5 shows Amazon (AMZN), which is one of the world's juggernaut companies. By dominating one particular space so well, Amazon has been crushing everyone in its path. But Amazon investors have ridden some massive swings.

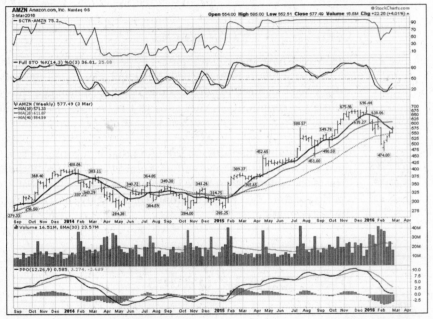

FIGURE 20-5:
Support for
Amazon.

For example, in 2014 the Federal Reserve had lots of stimulus going on to help the economy heal from the financial crisis. The market was roaring higher until the oil business struggled in late 2014. But Amazon was a dog all year, after years of running higher. The chart in Figure 20-5 shows a few big things:

>> **Moving averages:** As an investor, what will you hold through? Working from the left to the right, Amazon was finding support at the 10-week moving average. As 2014 started, Amazon had a big down week that wiped out about ten weeks of price gains. The stock dropped into May, losing $125/share before finding support at $285, which was the January high of 2013.

>> **Indicators bounce from oversold levels:** The stock continued to wobble and make lower highs all year. The support level of $284 held, but investors holding the stock throughout the year were staring at losses for the year of 30 percent. Was Amazon's long-term top finally here?

>> **Trend lines:** Use previous run-ups in the stock price to find a similar slope for trend lines. A short, sudden burst is not a good trend line slope, but one with a reasonable angle (45 degrees or so) is a better place to watch for support.

>> **Price support and new 52-week lows:** All the moving averages collapsed together in 2014, and Amazon struggled. Heading into 2015, Amazon risked gapping to new 52-week lows. Great stocks make higher 52-week highs, not lower 52-week lows. On the January 2015 earnings call, the stock roared! It broke above all three moving averages; the moving averages were in a bullish alignment, with the short-, then medium-, and then long-term averages above each other; and Amazon more than doubled in price in one year. Price support held!

Thinking about trading styles

Depending on your investment style, what works for you? If you're a very short-term trader and hold stocks for only a few days, you use much shorter time periods on your charts. If you want to hold a stock for weeks and even months, you aren't going to sell just because the stock made new four-day lows, whereas a short-term trader would have already exited a trade.

Refer to the Amazon stock shown in Figure 20-5. Traders out below the 10-week moving average and back in when the stock rises above had a choppy year after a solid 2013. The same applied to the 20-week moving average traders. The traders who sell when the stock moves below the 40-week moving average spent most of 2014 ignoring the stock. When they did get in (July and November), the stock immediately went back down. Ouch. While the example highlights whipsaws (failed breakouts) above the 40-week moving average, there were only five weeks of whipsaws in 2.5 years.

One big consideration is taxable gains. If you have to pay some tax to the government every time you sell, you may choose to hold through larger down-trends on big juggernaut stocks. The issue comes when the stock continues down for three years and you have given up all your gains. (Microsoft did exactly that in 1999 and lost 70 percent from the highs.)

There is no sign at the top saying "Exit now." If there were one, everyone would sell and there would be no buyers. The January 2014 plummet for Amazon in Figure 20-5 was a sell sign near a top. But as a shareholding investor, you have to decide what to do based on your time frame. Stocks don't usually recover quickly when they drop past ten weeks of previous price action.

If you decide to trade in and out, you'll need to pick the level of moving average or support at which you will actually sell or buy. You could also make your decision based on the RSI or full stochastics (see Chapter 11), the SCTR (see Chapter 12), or any number of other indicators.

Considering big picture trends

If the 40-week moving average has positive slope (pointing up), that can be part of the signal. If the 40-week moving average has a negative slope (pointing down), avoid the stock.

The best way to find your way is through experience, but you have to start with some ideas. Being aware of momentum and how the stock is behaving compared to others in the industry group is valuable. You need to watch the strength of the industry group to decide whether your stock is showing short-term weakness in a strong group or whether the whole group is starting to weaken. When your stock's industry group starts to weaken and other industries and sectors start to outperform, locking in profits may be worthwhile.

Selling Stocks Before They Head South

Selling stocks for a loss is part of technical trading. Obviously, the preference is to sell stocks when they're winners. The worst trades are the ones that immediately reverse when you enter into them and take you to a loss position. Taking small losses rather than large losses is akin to paper cuts versus amputations. If you can keep that discipline to keep losses very small, you will make a lot of money in the markets. Some very profitable traders lose money on 40 to 60 percent of their trades.

Some settings on StockCharts.com can help with exiting a stock based on technical indicators, as you find out in the following sections.

Chandelier exits

Chandelier exits can help indecisive investors. *Chandelier exits* are placed as a line on the chart that is a maximum retracement off the most recent high. As the price moves up, so does the line. Eventually the stock drops in price and kicks you out.

Put the overlay on the chart by selecting Chandelier Exits from the Overlays drop-down menu and click Update (flip to Chapter 3 for an introduction to overlay settings). Check to see whether the price goes below the line too often. If so, increase the range from 3.0 to 4.0 until the line fits the stock better. Two chandelier exit lines are shown on Figure 20-6 on the panel with the price bars.

The Cabot Oil and Gas (COG) weekly chart is shown in Figure 20-6. The chandelier exit set at 3.0 would have kicked you out in October 2016, but the setting of 4.0 would have been okay. In that example, changing 3.0 to 4.0, which is four times the average range for a week rather than three times the average range, works better as a setting. However, for most of the downside moves in 2014 and 2015, getting out earlier would have been better.

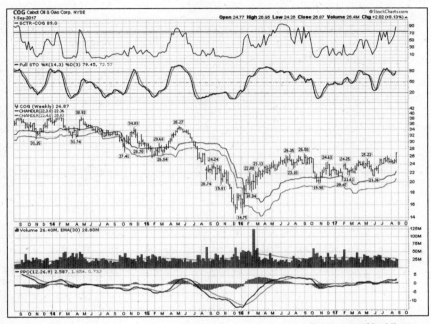

FIGURE 20-6:
Chandelier exits.

TIP

You may need to eliminate the other moving averages to clearly see the chandelier exit line on your charts, but the actual price level is shown on the legend.

Parabolic stop and reverse

Parabolic stop and reverse, commonly called parabolic SAR, moves the stop closer to the price as the advance continues. Eventually, the stop is very close to the price and kicks a sell signal. Parabolic SAR is found in the Overlays area. Figure 20-7 shows the default settings for the parabolic SAR. The parabolic SAR dot will move up above the highest price recently recorded and move the system to a sell signal. This system works well on strong trending stocks, but is terrible during sideways consolidations.

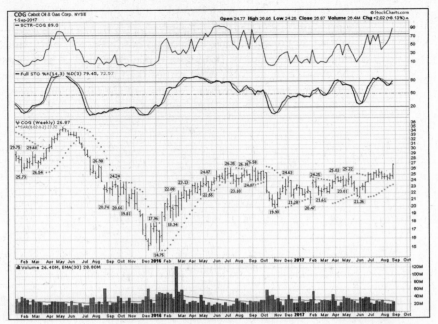

FIGURE 20-7:
Parabolic SAR.

Chart courtesy of StockCharts.com

For Cabot Oil and Gas, the parabolic SAR was on a sell signal for most of 2015. In 2016, it switched to a very profitable buy signal. However, from June 2016 through most of 2017, the sideways chop was an awful solution, with every trade losing money as a buy-high, sell-low trade. In a full parabolic SAR system, you would short the stock when the system reversed, until the price of the stop was hit to the upside, telling you to go long on the stock. In this example, shorting the stock would have only doubled your losses in the sideways chop. You don't have to short the stock; you can just sell the shares you have and wait for another buy signal to trigger on the parabolic SAR or use other indicators you like. For this reason, use the parabolic SAR on strong trending stocks only.

REMEMBER

The best rule in trading is to have a stop somewhere. If you don't have a stop, a downturn can really hurt your year-end profit despite all the wins you may have racked up during the year.

Chapter **21**

Putting It All Together

I n earlier parts of this book, you discover how to build stock charts and explore all the tools you can add to those charts. In this chapter, we take a closer look at how you can put all this information together to improve your stock trading decisions.

TIP

To get started, you may want to take advantage of the 30-day free trial at StockCharts.com so you can try out all the advanced options we talk about in this book. To sign up, go to StockCharts.com and click the green button that says, "Free 1-Month Trial." You can access the analysis tools we show you from the Members page. The Control Center resides on the left side of the Members tab. Some of the tools described here are for Extra members and PRO members. During the 30-day free trial, try to use the PRO-level tools. If you decide you don't need them, you can start as a basic member. The advanced tools will be grayed out on the Control Center.

TIP

There is a lot of science around risk management and trading strategies. This book gives you a strong base to start your charting. For trading strategies and risk management ideas, consult other books in the *For Dummies* series. In particular, *Trading For Dummies*, 4th Edition, by Lita Epstein, MBA, and Grayson D. Roze (Wiley) also uses all StockCharts.com methodologies.

Gauging the Market's Direction

To gauge the overall direction of the market, watch two indexes: the NASDAQ 100 and the S&P 500. The NASDAQ 100 ($NDX) is typically associated with high technology and rapid growth. The S&P 500 ($SPX) is a broad, stable index with massive companies that market products around the world. Understanding how these two indexes are performing will go a long way toward managing the upside opportunity and the downside risk in the market. Asking these four questions is a great start to analyzing the market direction:

>> Is the market topping?

>> What are the leading sectors?

>> Is market breadth healthy?

>> Are the two main indexes above the 40-week moving average?

In the following sections, we take a closer look at how to spot a market top, discover which sectors are leading, and determine the strength of the market.

TIP

With the massive market corrections in 2000–2002 and 2007–2009, you have some of the best training examples for researching how major markets top out and warning signs to watch for. Sudden, unknown world events can never be priced in.

REMEMBER

Nothing guarantees a stable market, but the market direction tools in this section can definitely help keep you aware of a strong investing backdrop when the market structure is largely supportive for going higher.

Market tops

One of the main issues to review as you gauge the market's direction is how to avoid being invested in terrible stocks when a market correction occurs. You don't want to put money to work only to lose money right away, so understanding what makes a good backdrop is important.

Market tops (introduced in Chapter 9) take time to develop. Some sector has to get crushed to start breaking down the market. Using stock charts, you have a better chance of finding that market top and getting out before the stock sector collapses. By avoiding weak sectors, your portfolio has time to adapt to changing market conditions.

Here's an example: In 2000, the technology sector collapsed in March, which is the obvious one you hear about. However, the number of advancing stocks versus declining stocks on the New York Stock Exchange (NYSE) was falling for two years before suggesting a bubble in technology. In the early days of March 2000, only a few technology stocks were carrying the NASDAQ market higher.

Six months later in September 2000, the S&P 500 ($SPX) was very close to making new highs, but the NASDAQ was down by 50 percent. The chart in Figure 21-1 can be created by changing the chart type to cumulative from candlestick in the Chart Attributes area and using the ticker symbol $NYAD (the symbol for the NYSE) for the main chart. The cumulative chart forms a smooth curved line, called an advance/decline line, rather than a candlestick chart, which can look spiky and hard to read. This chart just gives you another way to look at the advances and declines of the market. Figure 21-1 shows you the advance/decline line from 1993 to 2017 for the S&P 500 Large Cap Index, the NYSE, and the NASDAQ 100.

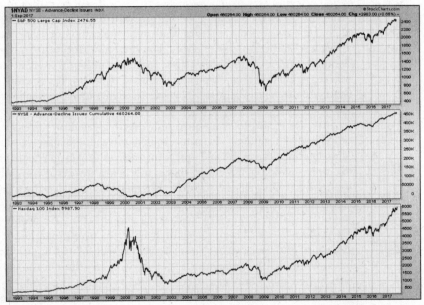

FIGURE 21-1:
Advance/decline
lines.

Chart courtesy of StockCharts.com

Looking at advance/decline lines, you can quickly pick up some clues about stock market changes. Here are some examples of what you can see using an advance/decline line.

In 2005, the housing sector collapsed. It eventually spread into the construction materials. Then the financial sector came under pressure, with mortgages valued much higher than the property values in 2007. It took multiple years to take down the overall market. When banks are weak, there is usually some indication of a bigger problem as the bankers are the first to know who can't pay their bills. Notice when the S&P 500 made its high in October 2007, the advance/decline line was already making lower highs and lower lows as well as breaking a long multiyear trend.

In 2011, raw materials topped out. The rare-earth metals, which had been great performers, collapsed. Precious metals topped out in 2011 as well. The energy sector collapsed in the second half of 2014. With both the raw materials and the energy sectors weak, the slowdown migrated eventually into railway stocks, trucking, steel, and finance. Once again, the advance/decline line was going lower, confirming the problem. When crude oil bottomed in 2016, it marked the lows for the market and the rally began. You can see the advance/decline line start to climb in 2016, showing the start of the rally.

REMEMBER

When one industry group collapses, there will still be rallies in other sectors. The issue comes as more and more sectors start to break down. The goal of investing is to stay away from sectors that are weak and focus on strong sectors. By staying with the top three sectors, you can outperform the market and avoid being derailed. When all the sectors are breaking down, that is a major clue that the market is in trouble and you should move to safety. If you can't find a sector that you watch in a strong position, move to cash and wait out the storm.

In 2017, for example, the entire retail sector was under pressure by Amazon and other online retailers. The retail industry weakness may eventually cause problems in shopping malls and spiral into something larger in 2018. Using this as an example, avoiding the retail space and being aware of the potential for related industries (mall owners) to suffer is a method of protecting a portfolio.

TIP

Being aware of which sectors are weak and watching for problems spreading into other industries is a high-level analysis of the overall market. If investors start to sell more and more industries, the charts will be making lower highs and lower lows. While that is happening, it is okay to be invested in the top-performing sectors. When more and more sectors start to break, the problem expands, pulling the overall markets down. The Industry Summary discussed in Chapter 20 can keep you aware of industries that have negative performance over different periods, but a three-month period is an important timeline to consider.

Leading sectors

Of the ten sectors, some are aligned with growth while others are aligned with defensive positioning:

>> **Consumer discretionary:** Growth

>> **Information technology:** Growth

>> **Telecommunications services:** Growth

>> **Materials:** Growth

>> **Energy:** Growth

>> **Utilities:** Defensive

>> **Consumer staples:** Defensive

>> **Healthcare:** Used to be defensive, but biotechs, medical equipment, healthcare providers and pharmaceuticals have been some of the most aggressive stocks in the last ten years

>> **Real estate:** Defensive, typically associated with income stream investing

>> **Financials:** Both defensive and growth

Because investors age over time, the income streams from utilities, real estate (especially real estate investment trusts, or REITs), and financials are important ballasts in a portfolio. While these defensive areas may perform in line with the S&P 500, they have a place in portfolios that need an income stream. Using the strongest stocks in those sectors can also help get capital gains as well as income. Avoiding weak stocks chosen for income stream investments is just as important as owning strong stocks in growth areas.

In the following sections, we describe two tools you can use to determine which sectors are leading the market.

Performance charts

A performance chart (also called a PerfChart on StockCharts.com) is used to compare multiple stocks on one chart; we introduce these charts in Chapter 12. Figure 21-2 shows a PerfChart in the middle of a big bull market, looking at performance from July to October 2016. Notice how the growth or aggressive sectors (like technology) are doing very well and the defensive sectors (like consumer staples and utilities) are not.

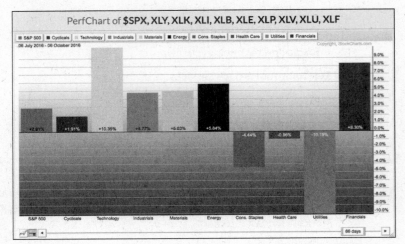

FIGURE 21-2:
A bull market profile.

Chart courtesy of StockCharts.com

TIP

By selecting the Histogram button in the bottom left, you get histograms rather than line charts. You can switch back and forth as you like.

If consumer staples (XLP) and utilities (XLU) are becoming the top-performing areas of the market, the market is probably getting weaker and more research needs to be done. PerfCharts in Histogram mode can show you which sectors are leading. Figure 21-3 shows the defensive groups performing significantly better than the growth areas of the market. While utilities were positive and consumer staples flat, they are holding up better than the other sectors. This chart examines November 2015 through February 8, 2016, which was at the final low.

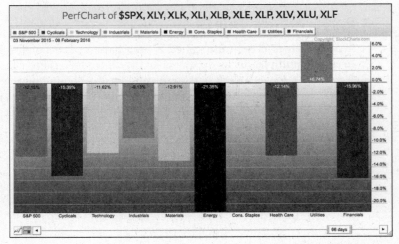

FIGURE 21-3:
Defensive groups perform better during a market correction.

Chart courtesy of StockCharts.com

TIP

You can also use the PerfChart to compare sectors relative to the S&P 500 ($SPX). This makes the $SPX the zero level, and some sectors outperform while others underperform. To compare relative to the $SPX, click on $SPX on the top left. In Figure 21-4, the $SPX button is grayed out. This chart shows you how a sector is comparing relative to the broader market.

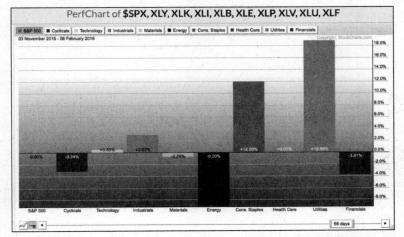

FIGURE 21-4:
Sectors relative to
the S&P 500
($SPX).

RRG charts

A Relative Rotation Graph (RRG chart; see Chapter 12) is a visual model of sector rotation relative to a common reference point; these charts are accessible from the Control Center on the Members page on StockCharts.com. Figure 21-5 shows the XLP and XLU sectors advancing and the XLE energy sector plummeting shortly after the market top in 2015. The date is in the white space in the middle (July 24, 2015), and the shading on the small $SPX graph on the right shows you what time period is being shown. The market started to break down in August 2015.

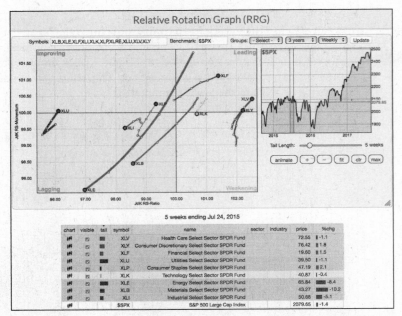

FIGURE 21-5:
RRG sector
alignment.

REMEMBER

While it may not always be this obvious, if these two defensive sectors are improving and other sectors are breaking down quickly, this can be a good clue for market weakness. If the defensive situation is starting to show up, you can do more investigative work and add some strong stocks in the defensive industries. Otherwise, you want to be looking for stocks in growth sectors that are pointing toward the top right corner. In this example, you would be looking for stocks in the defensive sectors of utilities and consumer staples, and selling stocks that are starting to weaken. Energy, technology, materials, and industrials are all pointing down to the left, which is not the direction you want your stocks to be going.

Market breadth

Market breadth can be a helpful indicator warning of weakness; we explain how to conduct breadth analysis in Chapter 15. You can check the bullish percent indexes and the percentage of stocks above the 200-day moving average indicators to understand how many stocks are participating in a positive way in the market. The NASDAQ 100 bullish percent index chart along with the percentage of stocks above the 200-day moving average is shown in Figure 21-6. The actual trend of the NASDAQ 100 is shown in the top panel.

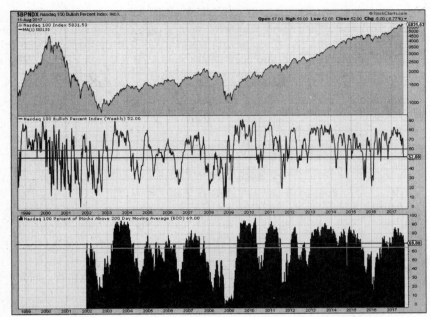

FIGURE 21-6:
The price trend of the NASDAQ 100, the NASDAQ 100 bullish percent index, and the percentage of stocks above the 200-day moving average.

Chart courtesy of StockCharts.com

As long as more than 65 percent of the stocks are on buy signals, the market has enough breadth to move higher. The percentage of stocks above the 200 DMA should also be better than 65 percent. When they dip below these levels, watching to see whether they can bounce back to a strong market position again is important. If they fail to improve, the market is susceptible to falling lower after brief rallies.

TIP

Watching the NASDAQ 100 ($NDX) and the S&P 500 ($SPX) breadth charts is most important, but being aware where the NASDAQ Composite ($COMPQ) and the NYSE Composite ($NYA) levels are can alert you to early weakness. You can see weakness in the NASDAQ 100 bullish percent index chart in the middle of Figure 21-6, where the index falls between 60 percent and 52 percent.

Position of the indexes compared to the 40-week moving average

If the $SPX or the $NDX is below the 40-week moving average, the market could be sensitive to falling farther. (See Chapter 10 for an introduction to moving averages.) Investors should be aware of the weak condition. Great buying opportunities come from these extreme lows, so investors should continue to watch for strong stocks in growth sectors that can accelerate when the markets turn optimistic again. Figure 21-7 shows the benefit of being invested above that level and cautionary below that level. You can see on both the chart for the S&P 500 (at the top) and the chart for the NASDAQ 100 (at the bottom) that there were periods between 1996 and 2017 where the index fell below the moving average line. But starting in the middle of 2016 through 2017, both indexes are well above the line, and it's been a good time to be in the market.

FIGURE 21-7:
The $SPX & $NDX indexes.

TIP

The slope of the 40-week moving average is also helpful. If the slope is positive (pointing up), the market usually bounces back above the moving average. If the line is pointing down (negative slope), more caution is advised.

Narrowing Your Focus to Certain Sectors

In order for the $SPX to be average, some sectors have to be moving faster than the index and some slower. They can all be going up, but they move at different rates. The $SPX reflects the average. Figure 21-4 illustrates this point.

Focusing your investment activities on leading industries (with the help of this section) is one of the most important methods for beating the overall market. Strong stocks in the top three sectors can be your growth stocks. While you may also need income from dividends or REIT distributions, you can also find some strong stocks in these defensive sectors to help your income. Flip to Chapters 13 and 20 for more about sectors and industries.

Choosing your fishing holes: Sectors with promise

Drilling down through the sectors can help you find strong industries. Click on the Sector Summary tool in the Control Center on the Members tab of StockCharts. com to quickly access the top-performing sectors. Sorting the Sector ETFs by SCTR ranking shows the strongest sectors from the highest-ranked SCTR declining to the lowest-ranked sector. (ETFs are exchange-traded funds. SCTR stands for StockCharts technical ranking; see Chapter 12 for more information.)

Figure 21-8 shows the top three sectors as technology, healthcare, and utilities, sorted by SCTR ranking. While these may move around from week to week, your strong sectors should have SCTR rankings above 50. Choose the top three industries as discussed in Chapter 20, and continue to drill down to choose three or four stocks in each of the strong industries.

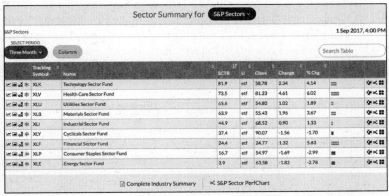

FIGURE 21-8: Sector ETFs sorted by SCTR ranking.

Chart courtesy of StockCharts.com

Use the SCTR peer group column to the right of the SCTR column (headed with a U) to focus your investments on the market-cap of stocks you like. Choose from large-cap, mid-cap, and small-cap. As an example, scroll down until you find strong-performing, large-cap stocks. If you don't find any strong-performing, large-cap stocks, find a different industry group or go to a different sector and drill down into the industries and stocks.

Investing in different sectors for ballast

REMEMBER

Having all your investments in the same area of the market can be treacherous to your investing health. If the three top industries are all in the materials sector, that can be too narrow. For diversification, take three stocks from strong industries in each of the three top sectors.

As an example, you might choose the software industry in the technology sector, healthcare providers in the healthcare sector, and gas utilities in the utilities sector. Then choose three strong stocks in each industry. You can also pick one strong stock from each of the top three industries in each leading sector. This would give you nine stocks in your portfolio. As you get sell signals in a stock, you should rotate into new stocks.

Using SCTR reports

One other method for quickly seeing where the strong stocks are can be using the SCTR reports for ETFs. SCTR reports are covered in Chapter 12. Go into the large-cap SCTR reports and click on the SCTR column header, then the Industry column header, and then the Sector column header. This sorts the entire report by sector, by industry, and then in descending order for the SCTR. See the report in Figure 21-9. Notice the drop-down at the top to select SCTRs for different groups, including ETFs. In this figure only stocks are near the top, which is common when the market is booming. ETFs tend to smooth out the trend because they include a basket of top-performing stocks and some that are not doing as well.

	Symbol	Name	Sector	Industry	SCTR	Chg	Close	Vol
	PCRFY	Panasonic Corp.			72.3	-4.0	13.32	75035
	HEINY	Heineken NV	Consumer Staples	Brewers	88.4	-1.5	52.41	15809
	ABEV	Ambev SA	Consumer Staples	Brewers	76.7	-0.9	6.24	14749914
	BUD	Anheuser-Busch InBev ADR	Consumer Staples	Brewers	57.7	-1.4	118.63	862094
	TAP	Molson Coors Brewing Co.	Consumer Staples	Brewers	22.7	0.7	90.03	942548
	STZ	Constellation Brands, Inc.	Consumer Staples	Distillers & Vintners	90.5	0.3	200.23	992590
	DEO	Diageo PLC	Consumer Staples	Distillers & Vintners	89.6	0.1	134.83	406492
	BF/B	Brown-Forman Corp. - Class B	Consumer Staples	Distillers & Vintners	82.1	3.3	53.38	922159
	PDRDY	Pernod Ricard SA	Consumer Staples	Distillers & Vintners	58.7	-9.4	26.93	25900
	WBA	Walgreens Boots Alliance, Inc.	Consumer Staples	Drug Retailers	26.8	-4.8	81.22	5335530
	CVS	CVS Health Corp.	Consumer Staples	Drug Retailers	26.1	1.8	77.92	4653775
	DANOY	Danone	Consumer Staples	Food Products	71.4	-4.3	15.64	136139
	NSRGY	Nestle SA	Consumer Staples	Food Products	54.0	-6.3	84.17	159017
	TSN	Tyson Foods Inc Cl A	Consumer Staples	Food Products	49.6	8.3	64.53	2893900
	HSY	Hershey Foods Corp.	Consumer Staples	Food Products	30.0	2.0	105.61	1173319
	MKC	McCormick & Co., Inc.	Consumer Staples	Food Products	28.3	2.7	96.14	780185
	ADM	Archer Daniels Midland Co.	Consumer Staples	Food Products	28.0	6.2	42.20	3007061
	MDLZ	Mondelez International, Inc.	Consumer Staples	Food Products	13.5	-0.3	40.88	6811733
	GIS	General Mills Inc.	Consumer Staples	Food Products	12.6	0.7	53.72	3912688
	K	Kellogg Co.	Consumer Staples	Food Products	11.4	-0.9	65.45	2474695
	KHC	Kraft Heinz Co.	Consumer Staples	Food Products	11.3	-0.7	80.85	4890208

SCTR Reports for **Large Cap Stocks ∨**

Select Period: Intraday   4 Sep 2017, 6:13 PM

Columns   Entries: 100   Search Table

FIGURE 21-9: SCTR reports.

Chart courtesy of StockCharts.com

TIP

An extremely attractive way to find industries that may be performing well, even though the sector is not, is to look for entire industry groups pushing above 75. With 186 industry groups, hidden gems can lurk underneath the sector strength.

An example of a hidden gem may be healthcare providers. Humana and Aetna have outperformed Facebook from the lows on February 1, 2016, to September 1, 2017. While Facebook is all the rage, two healthcare stocks sit relatively unknown to the wider audience. Seeing this strength by scrolling through the stocks in a sort order can really help diversification.

This is one of the major strengths of the SCTR. It uses price action to determine the rating, not overall sector strength. Plotting the stock's strength compared to its peer group is one of the most important indicators for a stock in our opinion.

Considering income stream investing

Not everyone invests for growth. Some investors prefer to focus on preserving capital and buying stocks and bonds that give them the highest income stream. This situation is very common when a person is approaching retirement or living in retirement.

TIP

If you need income from your investing, you can also search the market by dividend yield. Extremely high yields are usually available on terrible stocks. However, by scanning the market using some of the scan tools on StockCharts.com (see Chapter 14 for an introduction), you can pull up stocks that have a yield greater than 4 percent and an SCTR score higher than a level of 60. You can output the sort result by highest yield. Figure 21-11, later in this chapter, shows a scan table with the yield on the right-hand side. You would use this method of analysis for stocks to invest in to help meet your income goals. If the SCTR weakened, you would sell this stock and look for other high-yield stocks. You can use the Advanced Scan Workbench to do this.

Using Targeted Scans

After you've determined your portfolio's goals, you can set up personal scans and alerts (introduced in Chapter 14) to help you monitor your portfolio hourly, daily, or less frequently; the frequency depends on your goals. If you're actively trading each day or week, you'll check this information much more frequently than if you're managing a longer-term portfolio. Each time you log in to your StockCharts.com account, your scans and alerts will be waiting for you.

Scans are a way to look for a specific set of conditions. Rather than looking through thousands of stocks every day, you ask the computer, via lines of code, to go look for all the stocks with a specific set of conditions and give you a list. The Advanced Scan Workbench link in the Control Center takes you to the setup area shown in Figure 21-10.

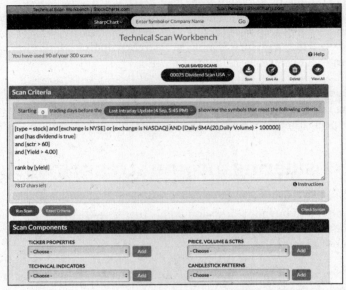

FIGURE 21-10:
Using the
Advanced Scan
Workbench.

As discussed in the earlier section on income stream investing, you may want to develop a model that will help you monitor the best assets to meet your income stream goals. Using the income stream investor model, you can use multiple individual components to create your scan. You want U.S. stocks with a strong SCTR and a dividend yield above 4 percent.

Start broadly by defining the country or the exchange, and work to smaller conditions. Define which exchanges you want to see and how much volume is a minimum volume for you. Investors in the United States would likely choose the New York Stock Exchange. Canadian investors would select the Toronto Stock Exchange, whereas British investors could choose the London Stock Exchange. Many investors deliberately choose an international mix for their portfolios to reduce the effect of poor economic conditions in one country. For example, if the economy is sluggish in Canada but doing better in the United States, a Canadian may mix his or her portfolio with both U.S. and Canadian assets.

TIP

You can select each coding line from drop-down menus on the lower half of the Advanced Scan Workbench page so you don't actually have to write any computer code. Then just change the settings within the code box.

You want stocks that have a dividend, so add that from the Ticker Properties drop-down menu below the coding area. Select "Has Dividend" and click Add. The SCTR greater than 60 means the stock is behaving pretty well, and the Yield threshold can be set by you. Lastly, you can ask it to sort the results using the "rank by" command on the last line. Here's the final coding:

[type = stock] and [exchange is NYSE] or [exchange is NASDAQ]

and [Daily SMA(20,Daily Volume) > 100000]

and [has dividend is true]

and [SCTR > 60]

and [Yield > 4.00]

rank by [yield]

Click Run Scan. A separate tab will appear with Scan Results. (Notice the tab header at the top of Figure 21-10.)

Figure 21-11 shows the scan results with the Rank by [Yield] information on the far right. You will want to put the scan results into one of your temporary ChartLists you created in Chapter 13. Use the drop-down menu above the scan results on the upper-left where it says Available Actions.

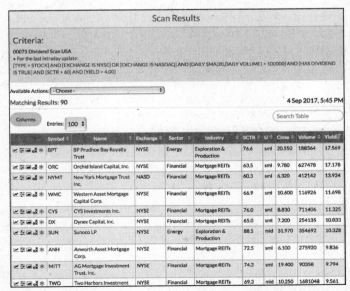

FIGURE 21-11: Scanning for yield.

Chart courtesy of StockCharts.com

TIP

The Dividend Yield column will disappear when you save this into one of the temporary scanning ChartLists, so check the "preserve the sort order" button as you move the scan you create to a ChartList. When you look at the results on a chart, click the full quote panel toggle in the Chart Attributes area. The dividend yield will show in the full quote panel above the chart. Click "apply style to all" at the bottom of the page under the chart to install the full quote panel on every chart in the temporary ChartList or add the full quote panel to your default view. You can see how to do this in Chapter 17.

Working with Price Displays, Overlays, and Indicators

Throughout this book we introduce you to price displays, overlays, and indicators. Now it's time to start fine-tuning these tools to better match your personal trading or investing style.

Price displays

Chapters 4, 5, 6, and 7 discuss different price display styles, such as candlestick, bar, and line charts. Chapter 8 discusses time periods, such as daily or weekly. Each investor has a different style and level of detail she wants to see. It is very important to set up the chart with your personal preferences so you enjoy the experience of managing your stocks. For example:

>> As a refresher, you can use candlesticks (see Chapter 4) on all time frames, but they have a lot of detail. Filled candles tend to highlight the negative. Typical candle patterns use one to three candles to form a pattern that plays out over the next five to ten candles.

>> Price bars (see Chapter 5) have detail, but the charts look a little smoother. Use your choice of single-color, two-color, or Elder Impulse three-color bars. Open-high-low-close (OHLC) bars are the typical choice for price bars.

>> Line charts (see Chapter 6) lose a lot of detail, but the trend is much cleaner. Area charts (mountain charts; see Chapter 7) amplify the line-chart information, and both of these displays work great for long-term charts of weekly or monthly data.

Chapter 9 discusses the analysis of a trend. Understanding what you want to see on the chart is the first step to successful investing. Support/resistance, trend lines, and price channels all play important roles. Depending on your style of investing, these tools enable you to monitor the price for higher highs and higher lows within your time frame.

Chapter 8 discusses time periods, such as monthly, weekly, daily, and 60-minute charts. Great investors usually trade in the same direction as the long runs shown by the monthly and weekly charts. When the momentum starts to wane on monthly and weekly charts, the daily charts may be more susceptible to breakdowns.

Watching the larger trends in momentum (see Chapter 11) on the monthly and weekly charts is a great tool to help you invest successfully.

Overlays and indicators

Chapter 10 discusses moving averages and overlays. Chapter 11 discusses indicators to help improve the timing of entries and exits. These tools have been built over time to help investors manage their trades.

Without question, choosing indicators you like is more difficult. Start with three or four and volume. Then if you would like to try a new indicator, add one and take one out. Charts with too many indicators make analysis impossible. By the time all the indicators line up, the trade is half over. If all indicators gave the same signal, you would need only one. Start with some of the indicators suggested and change one out to see whether it helps you make better decisions.

TIP

One recommendation is a relative strength indicator, a momentum indicator, and one other panel like Chaikin money flow or on-balance volume. You may like RSI or stochastics. Chapters 17, 18, and 19 present strategies for pairing overlays and indicators with different types of investing.

Coauthor Greg's default daily chart has SCTR and relative strength to $SPX on top. The moving average convergence divergence (MACD) indicator and volume are plotted below. On a weekly time frame, the SCTR, RSI, full stochastics, and PPO are the chosen indicators.

SCTR and the relative strength rankings

As long as the SCTR on each chart is above 75, that's a good indication that things are okay. Because of the way the SCTR is calculated, it doesn't give a move below 75 quickly if the stock is a fast-rising stock. You may have to sell before the SCTR falls below a minimum level. Use the relative strength compared to the $SPX as an earlier indicator for exiting a stock than the SCTR.

Breaking trend lines on the relative strength compared to the $SPX chart are cautionary as the stock was really outperforming the $SPX before. If the relative strength chart starts to make two-month or three-month lows, you probably need to make some strategic decisions.

Use options to protect the position, sell part of the position to lock in gains, or sell all if the industry is starting to underperform as discussed in Chapter 12. Each investor has different sell points depending on his timeline. Some investors may sell as the price touches a top weekly Keltner channel. Other investors want to hold even if the stock is above the Keltner channel, but when it starts to come back inside the Keltner channel, they sell. Keltner channels are covered in Chapters 10 and 14.

Taking Away Lessons from Your Wins and Losses

You've heard the old adage "learn from your mistakes," but you also want to learn from your successes. The only way you can do that is to keep a good history of your past successes and failures. As you begin to trade, keep a journal of all your trades and analyze all your winners and losers. Not only will you take time to figure out what went wrong or right, but you will also have a history to go back to if you want to review what happened with a gain or a loss.

Journaling about the market and your trading

When you buy a stock, annotate the chart to keep all the details on the display. Chapter 17 demonstrates the annotation tool. Enter the exact price, number of shares purchased, and date on the stock chart as a text box. Save that information. If you're investing for dividends, select the Events overlay in the Overlays area. This will put a little vertical dashed line on the chart, marking your dividend dates. You may want to draw little lines or arrows where your stop is. You can also add notes under the charts by using the ChartBook View rather than 10 per page, CandleGlance, or Summary view. There is a small box for journaling about each stock chart as well as a place to journal about the overall ChartList.

TIP

You can either journal your trades on the StockCharts.com platform on each chart or use a separate Word document and just make a few notes whenever you get the chance about what you think. It's your trading journal, so write it like a diary. Your notes may include descriptions like bullish, bearish, worried, happy, sad, or confused; market performance that day; what types of trades are working better; industry groups that are leading; or odd things in the market, such as a sudden plunge or surge in a sector or industry.

New trends in the market are interesting to keep track of. An example in 2018 may be keeping updated on crypto currencies like Bitcoin, new investment ideas like Autonomous Vehicle Technology, or social phenomena like marijuana stocks or social media.

Understanding how IPOs trade is important, and there's usually a pullback or base-building process that allows you to get on board after the original IPO. Journal how these stocks behave to give you confidence in handling highly speculative stocks with no real trading history.

REMEMBER

By journaling how you handled a trade, you can apply the knowledge you gain the next time.

Tracking and analyzing your winners and losers

After you own a basket of high-performing stocks, you can save them into your current stock ChartList to keep them all together. (Find out how to create ChartLists in Chapter 13.) You may want to make a bookmark on your browser to link to your current stocks ChartList. Instantly, you can see how they are performing through the day or the week.

Set up ChartLists to move your closed trades into and keep a spreadsheet of your wins and losses. Chapter 13 explains how to create ChartLists, numerically control the order of your ChartLists, and move charts into a ChartList.

To move a chart from one ChartList to another, click the Save As link on the top center of the chart. This is shown in Figure 21-12.

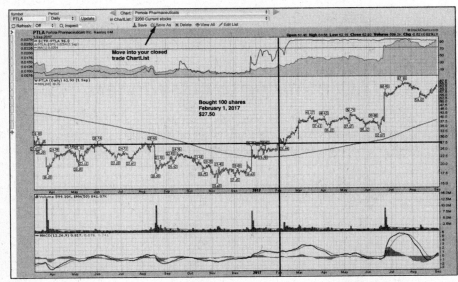

FIGURE 21-12:
Moving charts to your closed trade ChartList.

Chart courtesy of StockCharts.com

When you close a position, click the Save As link and move the stock to your completed trades. Analyze the trade when you close it. You may want to write notes documenting events like those in the following example: Staying with Figure 21-12, say that when the SCTR moved above 75 on February 1, 2017, you bought the stock of Portola Pharmaceuticals (PTLA). The stock was breaking to new 11-month highs. Biotechs were starting to move as an industry group. Price continued to move right away, which was a good sign. On March 1, stock had a huge range day but closed near the high end of the range. The stock consolidated sideways for three months.

On May 26, the stock made new two-month lows in relative strength. The SCTR was still very strong, and this was the first pullback on the chart, making this a stock to watch closely. The stock rallied 10 percent off the lows to $39. It reversed and spent one day below support (June 16) but closed in the top third of the bar — definitely the weakest moment on the chart so far. The following Monday, the stock opened, tested lower, and closed higher with an outside day — bullish. Then it continued higher again. On June 23, the stock soared to $57.50. The stock continued higher and was consolidating in a wide range.

A wild stock to ride, but then a stop at $42 (former support/resistance) was a long way below, but that was the last support/resistance level. As long as the SCTR continues to be strong and the relative strength continues to hold up, keep owning the stock. If they break down, don't wait until $42 to sell.

Stocks aren't always this easy or this rewarding. But in this example, using simple technical tools in an improving industry group gave a great result. Now that the stock is above a double, there is a tendency to want to sell. The stock continues to outperform the $SPX, so try to resist the temptation to close the position. There would be nothing wrong with selling half, locking in a profit, and allowing the rest to ride until a technical condition hits to sell the stock.

Continuing to buy winners

TIP

Stocks in an uptrend that pull back can be very attractive. Using some form of channel trade (see Chapter 10) or stochastics (see Chapter 11) can help buy winning stocks. Here is a list of tools to help:

>> **Full stochastics:** These help you pick out wide swings in stock price. Not every trade is guaranteed to work, but this is a lot better entry than buying the stock at previous all-time highs after a huge run.

>> **Keltner channels:** These can help you find stocks at the low end of their uptrending channel. Playing the range between the bottom of a Keltner channel to the top can generate 25 percent trades because the channel continues to move up over time. Use the Advanced Scan Workbench to find these stocks.

>> **Stocks with SCTRs moving above 75:** This movement suggests something is improving. Looking through the SCTR tables or using the drill-down tools in the Sector Summary can quickly help you identify strength. Use the Advanced Scan Workbench to search for stocks crossing above 75. (Flip to Chapter 12 for more about the SCTR.)

>> **Breakouts to new highs:** Understand that no one who owns the stock wants to sell because owning the stock is comfortable now. If institutions start to hit the buy button, this can propel the stock. Use the Predefined Scans or the Advanced Scan Workbench to find these stocks.

>> **Pullbacks to horizontal support/resistance levels:** In Figure 21-12, the two moves just below support were critical to test shareholders. Give a little room around the support level, but if it holds, you probably want to keep the trade.

>> **Pullbacks to moving averages:** Stocks can pull back to common moving averages and then bounce. Use the Advanced Scan Workbench to find these stocks.

Refraining from holding losers

Losing stocks have two costs. One is the fact that your capital is disappearing, and the second is the lost opportunity of not being in something going up.

Have an exit strategy if the trade doesn't work. Here is a chart where human emotion keeps you in the trade. Stops would have kicked you out. Figure 21-13 had all the setups. The purchase date was June 8, 2017. Notice the vertical line is just to the left so you can see the price action clearly. The stock was breaking out to new ten-month highs. After pausing at resistance at $5.80, the stock surged. The trade entry was $6.04. The MACD was positive, the SCTR was above 75, and the stock was making new six-month highs in relative strength compared to the $SPX. Volume was well below average as the stock consolidated. The stock was making higher highs and higher lows. It was well above the 200-day moving average. Another gold stock was bought the same day (the chart for that stock isn't shown).

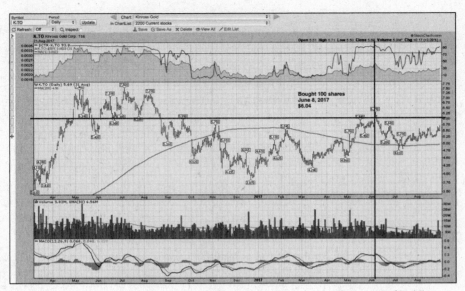

Bought 100 shares
June 8, 2017
$6.04

FIGURE 21-13:
Trading
without a stop.

Chart courtesy of StockCharts.com

The problem came when Kinross (K.TO) stock reversed in the next few days and $5.80 did not hold. Within a week, losses were 10 percent. The brief bounce suggested maybe the stock could resume the uptrend. It immediately dropped down to the 200-day moving average with 20 percent losses. The stock chart showed a strong rally back to resistance by September 1. There was a trend in higher lows from December 2016. The loss position got reduced to 10 percent, and the September 1 high was where the stop should have been put in June.

Wasting months in a losing position and depleting capital is not the best way to grow your portfolio. On September 1, the industry group was improving. Gold stocks accelerated at the end of August. The gold stock industry group was overbought at the end of August, so this may be the end of the run.

While another gold stock bought at the same time pulled back to horizontal support and held, Kinross did not. Each trade has to be managed separately. When the Kinross trade was put on, it was the better-looking opportunity. The influence of the other stock led to mismanagement of the Kinross trade.

7

The Part of Tens

Avoid ten common trading errors with the help of charts.

Find tomorrow's great stock on today's charts.

Chapter **22**

Ten Common Investing Mistakes and How to Avoid Them

E veryone makes mistakes when investing or trading in stocks. The key to success is to find out how to avoid them as much as possible. In this chapter we focus on ten common mistakes and discuss ways to avoid making them.

Trying to Fight the Market Instead of Following It

Some contrarian investors always look for the top of the market. Others always look for the bottom in the worst stocks. In some industry groups like commodity-related products, trading with the main trend is important but being fussy as weakness appears can be prudent. For the most part, it is much more important to decipher the most recent trend and try to stay with that trend.

Rarely is an overnight hold against the trend a worthwhile endeavor. The stock market has traditionally had long bullish periods and rather short bear periods. The bear periods may have been major, but they were not very long. Even in the huge bear market in 2008, the market dropped 800 points one day and closed on the lows. The next day it opened up 800. Many new investors stayed short overnight thinking they were finally going to be right about the market falling, only to have their hearts handed to them on the open in the morning.

TECHNICAL STUFF

A lot of the major institutions don't short the market. They have the firepower to own things going up and to hold winning positions up, which means adding to positions when some investors are selling off a good stock.

REMEMBER

In general, when the S&P 500 is above the 200-day moving average, you want to be invested in the market, expecting the market to go higher. When the market finally tops, and it will, you'll have a short period of time where your trades stop working. By following the leadership into the stable sectors of consumer staples and utilities, you can also protect parts of your portfolio. The bottom line is that the market is usually going up, and being in the rising areas of the market will make you a lot more money than being in the falling areas.

See Chapter 10 for more on moving averages; Chapter 9 for more on topping patterns; and Chapters 12, 13, and 20 for more on sectors.

Buying a Loser

One of the hardest things for investors to do is to buy winners. Many investors like to buy stocks on sale; the closer the stock is to the bottom corner, the higher the attraction for them. Unfortunately, in the stock business, it can take years for a stock to right the ship and to start making positive gains for the portfolio when you try to buy it in a downtrend.

WARNING

The most important part of understanding the stock market business is the recognition that a great company being sold off by millionaires who manage money for billionaires shouldn't be your first choice for a stock pick. If a stock has been trading lower, it will have sudden bursts that actually start to make the stock look better. These are what we call bear market rallies. These rallies can be a few days to a few weeks long. While in a downtrend they will suddenly spurt higher.

Something that should happen in a lousy, good-for-nothing, beat-into-the-trash stock is that some news should start to improve in the stock. Unfortunately, the first piece of positive news in a really bad stock is a significant change in management. The stock will usually jump on that news. If the stock doesn't improve on new management being announced, a total chaotic mess ensues and will usually need months if not years to be fixed.

TIP

You can avoid a mistake here by allowing a base to be built sideways and try to buy somewhere in the base. Chapter 9 has an important section about bases.

Chasing a 25–35 Percent Off Sale in Great Companies

The Dogs of the Dow (the worst five stocks in the Dow 30) are under tremendous pressure to fix the problems and get the stock moving north again. Some of the world's biggest companies go on sale for 25 percent off every now and then. When a company is in a huge stock slide, owning it is very risky. Somehow there must be a strategy for expecting great companies to fix what ails them. You can watch these dogs and look for moves made by the company to stop their downtrend.

You can also use the strategy of looking for very high volume in one day or week. This is usually referred to as capitulatory volume. Anyone who was so frustrated with the downtrend throws in the towel and capitulates from holding to selling the stock. Remembering that someone has to buy all those shares being thrown up for sale is an important piece of the stock market. Who else would be buying when someone is selling? Who else could buy millions and billions of dollars of stock on very, very bad days?

Large institutions step up to support the stock when they also own shares. This may be just long enough for them to get out of the position over the next few weeks, but it can also mark a level at which they will continue to buy the stock. For example, Apple had three dips to $90 in 2015 and 2016 — huge volume on the first, less volume on the second, and less volume on the third. The first (August 2015) had a huge price move, the second (January 2016) had a huge price move, and the third (May 2016) had almost no movement.

TIP

On a weekly chart, the momentum (depicted by indicators like the PPO, KST, MACD, and PMO; see Chapter 11) usually starts improving and makes a higher low on the final low. If the momentum starts to break trend lines on the momentum chart and you really like the stock, you can start to enter the stock near the lows. If the lows don't hold, you should sell the stock with a small loss because the institutions aren't willing to step in and support the stock at that level any more.

REMEMBER

The first rule is it has to be a *great company* that was formerly in a big uptrend and is now building a base to do it again. Avoid making a costly mistake by being prepared to sell quickly if the trade goes the wrong way.

Falling for a 75 Percent Off Sale

A ravaged stock that was a former great company presents an important lesson. Very rarely do these stocks ever climb out of the hole. When a major stock falls 75 percent off, whatever was driving the stock no longer is. Because the corporate structure is broken when the stock plummets, it takes years to rebuild the company morale, and management is consumed by the lawsuits of the past.

One of the problems with buying these stocks is the assumption that at some point they will resume their former glory. Technology stocks in the year 2000, for example, crashed from over $1,000 to less than $1. The largest companies were gravel on the road to ruin.

Investing in a formerly reputable stock that's being swept away in an industry crash is very risky. For all the stocks that made it through that crisis, many were sold or collapsed under the weight of the debt compared to the stock value. Merrill Lynch, Lehman Brothers, Washington Mutual, and Bear Stearns come to mind. JP Morgan's president, Jamie Dimon, said buying a house and buying a house on fire are two different things. He offered $2 a share for a company trading $170 only 15 months before. He regretted the purchase, as it cost $13 billion in legal fees and $4 billion in losses to close the trades JP Morgan acquired as part of the deal.

REMEMBER

Probably the best thing to do with this type of stock is to remove the cliff from the left side of the chart and trade it as if it were a new company. If the stock is climbing, own it, and when the stock quits climbing, sell it. Forget about what it was and remove yourself from the thoughts of any hope of former glory. Be very, very quick to sell and very reluctant to buy.

Forgetting That Commodity Stocks Are Very Volatile

Commodity-related stocks, such as oil or gold, are extremely volatile. They rise like sails on a sailboat and fall as fast as a stone. While they can be extremely profitable, they can also damage your portfolio quickly if you don't exit.

Some background may help your understanding of commodity-related stocks. For example, the oil business has had a complete crush in each of the last four decades. Oil was $147 in May 2008, and months later, it was $49 in January 2009. Natural gas was over $12 in June 2008, it dropped under $1 in April 2016, and it is profitable closer to $3 or $4.

Other popular commodity options can be gold and silver. These can be all the rage, or they can continually twist and turn, frustrating investors over and over. Gold was over $1,800 in 2011, had four massive swings, and ended up under $1,100 in 2016. Trading it was fine; holding it was brutal.

TIP

The important piece of working with commodity stocks is to trade them; never invest in them. They can usually produce massive profits in swing trading but massive losses in holding. This is not to suggest that you shouldn't trade them, but rather that you should own them when the underlying commodity and the exchanged-traded funds (ETFs) are above the 50-day moving average and sell when they are below. (Chapter 10 introduces moving averages.)

Buying a Story Instead of a Stock

Understanding that every stock has a story, each corporate leader is going to highlight what is going well and try not to spend any time talking about the problems. Every company has problems, but management's job is to keep the team moving forward. The analyst community is trying to glean information from the company and is happy to publish good ideas coming from the company. Most stocks have a buy or hold rating, but very few have a sell rating.

As we note in Chapter 2, the basic premise for using a price chart rather than using solely fundamental data is to enable you to be nimble and move into a company stock and leave without emotion getting in the way. Behavioral investing or behavioral analysis is the same as chart analysis. You keep an eye on what the large investors are doing with the stock. What is going on with real dollars? What is the general psychology toward this stock?

The institutional investors keep track of the rate of change of growth. When the growth is still accelerating, they are happy to own the stock. When the growth is still positive but declining quarter over quarter, the large investors will trim their position size. By the time the stock actually has a negative quarter where earnings declined but were still positive in a high-growth industry, the stock is well off the highs. When the stock starts having a losing quarter, which is what most investors would consider a problem, the stock is already way off the highs.

REMEMBER

All of this makes it more difficult to understand the story. The company is still growing, but the stock stops going up. The company keeps growing, and the stock is down 20 to 30 percent. As an investor, you need to sell your shares to someone else at a higher price than the price at which you bought them. If you need to deeply examine the company to do that, that will be part of your investment strategy. Remember to sell soon enough that you can sell to someone who is willing to pay more.

Investing in a Sick Sector

Warren Buffett has a famous quote: "When a management with a reputation for brilliance tackles a business with a reputation for bad economics, it is the reputation of the business that remains intact."

REMEMBER

It is very difficult for a company to post good results in a bad business environment. This underlying theme can't be overstated. Industries go through good times and bad times. Your role is to invest in the good times and find another business that is also having a good time. You don't have any loyalty to staying in a weak industry group. Your kindness will cost you capital.

Warren Buffett likes to buy and hold consumer staples stocks because they are something we need every day. The business may come and go, but because he never sells the stocks, he never pays taxes on the capital gains, only on the dividends received.

Industries like retail, automobiles, trucking, and airlines have growth periods and big periods of contraction — like commodities, but not usually as severe. The bottom line is that missing the downturn is way more important than holding the stocks through severe cycles.

The 2014–2017 period has been very hard on retailers in malls. Trying to find winners in a losing sector is exactly what Warren Buffett was talking about. Until the industry improves, there is no need to put your money to work there when other industries such as semiconductors, healthcare providers, and biotech are doing well. Eventually those industries will roll over or slow down and you can rotate into others.

Selling a Winner Too Soon

Selling losers is hard, and selling winners too soon is easy. The temptation is to lock in a gain, but your winners have to have some room to run. Using relative strength indicators, introduced in Chapter 12, can help you stay with strong trades.

Check the sector and industry performance. If the industry group is still outperforming the S&P 500 ($SPX) over a three-month time frame, you want to continue to hold. Don't make the mistake of selling too soon.

TIP

Here's a methodology to help you avoid this mistake: On StockCharts.com, use the Price indicator with ratios in the Parameters setting to help watch $INDUSTRY and $SECTOR strength. This ratio works when you have a stock with defined sector and industry group data showing in the top left corner of the full quote panel.

>> $INDUSTRY: $SPX

>> $SECTOR: $SPX

>> Actual stock: $SPX

REMEMBER

Draw trend lines on the ratio graphs in the Indicator area. Then consider the following:

>> As long as the sector and industry are holding above two-month highs and you're in one of the strongest stocks in the group, you should be able to keep holding during periods of volatility.

>> If a long uptrend is breaking in relative performance, you want to be aware of the break. As long as the stock continues to outperform the $SPX, you want to try and hold the position.

>> If the overall market is breaking down, keep your stops close so that it does take you out of the trade. Market breadth information keeps you aware of the condition of the overall market. You can find more information on market breadth in Chapter 15.

>> If it is a really strong stock that has outperformed for years, you probably want to maintain your position in one of your biggest winners. Using options can also give you some time to make decisions.

Continuously Avoiding What's Worked

One of the biggest regrets in most investing careers is not staying with what worked early on. Continuously grabbing some new methodology to try can just be a waste of time and create problems.

Don't allow a new charting indicator to absorb your time for months. Keep what is working. Take ten stocks from a scan result (see Chapter 14) and add the new indicator. Make a paper trading log of the entry and exit improvements of the new signal. Keep the analysis to a few hours per week. Otherwise, you'll never trade well and you'll never stabilize on what is working. Paralysis by analysis is a problem for chartists. Use stops and keep trading. Work through your winners to see what worked. Work through your losers to see what went wrong. Sometimes, it just went wrong. Exit with a stop.

Read the commentary from the StockCharts.com blogs (visit stockcharts.com/articles). There are lots of good market analysis ideas from technical analysts.

Not Buying Stocks in Falling Markets

One of the hardest buys to make is buying when markets are falling. You actually don't want to buy in falling markets, but you do want to buy when stocks stop falling. The more major the market low, the better the buying opportunity on strong stocks.

As the indexes fall or pull back, your time should be spent trying to get an unbelievably good list to reenter the market. Other traders and institutional investors are going to be looking for horizontal support levels on the S&P 500 ($SPX) or the NASDAQ 100 ($NDX) where price held before. Know what levels the 100, 150, and 200 daily moving averages are at. They also move every day, so keep aware of the changes. (Flip to Chapter 10 for details on moving averages.)

Even in a gigantic bear market, there will be ripping rallies that are very profitable. More important than buying weak stocks near the lows is buying strong stocks near the lows when the overall market is selling off. Watching for stocks making new highs while the market is making lower lows is a great way to find good stocks.

TIP Scans and alerts are explained in Chapter 14. Watch for growth stocks that are breaking out to new three-month, six-month, or 52-week highs. Review this information to help you develop strategies to avoid making the mistake of staying out of a falling market and missing some good buys.

REMEMBER When everyone else is scared of the market, you should be leaning in, looking to buy. Take action when the price action confirms, not before. And don't forget: Have fun. Enjoy studying the market, customize your charts, and realize how much you have learned in a short span of time.

Chapter **23**

Ten Tips for Cashing In on Tomorrow's Amazingly Great Stock

The only guarantee you have about the stock market is that there will be crazy days. You want to use charts to tame those crazy days by anticipating the swings, buying at good entry points, and selling at good exit points. Notice that we didn't say the *best* entry or exit point. No one can consistently do that, but using stock charts wisely, with the help of this chapter, can help you manage your portfolio more prudently when the market goes wild.

Being Prepared for Big Moves in a Short Time

Financial reporters enjoy talking about stocks on a panic run. Don't join the panic; instead, try to understand the ways these stocks trade to maintain your financial health.

One key example in 2017 was a Bitcoin trust (GBTC). From April to September it rose over 1,000 percent. Within seven trading days in May, it rose $275. Within 20 days it rose $400. The final three days of the surge in May, it was up 127 percent. Within three weeks, it had lost almost 50 percent from the highs.

In mid-July, the Bitcoin trust plummeted to $250. It took off to the upside, and in 30 trading days, it had gains over 300 percent from the lows. Yes, it tacked on $760! Within three days it lost 40 percent from August 31 to September 4.

TIP

Picking the top when a big move is happening can be difficult. Take off money on the way up by selling some shares to preserve gains, then try not to enter when the price is moving 10 percent a day. Wait for very small bases in the chart where the candles aren't so long. You can review Chapter 9 on bases to get a better handle on big movers and shakers.

Understanding That You Don't Have to Be First to Buy

Don't jump in on a ballistic rocket. Moving into these stocks when they don't have a base is wilder than kids on a sugar high.

When a stock is moving straight up or straight down, there are no horizontal support/resistance levels (see Chapter 9). In an initial public offering (IPO), as the stock starts to trade, the charting software picks the high and the low of the chart and plots them. That can make the first few initial bars very long. It can be helpful to use 30-minute bars for the first few days as the stock starts trading and then expand to 60-minute and then to daily. On the 60-minute chart, plotting the 100-period moving average can be helpful, but that is very short-term.

TIP

In general, the 20-day moving average supports the stock on a quick rise. It is still in a good uptrend when it trades above the 50-period moving average after the stock has traded for three months.

If you are in a parabolic stock, the whole thing usually ends in less than two to four months. The Internet blow-off in 1999–2000 went almost a year, which is very rare. You can use a moving average convergence divergence (MACD) indicator on a 60-minute chart or daily chart to help with momentum trend lines, but the bottom line is that all the indicators will be very short-term until the stock has some trading history.

Review Chapter 8 for more on charting different time periods, Chapter 10 for more on moving averages, and Chapter 11 for more information on MACD.

Waiting on the Big-Name IPOs

Every now and then, a highly touted stock, such as Snap or Spotify (two highly anticipated public offerings in 2017), has an initial public offering (IPO) and the media talks through the deal a thousand times more than the average investor needs or wants. The conversation becomes all-consuming during the weeks leading up to it, when it first starts to trade, and during the weeks that follow.

With all that hype, who can resist owning such a wonderful stock? While every one of these stocks will have a different start, Facebook represents one of the largest-ever IPOs. On the first trade at $38, the company was valued at $104 billion. The stock soared on a weekly chart on the first day, and by the end of the week, the entire surge was gone. Within a month, the stock was 30 percent off the IPO price, and within four months, the stock was 60 percent off its highs and less than half of the first trade on IPO day. This is a very common pattern for IPOs.

REMEMBER

Don't get caught up in the IPO hype. Wait for a small one-month base to set up.

Seeing Huge Gaps on Earnings

Earnings gaps on charts range from little to huge. The big earnings gaps are great to watch for. An example might be a stock that rises 5–7 percent on big earnings and changes the chart trend by breaking above a previous level of resistance.

You can tell they are earnings announcements because they usually occur in three-month increments on a chart — most likely January, April, July, and October, but they can be any three-month intervals.

TIP

Putting stocks with big earnings gaps in a separate watch list and trying to find attractive entry points is a worthwhile endeavor. If the stock gapped up and then continued up throughout the day, the bottom of that bar is your support. The bottom level of the price bar on the day of the earnings announcements should hold. If price doesn't keep closing above the level, be cautious. It may close below by one day, but it shouldn't close the week below.

Earnings gaps that occur on high-leverage businesses like Internet software can really start a new trend. Use the Predefined Scans for Gaps. You can review information on scans in Chapters 14 and 21.

Watching for Crisis in a Stock

All companies face a crisis at some point. For example, a competitor may make moves to acquire the company; there could be a company scare, such as Equifax announcing millions of records were compromised; or there could be a shakeup, such as a change in CEO.

These crises can impact more than just the company involved. The entire industry may be impacted. The companies that fall will likely have some sort of bounce. After the crisis, other news may break about the stock. Watching the amount of selling that happens on the next piece of news is more important.

When the crisis is built into the stock, two obvious things will happen. First, the company will go into a tailspin with the stock making lower lows and lower highs. In that light, you need to wait for a proper base to set up (see Chapter 9 for more about bases).

You may also start watching the stock for the sign of a support level. For example, after the first sell-off, the stock rallies. On the second sell-off, it makes another low near where the first sell-off went. This is now a support level. It may have gone slightly below the previous levels, but when this support level has held for multiple pieces of bad news, it is much stronger as a place to enter. If the price falls below it in a few weeks, sell the stock and step aside until better price action occurs.

TIP

The second news event is better to trade on than the first. When the second or third set of bad news fails to change the stock and the recent lows hold, this can be a great opportunity. Use the recent low as your stop-out point, and enter the stock with a small position. If the stock starts to improve, that's a good trade entry that could be the start of a very strong run.

Using Volatility to Warn the End Is Near

Volatility can be measured in different ways. *Volatility* is how much the stock price moves around. Does it trade in a range of a few dollars per week or change dramatically as discussed about Bitcoin in the earlier section "Being Prepared for Big Moves in a Short Time"? The higher the volatility of a stock, the more difficult it is to own large positions.

A simple way of monitoring volatility is to watch the length of the price bars or candles. It's not quite as obvious on a daily chart, but the weekly chart really shows the changing character of a chart. (Review Chapter 4 on candlestick charting for more information.)

Seeing increased volatility at the end of a major run is very normal. It's a good clue to be aware of the change in investor stability. It also happens in the index sometimes. It's more likely to be seen on sector charts or industry group charts.

REMEMBER

After a nice long uptrend, when you suddenly see the largest down candle in years, that's usually a significant trend change and the new direction should be assumed to be down. It's a great place to make decisions.

Measuring Volatility with the Average True Range

One of the indicators that you can plot on stock charts is the average true range (ATR), which can help you see changes in volatility of the stock or commodity. Select it on the Indicators drop-down menu on StockCharts.com. (For more information on indicators, review Chapter 11.)

Do a little research to find some major stocks that topped out a while back, and look to see whether any clues were provided by the ATR indicator. Sometimes the volatility picks up because of a bad earnings call. When the ATR is relatively constant, it's normal for the stock to bounce around a little. While the stock is trending higher or sideways, the ATR can change somewhat. When the true range shrinks or expands meaningfully, try to do more work on the stock chart by analyzing other indicators for other potential sell signals.

Realizing That the SCTR Won't Help Find Exits

Because the two main components of the StockCharts technical ranking (SCTR) are based on longer-term moving averages, in a fast-rising stock, the SCTR will be slow to turn down. You can review details on the SCTR in Chapter 12.

The SCTR is much better at finding entries than exits in fast-moving stocks. If your goal is to outperform the market, you usually have to be in high-performing stocks. This doesn't mean that the volatility has to be higher. A strong stock can trend higher with the same sort of percentage move each week for months. The stock doesn't have a sudden change in volatility, so it is still smooth.

In combination with the relative strength (see Chapter 12) compared to the S&P 500 using the ratio tool, and the volatility picking up on a weekly chart, these can be additional tools. Using the ATR can also help (see the preceding section), but the SCTR will be too slow to help find exits on rapidly rising stocks.

Working with Bollinger Bands

Bollinger Bands (covered in Chapter 10) are also associated with volatility as they flare out and narrow based on the recent volatility of the stock. While this can be helpful to look for, sometimes the Bollinger Band width (the distance between the Bollinger Bands) is more important than the actual Bollinger Bands.

Bollinger Bands can be selected as an overlay on the stock price on StockCharts. com. Bollinger Band Width is an indicator selected in the Indicators drop-down menu and plotted as an indicator below the stock on a separate panel.

When the Bollinger Bands pinch in, that's a reduction in volatility. When a stock or an index trades in a tight range for a few weeks and suddenly breaks out to the upside, that's usually a positive signal of increasing volatility.

Conversely, trading in a narrow sideways range and then breaking down is usually due to a lack of momentum to push it higher. This sudden change in volatility based on the price change may also show up in the volume, where it accelerates as the Bollinger Bands expand.

TIP

The Bollinger Bands are a great indicator of volatility. The best clues appear from a long narrow channel of the Bollinger Bands. A sudden breakout or expansion can be very meaningful. This may happen because of earnings-related gaps or sudden industry problems, but these narrowing bands that suddenly expand are available in the Predefined Scan results. The Predefined Scan Name is "Moving Above Upper Bollinger Band." There is also a bearish scan for a volatility breakdown called "Moving Under Lower Bollinger Band." Review how to set up scans in Chapters 14 and 21.

Using the U.S. Dollar as a Guide

When the U.S. dollar is dropping, that favors exporters as their goods are less expensive for other countries to import from the United States. For importers, the goods that they resell have higher costs because they bought them from other countries in a currency that is rising. That makes their profit margins thinner unless they have some ability to raise and lower prices to reflect this.

For industrial manufacturers that export, a falling dollar is helpful. For retailers that import, a falling dollar is a headwind. On a macro picture basis, a falling dollar is helpful for commodities. That does not make the day-to-day correlation work, or even the week-to-week correlation fit perfectly. However, on a big macro trend, expect weakness in the dollar to help commodities. Review Chapter 13 to see how to organize your charts by industry groups or sectors.

REMEMBER

Obviously, the dollar is always moving around, but in general it trended up from 2011 to the end of 2016. For most of 2017, the dollar has been getting weaker. A major trend change in the dollar can affect the sectors that are sensitive to the value of the dollar.

While the SCTR (see Chapter 12) helps point out strong-performing industries all the time in real time, watch for correlations across industries that may also be because of the direction of the dollar.

One of the common themes is international investing. When the U.S. dollar is falling, these other markets will perform fabulously in U.S dollar–priced exchange-traded funds (ETFs). For example, EWG is the ETF for Germany traded in U.S. dollars. If the German stock market is going up in local currency, the $DAX index is going higher. But if the U.S. dollar currency is falling, a U.S. investor will get the currency gain on top of the stock market gain by owning shares of EWG.

If the U.S. dollar is rising but other markets are outperforming the U.S. markets, then you need to use ETFs that have the word "Hedged" in the name to actually get the gains (for example, HEWG). This removes the impact of currency for the most part, and you just have the performance of the ETF.

Index

M

About the Authors

Greg Schnell, CMT, MFTA, has presented across the United States and Canada, educating traders and investors on how to use stock charts. As a senior technical analyst for StockCharts.com, he writes several blogs, including "Don't Ignore This Chart," "The Canadian Technician," "ChartWatchers," and "Commodities Countdown." He serves on the board of the Canadian Society of Technical Analysts (CSTA) and is a member of the CMT Association.

Greg received the award for Top Trainer/Educator for Technical Analysis by the Canadian Society of Technical Analysts in 2016 and presents regularly online to audiences of StockCharts.com, the CMT Association, and the CSTA. In 2017, Greg was named the Top Technical Independent Analyst by the Canadian Society of Technical Analysts. He specializes in both the U.S. stock market and the Canadian stock market, as well as commodities markets.

When Greg takes a break, it usually involves travel as he has roamed the world extensively on five continents and lived in Europe for four years. Married with two daughters, he enjoys painting, golf, and other seasonal sports.

Lita Epstein, MBA, who earned her MBA from Emory University's Goizueta Business School, enjoys helping people develop good financial, investing, and tax-planning skills. She designs and teaches online courses on topics such as accounting, reading financial reports, investing for retirement, and getting ready for tax time. She has written more than 40 books, including *Trading For Dummies, Bookkeeping For Dummies,* and *Reading Financial Reports For Dummies,* all published by Wiley.

Lita was the content director for a financial services website, MostChoice.com, and managed the Investing for Women website. As a congressional press secretary, Lita gained firsthand knowledge about how to work within and around the federal bureaucracy, which gives her great insight into how government programs work. In the past, Lita has been a daily newspaper reporter, magazine editor, and fundraiser for the Carter Presidential Center. For fun, Lita enjoys scuba diving and is even certified as an underwater photographer. She hikes, canoes, and enjoys surfing the web to find all its hidden treasures.

Dedication

Greg Schnell: To my beloved wife Cherry, and my daughters Dayna and Kaylyn.

Lita Epstein: To my mom, who encourages me every day.